Getting It, Having It, Keeping It Up

Getting It, Having It, Keeping It Up

Straight Men's Sexuality in Public and Private

BETH MONTEMURRO

RUTGERS UNIVERSITY PRESS
NEW BRUNSWICK, CAMDEN, AND NEWARK,
NEW JERSEY, AND LONDON

Library of Congress Cataloging-in-Publication Data

Names: Montemurro, Beth, 1972– author.
Title: Getting it, having it, keeping it up : straight men's sexuality in public and private / Beth Montemurro.
Description: New Brunswick : Rutgers University Press, [2022] | Includes bibliographical references and index.
Identifiers: LCCN 2021011642 | ISBN 9781978817821 (paperback) | ISBN 9781978817838 (cloth) | ISBN 9781978817845 (epub) | ISBN 9781978817852 (mobi) | ISBN 9781978817869 (pdf)
Subjects: LCSH: Masculinity—United States. | Sex—United States. | Man-woman relationships—United States. | Performance anxiety—United States.
Classification: LCC BF692.5 .M64 2022 | DDC 155.3/32—dc23
LC record available at https://lccn.loc.gov/2021011642

A British Cataloging-in-Publication record for this book is available from the British Library.

∞ The paper used in this publication meets the requirements of the American National Standard for Information Sciences—Permanence of Paper for Printed Library Materials, ANSI Z39.48-1992.

www.rutgersuniversitypress.org

Manufactured in the United States of America

Dedicated, in memory, to
Dr. Mary Ann Groves (Manhattan College) and
Dr. Barry Schwartz (University of Georgia),
two wonderful mentors
who guided and inspired me

Contents

Getting It, Having It, Keeping It Up

CHAPTER 1

Introduction

We can't always perform. But we still want some woman to take her clothes off and show us that we still matter.

—Wesley, 68

Wesley, a single white upper-middle class real estate professional, lives in a large city in the northeastern United States. Born in 1947, he came of age in the late 1950s and early 1960s, a time during which public attitudes about sexuality were still fairly conservative. Wesley spent his adolescent and teen years in a New York City suburb, after his parents moved out of Manhattan when he was 10, because they wanted a safer environment for him. Before relocating, Wesley frequently got into fights, finding that if he picked on other boys, other boys were less likely to pick on him.

All his life he felt different. As a teenager, he knew girls found him less desirable than other boys because he was legally blind, having been born with a degenerative eye disease. Being blind meant he couldn't play sports and critically, in his estimation, couldn't drive. He explained:

> My life really diverged at age 16 and a half. That's when everybody else got their learner's permit to drive a car. I never got a learner's permit. . . . And no girl would date a man who did not have access to—didn't have to be *his* car—could be his parents' car but he had to drive, ok? That

> was the basic condition that you were a credible adult. So . . . I didn't get a date. So if you don't go parking—most of what you learn about sex happens in the back seat of a Chevy—if you don't get that education, what do you do? Well, I got my education out of the pages of *Playboy* magazine.

If he could never pick someone up to go out, never have a place to "make out," how could he ever get anywhere with girls? On his own, he developed ideas about desirability and women's bodies from looking at the erotic imagery in *Playboy* and other magazines. Of course, the women in *Playboy* were merely images of fantasy. Having no real intimate experiences with girls and women, he saw them as objects of lust. He seemed to internalize this characterization of women because he consistently mourned the lack of both affection and validation that came from access to women. Not being able to date was emasculating to Wesley because he was not able to prove to anyone (including himself) that he could get the attention of women. He knew then—and to the day of the interview he still believed—that being seen as desirable was critically important in being seen as a man. He lamented, "Getting approval from a woman on any level was the single most important—it was the prize. It was the single most important thing. And I think it probably still is. Most therapists will tell you this: 'It's your own opinion of yourself that matters.' And that's a great line for a therapist. After a while I think it gets a little stale. We don't live in isolation. We live in a connected society and what other people think of you does matter."

Wesley's interview revealed that he consistently questioned his worth and longed for the approval of women. But it was always out of reach. In fact, he didn't have *any* physical or romantic contact with a girl or woman until he was in his 30s. He explained: "I did not touch a woman until I was 35 years old. My peers already had children in school and I was a virgin. At that point in my life I had pretty much concluded no woman was ever going to touch me. I married my job. . . . I did the things I was good at—which I know how to make money. I'm very, very good at that. And I did not do the things I wasn't good at—which was talking to women and getting them to go to bed with me."

Wesley resigned himself to a celibate life. He recognized his place in the hierarchy of men and felt he would come up short every time. What is more, he saw his blindness and smaller stature as a mark of failure as a man. He bemoaned:

> I'm asking a woman to choose me over a sighted man and that is kind of silly right on its surface. Because I have to be not only as good as a sighted man, I have to be better. That's a very tall order. And for most of the women I've met in my life, I just couldn't pull it off. I was never good enough. . . . It's this constant struggle of "Choose me! Don't choose that other guy." And you have to explain to the woman why I'm a better choice and there's not always a good answer to that question. . . . I couldn't drive. I'd have to take public transportation. . . . I'm 5'6. That's not tall enough for women. Maybe I didn't have a $6,000 Armani suit? Maybe the suit! Who knows?

For Wesley, never being able to get the attention of "hot" women, and instead getting only mild interest from women he described as those "other men won't date," stood as a defining element of his life. This left him feeling dejected about his manhood and self-worth, despite having made a successful career in real estate. He developed a sexual self in the shadow of failure, of not getting what he thought he should as a man. In his study of the unattainable criteria for succeeding at manhood in the United States, sociologist Scott Melzer found that when men cannot or do not meet these standards, "they internalize their failures and endlessly try to repair them or compensate for them."[1] Wesley certainly worked, throughout his life, to both fix and make up for what he lacked in his poor relations with women.

Wesley's story shows how lack of sexual success and affirmation from women made him feel like a loser in the hierarchy of men. U.S. culture shows which women are more desirable than others and teaches men that "getting" those women is meaningful and demonstrative of masculinity.[2] Short of having those women, having a woman, any woman, is necessary. So for Wesley and men like him, the lack of sexual intimacy and relationships resulted, in his view, in being an insufficient man.

Growing up in the 1990s, Issac, a 30-year-old married middle class Black case manager, had a very different experience from Wesley's. Although his parents were not open about sex and discouraged him from having it when he was a teenager, through friends, he learned about it at an early age and saw it as part of his Jamaican culture. Several times during his interview, he talked of how there was an expectation for Jamaican men to be strong sexual performers. He recalled exposure to pornography when he was about 7 years old and "playing house" or fooling around with girls in his neighborhood, around that same time. But as he got into his teens, sex became "more of a competitive thing like, 'Oh, I had sex with three girls. Oh, I had sex with four'. . . . And this is the sad thing—it wasn't about, how well to do it, or how to do it well. . . . Everything was over-glorified, or 'My dick is as big as this,' or 'I just want a lot of it.'"

From these types of conversations with peers, Issac gleaned that sexual knowledge and experience were important currency. Friends talked about girls and sex in the way that they'd talk about sports, keeping track of "plays" and boasting about scoring. So, Issac sought out sexual encounters with the goal of conquest and securing status. And he never lacked opportunity. Girls liked him, he discovered, and were eager to please. He felt mature and manly because he was getting affirmation of his sexual and social worth.

When he was in high school, Issac recalled a summer he spent hooking up with a college girl. It was in this relationship that the way he thought about sex started to shift. He realized he had the capacity to satisfy his partner—that sex was not just about his own gratification and pleasure.

Before, he thought about his "needs" and never really considered what might feel good to his partner. He pinpoints this experience as setting him on the course to trying to perfect his techniques for satisfying women. He explained, "I was like, 'Oh, I can please you?' There's a competition in my head, and I wanna be the best at pleasing. And so that opened me up to learning."

Issac started to think about sex as a challenge and opportunity to be good at something that reinforced his masculine self-image. As he entered into sexual relationships, he was no longer proving something just to his peers but also to himself, in compliance with his internalization of what it means to be a man. He wanted to feel and be seen as both skilled and better than other men. Cultural ideologies of straight masculinity and strong sexual performance, particularly those for Black men, informed and influenced his sense of himself as a man and a sexual self—that is the way he sees himself as a sexual person. If he was good at sex, if he could "give" his partner a satisfying sexual experience or powerful orgasm, he achieved something important. Men, like Issac, who use a partner-centered narrative regarding sexual satisfaction do so not just as a means of showing that they care about their partners. Framing pleasing as accomplishment tells as much about men's sexual skill and pride as it does about partners' gratification.[3] When Issac succeeded at this challenge he succeeded at manhood. This was something he could *do* to show he was a man.

Issac's narrative helps us see how perception of sexual performance can shape sexual selves and how women partners play the significant role of affirming manhood throughout men's lives. First, as was evident in both Issac's and Wesley's stories, girls and women serve as entities that boys and young men can use for gratification, objectification, and conquest. In early experiences, girls and women also act as intimate partners who help men gain valuable experience that they can then use in interactions with male peers. But later, as men move out of public displays of masculinity with friends, when women choose them as sexual partners or react positively to sexual performances, sexual experiences can indicate or confirm manhood.

This was evident in most men's interviews. Issac, for instance, offered no shortage of stories of sexual proficiency during his interview. He said he frequently and easily garnered the attention of women, which enabled him to reinforce his sexual self-image as a desirable, skilled, generous sexual partner and as a straight man. His statement, "there is a competition in my head and I wanna be the best," shows the importance of striving to be at the top of an imagined hierarchy of men. Men are taught to envision other men as both audience and potential competitors to their sexual experiences.[4] Thus, their sex acts are always performances and opportunities to move up or down in rank. So, Issac wanted to be better than other men because this implies that he is more powerful and brings status. The competition aspect, characteristic of contemporary U.S. masculinity, suggests he must continually prove himself—his manhood, his sexual virility, his supremacy—to maintain that masculine status.

Although Wesley's and Issac's sexual experiences and lives could not have been more different, they both learned the same message—getting sex and maintaining the sexual attention of girls (and women) was critically important. When men could prove their worth by attention from or affiliation with women, they felt they were doing what was expected of them as men. Both in public with their men peers and in private with their women partners, throughout their lives, Wesley and Issac, like the majority of those interviewed for this book, stressed the necessity of sexual encounters and relationships with women in making men, men.

Over the course of several years, my research assistants (primarily John Jackson and Jonathan Magill) and I conducted in-depth interviews with ninety-four straight men to investigate how men's feelings about sex, sexual relationships, and their sexual selves changed during their lives.[5] What I found is that, for men, sex is an act of affirmation. Sex affirms manhood, while simultaneously confirming social and, often, personal worth. In other words, sex is what sociologists Douglas Schrock and Michael Schwalbe classify as a "manhood act"—an act "aimed at claiming privilege, eliciting deference, and resisting exploitation."[6] Through the use of women as both *objects* and *agents of affirmation*, men prove their manliness and their place among men.

I explore how sex functions as an affirmation of manhood by describing what men participants identified as the three primary areas of concern in their sex lives: *getting it*, *having it*, and *keeping it up*. *Getting it* is understanding and gaining access to sex; *having it* is doing it "right"—being solid if not strong performers who satisfy their partners; and *keeping it up* is being able to maintain an active sex life despite problems associated with aging, erectile dysfunction, infidelity, relationship transitions, or loss of intimacy. *Getting it*, *having it*, and *keeping it up* are not just about sex but also about *getting*, *having*, and *keeping* women, and *getting*, *having*, and *keeping up* masculine selves—all of which are precarious for many men throughout their lives.[7]

Worries about men who are better performers, whose genitals are bigger, who can provide greater sexual satisfaction to women, who can get the "hottest" woman loomed large—particularly for men earlier in their lives and for men without committed partners. Later, physical and relationships threats—declining energy, erectile dysfunction, divorce, aging bodies—were of concern. *Getting*, *having*, and *keeping up* with sex and *getting*, *having*, and *keeping* women sexual partners, allowed men to *show* their manhood.

Following the Masculine Script: Heterosexual Sex as an Act of Affirmation of Manhood

This books responds to calls for research that shows how gender identities shift in a variety of contexts or situations, as well as to Schrock and

Schwalbe's call to study the "practices and processes" involved in being seen as a man; those that "signify possession of a masculine self."[8] Men give off masculine impressions by complying with social expectations for manhood, including demonstrating power, status, and control over oneself and one's body. These acts maintain existing gender inequities—particularly when women are used as objects of leverage and validators of men's desirability, skill, and value—and when men who fail to *get*, *have*, or *keep it up* are seen as lesser men. Men used sex—sexual activities, talk about sex, talk about female bodies—to prove manhood to other men, to women, and to themselves, as well as to marginalize other men. In this book, I explore the way men learn about sex as a critical area of masculine knowledge and as a practice through which they can show off their manhood. By looking at the role of women in "manhood acts," I also address Schrock and Schwalbe's appeal for empirical explorations of "manhood acts" as collaborative. I do this, too, by looking at how men work together to signify masculine selves, as they police themselves and others when they fail to live up to masculine standards.

Sociologists who study masculinity have long reported that hegemonic masculinity—that dominant and culturally endorsed way of being masculine at a given point in time—is a very public thing.[9] And, displaying or confirming heterosexuality is a key aspect of complying with hegemonic masculinity. We also know from research that Western adolescent and teenage boys spend a great deal of time in one another's company and that there is an expectation for them to continuously demonstrate their conformity to dominant ideologies of masculinity.[10] Moreover, sociologists and masculinity scholars Tristan Bridges and C. J. Pascoe suggest that we need to think about the link between sexuality and masculinity as "discursive practice."[11] In other words, we need to look at how masculinity is practiced not just through behavior but also through dialogue. Plainly, it is not just through bodies that we convey and construct our sexuality. In everyday interaction, through the way boys and men talk to and about girls and women, the way men express entitlement to women's bodies, the way men position themselves among men, a particular type of masculinity is being articulated and reified.[12]

Girls and women are instrumental in these "manhood acts," not only as vehicles for the display of heterosexuality but also as people over whom boys and men can show power and control.[13] Essentially, straight manhood is affirmed by sexual interaction; females are necessary in the pursuit of sex. In the early stages of sexual development, girls serve as *objects of affirmation* or *objects of denial*. Female bodies are things that boys can talk about and act on as a way of signifying masculine selves. When men enter into committed relationships and their views on women and sex start to shift, women move from being *objects* to *agents*—from things to actors. As girlfriends, wives, and/or sexual partners they can be *agents of affirmation*—that is, women who can validate men's desirability and assuage concerns about performance. In this capacity, they also provide a space for expression of emotion and vulnerability, particularly when men's bodies no longer respond or function as they are "supposed to" or as they did when they were younger.[14] As potential sexual partners, women can also serve as *agents of denial* when they reject or criticize men. They can also be *agents of denial* as wives or girlfriends, when they no longer show interest in their partners or when they leave them for other men. In this way, women's response can be interpreted as judgment on manhood.

Schrock and Schwalbe noted that manhood acts vary based on context and "audience expectations."[15] Through socialization and interaction, men learn "sexual scripts," which guide them through sexual situations and allow them to prepare for the relevant audiences—whether peers or partners. Sociologists William Simon and John Gagnon defined sexual scripts as cultural narratives or ideologies that guide individuals in sexual situations.[16] Scripts facilitate interaction as they provide expectations for behavior in a given situation. Like actors in a play, we are given scripts that we study, commit to memory, and then act out when the time comes. Sexual scripts help actors anticipate the reactions and moves of potential and actual sexual partners. Sexual objectification of women and voyeurism are sexual scripts. Sex as a vehicle to intimacy is a sexual script.[17] Boys and men learn these scripts from popular culture, from pornography, from peers, and sometimes from parents.[18]

Sexual scripts operate on three levels. First, there are "cultural scenarios," which are at the societal or social group level. These are the notions that come through in films like *The 40-Year-Old Virgin*, *Weird Science*, or *Revenge of the Nerds*, which show us that boys' or men's status as "nerds" or "losers" can be redeemed if they are able to get the attention of "hot" girls. They also are evident in incel culture and cases like that of mass shooters like Elliot Rodger and Dimitrios Pagourtzis who ostensibly sought violent revenge on girls and women who did not want them.[19] In those contexts, the script is men's entitlement to female bodies and a sense of frustration if they cannot get what they feel they deserve.[20] Dominant cultural scenarios also include ideas like: boys will be boys, sexual conquest leads to status elevation, degrading or sexually objectifying girls and women is normal, men should initiate sex, men should not take no for answer, and heterosexuality is the norm. Cultural scenarios allow us to visualize how sexual situations typically proceed.

Second, sexual scripts also function at an interpersonal level (interpersonal scripts)—that is, between partners in sexualized situations. Potential sexual partners size each other up, taking in what they can see and sense, and pair that with gendered, heteronormative cultural expectations. The way they read each other shapes the plot going forward. So, individual men can study partners and, influenced by cultural scenarios, think about how they should act as men or teenage boys. They then construct a plan of action for initiating or not initiating sexual intimacy or trying or not trying a new sexual experience. Sexual scripts show us how private interactions have public influences. Actors imagine others' perceptions and expectations of them, which influences their sexual decision making.

The third way scripts play out is in our minds. These are called "intrapsychic scripts." Intrapsychic scripts are the conversations individuals have with themselves as they negotiate sexual situations and consider others' reactions to their behavior. Referred to as "internal rehearsals," it is through intrapsychic scripts that people fantasize about how their personal desires fit with social situations and expectations.[21] In that way, these scripts are also influenced by both interpersonal scripts and cultural scenarios. A man's desire to be sexually passive or to be dominated must be considered against societal norms for masculine sexual assertion. Internalized pressures about sexual performance, for example, may lead men to have sex in a particular way or expect a certain type of response from women partners.

At all levels of scripting for straight men, how to have sex is tied to how to "be a man." At the same time, although sexual scripts and particularly cultural scenarios provide abstract guidelines, men are not without agency or autonomy, and scripts can and do change over time. As boys and men have experience with actual sexual partners they may begin to see that the women they are intimate with do not (or do not want to) have sex like women in pornographic videos. They may create new scenarios when or if fantasies about aggressive domination are found to be unwelcome in practice. They may start to recognize that sex is not just about their own climax, but that women also want to feel sexual pleasure. And then they may focus on honing their sexual skills or redefining intimacy.

Hierarchies of Desirability, Hierarchies of Men

Research shows that men locate themselves in hierarchies of men—that is, they compare and rank themselves and others by sizing up who has more power, more assets, and more status.[22] Research on straight men's sexualities further reveals a *hierarchy of desirability*.[23] Because heterosexuality is a key aspect of hegemonic masculinity in contemporary U.S. culture, being seen as sexually desirable and having sexual interactions with women is important to men in situating themselves in the hierarchy of men.[24] One study, for example, studied online discussion among users on a pornography abstinence site and found that men privileged partnered sexual encounters over masturbation. In this case, site users constructed a hierarchy of desirability among straight men where those who relied on pornography for sexual release were cast as lower status men who could not get women.[25] Men encouraged each other to stay away from pornography and to find women partners instead. Sex thus functions as an act of affirmation not just when sexual release happens, but when it happens with female partners.

British scholars Janet Holland, Caroline Ramazanoglu, Sue Sharpe, and Rachel Thomson, authors of *The Male in the Head: Young People, Heterosexuality, and Power*, wrote that "Western male sexuality is characteristically competitive and assertive, and centers on men's desires and demonstration of potency."[26] By this they mean that men must *act* to be masculine and in that action, they show their power. Based on her ethnographic research on teenage boys, C. J. Pascoe called this "compulsive heterosexuality," wherein boys showed their "sexual dominance over girls' bodies" through teasing and harassment.[27]

This use of sex acts and talk as a demonstration of power has been documented not only among teens but also among men. Sociologist Brian Sweeney studied collegiate sexual cultures and found that men in fraternities followed what he called "player masculinity," which is the "homosocial peer culture of fraternity life [that] compels men to calibrate their personal sexual preferences and practices with an idealized group construction of masculinity based on heterosexual mastery and the domination of women."[28] The fraternity men he interviewed constructed some women as "sluts" and in so doing collectively demarcated them as objects unworthy of respect. Labeling women in these ways allows men to demonstrate authority over women and mark them as *objects of affirmation*—props for masculine posturing among peers.

The use of sexual mastery and knowledge to prove manhood also continues in adulthood, according to psychologist Gary Brooks, who theorized scripts for heterosexual men's sexuality that he termed the "Centerfold Syndrome."[29] In essence, Brooks said that the way men view women—as objects/like pornographic centerfolds—influences and inhibits intimate relationships and satisfying sex lives. He defined five linked schemas that men learn through popular culture, which cultivate this view of women. These are: *voyeurism*—which includes the "desire to look at women and images of women"; *objectification*, or viewing women as eroticized things rather than as subjects; *need for validation*—which is "men's perception that women have power to validate men as sexual performers" (with more attractive women viewed as more credible validators); *trophyism*—where men view women, and particularly the most desired women, as prizes that they can win; and *fear of true intimacy*—or a worry about sacrificing independence and the feminization associated with emotions.[30]

So, in Brooks's schema, heterosexual men are socialized to maintain a masculine detachment from women and to view sex as a competitive game played with other men, with women as both obstacles and channels to success. Empirical explorations of the "Centerfold Syndrome" find support for men's learning and internalization of these schemas (though some more than others).[31] One study found that men felt they were in competition with others for women and that highly attractive women served as markers of masculinity and success. This study also found that men believed in women's power for validation of "masculine self-worth" and linked rejection with emasculation.[32]

If having sex is an act of affirmation of manhood, not having it is an act of repudiation. Many of the men interviewed spoke of spending their lives on "missions" trying to prove themselves desirable enough, man enough, to both attract and keep partners. American culture is rife with instances of men lashing out in frustration, and often anger, when they've failed at manhood or do not feel validated as straight men. It is also filled with cultural messages about how to go about "getting" it. Men are taught to get sex by force or coercion; by "working out a yes" if the first response is no.[33] They are taught this by way of cultural messages suggesting that "good girls" resist before they give in and masculine boys and men push rather than accept rejection. They are taught this by the discursive expectation for sexually objectifying women that is a part of adolescent, teen, and young men's peer cultures.[34] They are taught this by the belittling and shaming of women who come forward after being sexually assaulted. In other words, we socialize boys and men in a culture that at the very least encourages (and often pressures) them to prove their manhood, heterosexuality, and social worth by using girls and women as objects, often with hostility.[35]

Because heterosexual sexual experiences and relationships function as evidence of both manhood and social value, the men we spoke with sought confirmation of these both directly and indirectly through sexual activity.[36] They sought feedback from partners. They read and responded to social cues and information from culture, from peers, from media and pornography about how to be good at sex. They pursued and received education from peers and family members. Why? They did so in an attempt to possess an arsenal of information and skills they could use to ensure fruitful sexual encounters and to demonstrate proficiency and competence in interactions with other boys and men.

Sexuality and Manhood in Public and Private

I wanted to write this book because I was struck by the disconnect I saw between cultural scenarios about boys' and young men's sexualities and the findings from interview studies about these same populations. In a patriarchal, heteronormative culture, boys and men must negotiate private, feminized feelings with public expectations for compulsive heterosexuality and hegemonic masculinity.[37] They grapple with seeing women as *both objects* and *agents of affirmation*—with knowing that men are supposed to dominate in sexual situations but also that women's reactions and satisfaction can signify something important about them as men.

Interview studies find that boys and young men express *public* sexual confidence, *public* condemnation of homosexuality and femininity, and *public* sexual objectification and harassment of girls.[38] They show how boys seem to internalize dominant cultural messages that sow the seeds of rape culture, with a masculinity grounded in using girls and women as *objects of affirmation* of manhood.[39] Yet, in the private context of interviews, the stories of men interviewed for this book, like the stories adolescent and teen boys and young men have shared with other researchers, show that men can view sex and women in very different ways.[40] Recent research confirms that boys and young men sometimes feel anxiety about early sexual experiences and fear doing something wrong.[41] At times, boys feel pressured and do not want to have sex and they sometimes wish they were not expected to take the lead in sexual situations.[42] Moreover, teenaged boys and young men can view first sexual experiences as acts of love and romance; virginity as a "gift" given to girlfriends or sexual partners.[43] Sex serves as a way not only to build self-esteem and feel affirmed as men but also to express care and love for partners.

And though there's not much research out there, there's also evidence that men do care about partners' sexual gratification, though more so as they mature, and more so in relationships than in casual sexual encounters (and perhaps for complex reasons).[44] There have also been some interesting findings regarding intimacy from studies looking at older (age 60+) men's sexualities. Social scientists who've spoken with men about how aging impacts their sexuality find that definitions of intimacy and sexual satisfaction in relationships shift with age and as men slip away from social visibility.[45] When men can't perform as they used to, they find other ways to express closeness to partners and redefine the meaning and act of sex. In so doing, they reconstruct manhood.[46] Sexual intimacy allows a private space for vulnerability, while still demonstrating masculinity through sex. In this way, women, as *agents of affirmation*, play the role of validators of emotion and self-worth in intimate relationships.

Throughout men's sexual lives, girls and women serve an important function in augmenting boys' and men's manhood, which in turn, maintains existing gender hierarchies. Even in private moments, partnering with women is an opportunity for confirming hegemonic masculinity. Thus, I look at how context impacts the expression of masculinity by examining the notion of *private masculinities*—that is the way men demonstrate masculinity in intimate situations, where they are less likely to be policed.[47] I suggest that the scope of the "audience" impacts the performance of manhood acts, as does the nature of the interaction. Intimate encounters set the stage for the performance of private masculinities, which can be very different from the way the same man is expected to or does perform masculinity publicly. In this context, men rely on women to affirm manhood because other men are not watching.

Twenty-First-Century Sex

Before delving into discussion of men's experiences, it's important to set the stage for the time period during which interviews were conducted. Although we talked about men's sex lives from childhood to the present, interviews were conducted between 2014 and 2016, and the era shapes thinking about sexuality. In the past sixty years we have seen significant changes in sexual norms. Premarital sex is more accepted, and sexuality is regarded as more fluid.[48] "Seduction seminars" and workshops as well as online tutorials teach men around the world how to attract and interact with women.[49]

Given lax regulations regarding the broadcast and dissemination of sexual images and the encouragement of self-branding and spectating generated by social media, sexuality in the twenty-first century is more public than ever before. We can access limitless pornography in many forms at any given time of the day. Because many Americans walk around with smartphones, viewing pornography is not confined to the privacy of one's home either. Access is only restricted by clicking a button saying one is old enough to view it—whether one is or not. Whereas in the past "adult" content, tame as it was, was confined to the evening on broadcast television, those standards have disappeared and cable and subscription channels make such content available "On Demand." Sexuality is a mainstay of popular culture where people share intimate details about themselves, their lives, and their bodies on social media and reality television. On the reality TV show *Married at First Sight*, for example, where couples are paired by a team of matchmakers and then meet for the first time at the altar on their wedding day, whether and when they consummate their marriage is a major topic of discussion. Although this is not the climate most of our interviewees were raised in, it is the one in which they live and think about sex.

At the same time, ironically perhaps, sex is also more private than it was in the 1960s and 1970s and even into the 1980s. In the 1960s and 1970s sex education provided specific information about how to have sex, and graphic sex-education films were shown in schools (both as a fear tactic and as acknowledgment of the reality of teen sex, depending on the era).[50] Now, however, abstinence-only sex-education programs dominate in public schools, as does a lack of direct discussion of sex.[51] Sex is something that is still rarely discussed among U.S. parents and children.[52] The tension between public and private sexuality on a cultural level mirrors the tension between public and private masculinity on the personal level, as communicated through men's narratives.

The heightened visibility of sex and the proliferation of images that provide scripts for how to do it also create a climate in which men's sexual functioning and bodies are under great scrutiny. Men are expected to be able to perform and resist the effects of aging or bodily decline. Men seek help if they do not "measure up"; looking for ways to enlarge their penises and improve their sexual performance.[53] The innovation, FDA approval, and mass marketing of Viagra and similar drugs have shaped the way men think about how their bodies are supposed to respond, particularly as they age.[54] Direct to consumer advertising of erection-enhancing products and medications reinforce the idea of "successful aging," in which individuals resist changes associated with aging bodies by defying age-related stereotypes, like that of sexual decline.[55]

One study found that while women fixate on changes in appearance during midlife, men are concerned with changes in bodily function.[56] Such concerns affect sexual relationships and can detract from feelings of desire and pleasure. Studies like this underscore the importance of more research understanding men's feelings about their bodies and sexuality. There is also a need for a wider scope so we can see how men, raised at a time when messages about erectile function overshadow messages about pleasure, negotiate these changing sexual scripts. Thus, this book is about *getting*, *having*, and *keeping* women as ways of demonstrating manhood. But, it is also about *getting* sex, *having* sex, and *keeping up* with sex as men age—as a way of signifying a masculine self.

The men whose stories fill this book come from a wide range of backgrounds.[57] They range in age from 20 to 68. About one-third of these men have never been married, one-third are currently married, and the rest were divorced or separated, engaged, or widowed.[58] We interviewed most of the men by phone and so were able to speak with men who lived throughout the United States, most in suburban or urban areas (see appendices for more detail on methods and participants).[59] About half of the men described themselves as middle class and about a third said they were working class. Compared to the U.S. population at large, they were well-educated. About half of the men had a college or graduate degree. Nineteen men had a high school education or less. All identified as straight, though some had had homosexual experiences during their lives. Approximately half of the men (52 percent) described themselves as white, 27 percent as Black, 9 percent were Asian, and 7 percent were Latino. Five men identified as biracial.

In the chapters that follow, I share the stories of the diverse group of men my research team and I interviewed. In Part 1, I look at how men *get* sex. First, in Chapter 2, I explore how men learn about and come to understand sex, as well as how they come to discover and construct their sexual selves. In Chapter 3, I focus on access to sex. Here, I share men's stories about "getting girls" and the importance of women in establishing manhood. In both of these chapters, girls and women exist primarily as *objects of affirmation* or *objects of denial*—they are tools that men use to convey or contest manhood.

Part 2 focuses on *having it*. In Chapter 4, I describe men's expectations for sexual performance and proficiency and the importance of their belief of a "right way" to have sex. Here women are mostly *objects of affirmation*, though at times their responses position them as *agents of affirmation* as well. The focus of Chapter 5 is having sex in relationships; I explore how committed relationships and feelings of love affect the way men have sex and how some men come to see women as sexual subjects rather than objects.

Part 3 of the book turns to *keeping it up*. In Chapter 6, I share stories of men's experiences with relationship issues and breakups as well as with life changes that affect their sex lives and sexual selves. Here, when men lack women as *agents of affirmation*, they often feel like failed men. Finally, in Chapter 7, I investigate what happens when men's bodies change as the result of aging or as they experience erectile dysfunction—when they literally cannot keep *it* up. In these times, long-term women partners can affirm manhood by staying with men. Throughout the book, I maintain emphasis on men's sexual stories. These are stories of triumph, failure, objectification of girls and women, accomplishment, anxiety, love, and heartbreak. They are stories of sex past, present, and future.

PART I

Getting It

CHAPTER 2

Getting It

UNDERSTANDING SEX AND BECOMING SEXUALLY AWARE

> *You kind of realize everything isn't Ninja Turtles and tree forts. There's a difference and you do lose— . . . I don't know if it's innocence, but somebody kind of drops the veil.*
>
> —*Randy, 35, engaged*

Before men have sex, before they understand themselves as sexual, they have to "get it." Getting it happened on two levels: comprehending sex and accessing sex. First, boys needed to grasp how sex actually works. This was not a straightforward task. In the early stages of sexual development, sex was a mystery to most of the men in this study. Although some had parents who sat them down for "the talk," most spoke of families where the subject of sex was readily skirted or viewed as taboo. Frequently, men told stories of surprising first erections and unforeseen nocturnal emissions. When this happened, most felt there was no one they could ask about what was happening with their bodies.

Such concerns were common among the men in this study, across generations. For example, Geno (65, married, retired executive, white) recalled, "My first date where I kissed a girl, I was 13. And the only reason I have the date was because all my friends were dating. . . . I was one of the later ones to come to that point." When I asked how he felt about his desire for this girl, he answered:

The first thing that popped into my head when you asked the question was embarrassed. . . . It was because of a number of things going on. Number one, the lack of information that I had, the lack of discussion at home about this. The lack of discussion other than the dating my friends were talking about as a 13-year-old. So there's a sense of confusion. Embarrassment. Lack of understanding. I didn't have a big brother to guide me. There was no role model or person I could ask . . . and uh, you know, the lack of TV, internet addressing this. There's no place to go.

For Geno, born in 1951, sex-education resources were scarce.[1] He recalled no cultural conversations or information about sex—even in media. Like other men of his generation, he was left to his own devices to figure out what sex was all about. At the same time, boys were supposed to be sexually knowledgeable.[2] The pubescent expressions of masculinity required *not* talking about what you didn't know about or pretending you did know about sex, even if you didn't. With this girl, in this moment, Geno was supposed to just know what to do without having been given any information or having talked to anyone about sex; hence, his embarrassment over his feelings of lust and over not knowing what to do.

School-based sex education proved no more useful. While most interviewees had it, none felt it prepared them for how things would actually go when they got down to business. Although men in their twenties and thirties more often described a sex-education curriculum focused on disease prevention and contraceptive use, men of all generations reported a lack of beneficial information from sex-ed courses. As Randy (33, engaged, trader, white) commented:

Their messages were so convoluted. I remember at one point they had us stand up and like, "Here's how you could get an STD: If you shake their hand and that passes to you and then you turn around and shake somebody's else's hands." And the handshake was effectively sex. You would transfer a[n] STD like that. And that was like the dumbest thing

> I ever heard. The way they presented it was really, really convoluted. And it was more of a "Don't have sex message" instead of a "Be safe about it if you're going to do it. Talk to somebody maybe before you do that" and stuff like that.

Like most participants, Randy wished he'd acquired some useful information from school about how sex worked. Sexual knowledge was valuable and getting it was part of the process of signifying a masculine self.

Getting It through the Grapevine: Pornography, Peers, and Parents

Socialization is the process by which we learn the norms or values of a culture. Part of that involves sexual socialization—which in U.S. society is learning the gendered ways boys and girls understand themselves as sexual and how they make sense of sexual behavior. Children are taught that heterosexuality is the norm.[3] Teenagers learn that a way to demonstrate normalcy is to get caught up in the world of crushes, flirting, and, for some, sex. Puberty is sometimes read as a "social accomplishment" for boys, as it makes them appear manlier among their peers.[4] Although there are multiple agents of socialization such as family, friends, popular media, schools, and religion, the men in this study learned the most about getting it from three sources: pornography, peers, and parents. These agents of socialization provided a lens through which boys learned how to view sex, how to perform masculinity, and, consequently, how to view girls and women.

Pornography

Pornography was the most salient influence on the sexual development of most of the men. More than half of the interviewees (62 percent, $n = 58$) specifically mentioned that they learned about sex from viewing pornography.[5] Many interviewees were keenly interested and actively sought out information about sex and women's bodies, because knowing what naked women looked like and how male and female bodies fit together in sexual acts was currency among adolescent boys from all generations of participants. The women in pornography were objects of affirmation, as boys could study them, be aroused by them, and talk about them as a way of demonstrating manhood.

Finding pornographic material was a challenge, as most of the men in this study came of age when internet pornography was not as readily available as it is now. Although most men expressed confusion about what sex was and how it worked before they had it for the first time, there were discrete differences between men who came of age prior to the online porn era and those who learned about sex in the digital age.[6] "Older" men, those born in 1985 or earlier ($n = 74$) expressed concerns about not knowing how to actually have sex or about being unfamiliar with female anatomy. Most said they had not seen a fully naked woman, either in real life or in print, before learning about sex. For them, magazines (and sometimes books) were critical in helping them feel prepared and developing sexual self-confidence, as well as in situating themselves among peers.

For the oldest men in the sample, this was particularly true. Jay (60, married, retired, white) explained the role *Playboy* magazine played in his sexual development. He said:

> When I was a young kid like every guy I knew had, through one way or another, got their hands on a *Playboy* magazine, and certainly they made the rounds. And that was like probably groundbreaking to go from, you know, being naive about sex to seeing it so directly and reading about it. So I would say, I mean things like *Playboy* had a huge influence. . . . It kind of legitimized and opened up the whole world of sex. You know, that was very, very mainstream and very ordinary, I think, and revealed a lot of information about it. I mean there were articles and things like that, too, it wasn't just pictures of women, but it kind of made it mainstream and it kind of made it normal and it kind of of made it okay.

Although Jay acknowledged that the women he saw in *Playboy* probably "weren't very normal or everyday people," he still emphasized how much sex was normalized for him from his exposure to the magazine. He learned that beautiful, busty women were the most desirable and that looking at naked women was something that he should want to do—that this was a "normal" and legitimate activity, part of the process of being a man. His comment that *Playboy* was passed around among his peers is an indication of this shared message about women's bodies and an example of manhood acts as collective action. So, as he learned about how sex works, Jay also learned about how female bodies are not only meant to be viewed but also how they are meant to be used—and I don't just mean sexually. The first influential women in shaping men's sexualities, for many men in this study, were the women in pornography.

For other men, *Playboy* sent messages about racial desirability. Tyrone (61, separated, entrepreneur, Black) said, "I do remember that there wasn't many Black people—Black women that you see, back then, so . . . it didn't represent my upbringing or women in my life at the time." Although he recognized that the women in the magazine were appealing, he says he never really felt too influenced by pornography because it was so far from his reality. He explained, "I just didn't—I just never had that mentality. I would much rather have the real thing in front of me. I was never that type of kid who got off on magazines and videos and stuff like that." So, though Tyrone didn't feel influenced by pornography directly, he still recalled, more than forty years later, which women were shown as sexy and alluring. Like Jay, he also learned about women's bodies and framing of desirability from *Playboy*. Part of getting sex for both of these men, was about understanding not only the mechanics of sex but which women were prized over others.

Gen Xers, Millennials, and Pornography. Getting it was not easy even for some men of the internet generation. Men in their twenties who were immigrants who had grown up in places like India, China, or Pakistan had little to no access to pornography. Others, born and raised in the United States in working class homes, did not have high-speed internet or smartphones. So, many of these men got it later than their more privileged peers. This lack of knowledge created a gap between boys, as those with no access to pornography or no desire to look at it were regarded as less mature and less masculine. Interest in getting it—that is, interest in seeing women's bodies and in how sex worked in action—was key in proving heterosexual manhood.

Yet, like the older men, for most participants in this study across social classes, understanding sex and discovering pornography started with *Playboy* magazine.[7] Craig (31, dating, East Asian), a project manager living in a large city on the West Coast, emphatically described his early interest in just seeing images of naked women's bodies, as means of both learning and gratifying his desire. He clearly viewed women as objects of affirmation that he needed to get a grasp on in order to feel and show himself as masculine. He explained how it was through pornography that he learned the way sex worked:

> It was friends and internet, you know? Learned about it from that movie, *American Pie* . . . Learning from them, learning from magazines. I remember one time specifically, this was again with uh, with *Hustler* magazine where they actually showed full vagina—you actually see everything, like the labia and the clitoris and everything (laughs). I remember . . . I was looking at it with my friend and my friend was like, "Where do you put your penis?" He was pointing at it and like, "I don't see a hole. I don't see a space where you can put it." The way he put it (laughs), "It just looks like a wound. It looks like an unhealed wound. . . . How are you supposed to place anything in there? You know? I don't see an actual hole." I was like, "I think you just push it in somewhere there." It was later on where we looked at more hardcore stuff where they actually showed penetration. . . . Watching videos online and stuff and . . . that's how we learn[ed].

Craig's comments reflect the lack of information about anatomy and sexual intercourse available to many American boys. Born in 1985, Craig came of age just prior to easy availability of internet pornography. But even after seeing images, he and his friends still had trouble discerning how exactly sex was supposed to happen. His narrative demonstrates the power of pornography in defining what sex is, particularly when used by boys and men as a visual aid for education.[8] It also shows how easily female bodies were constructed as things to act on, vehicles to figuring out a puzzle. Via pornography, boys' first interactions with women's bodies are passive and objectified.

Like contemporary teenagers and men of previous generations, Craig and his friends used pornography as a resource for both learning about female bodies and preparing themselves for sex.[9] Or preparing, at least, for conversations about sex. At that age, being able to talk about sex and women's bodies with confidence was important, possibly even more important than understanding exactly how to do it. Being able to "talk the talk" around peers is a key part of masculine performance for adolescents, teens, and young men.[10] Seeing images of naked women allowed boys to feel some level of competence when chatting with peers about sex or female bodies. This helped them avoid public emasculation. In this way, "getting" sex mattered not just for future or imagined intimate experiences with girls but also for interactions with other boys as a collective manhood act. There was more at stake with peers because there were usually more peers and more time spent with peers than there were sexual partners. This is an example of how the scope of the "audience" shaped manhood acts.

Pornography proved useful by helping men learn not just about female bodies but about their own as well. Viewing these images aroused them and helped them experiment with masturbation. In popular culture, there is a lack of reliable information about masturbation for boys and girls, and one study found that boys had little knowledge about how to do it before trying.[11] This was true for Jermaine (40, dating, unemployed, Black) who recalled first watching pornography when he was about 13. After viewing a few videos, he decided he wanted to see if he could do what they did. He explained, "I didn't know about ejaculation and that all that stuff would squirt. I was just looking at the TV and I see all kinds of stuff. . . . I actually didn't know that sperm and all that comes out of a real penis at that age. I wind up just experimenting and doing it. I did it and it came out and I didn't even know that. . . . I was like, 'Damn watch it do this amazing trick.'" Jermaine was able to capitalize on the availability of women in pornography as a source of arousal, which gave him the opportunity for sexual self-discovery. Knowing about masturbation and ejaculation was part of the process of getting it.

Culture and Pornography. Generation was not the only factor in how pornography influenced learning about sex. For men who grew up in more conservative cultures or who were first-generation Americans raised by non-Western parents, pornography opened the floodgates to a part of life they knew little to nothing about. For instance, when Shane (21, single, student, South Asian) moved to the United States from India as a teenager, he went from a world where there was no information about or discussion of sex to one where he could watch people engage in previously inconceivable sex acts online at any moment. He shared:

> When I was back in India the internet is like a dial-up connection, so no porn, nothing. And when I came here, pssh—it's right at my fingertips. So I want to say here it made me a more sexual person, I think, after watching a lot of porn, too. Because India, it's very limited and you don't get to know much about sex or anything until you have sex, which is not till you get married. But the thing is—I guess my first sexual experience, the first time I have sex with my girlfriend, the reason why I know what to do is because I've seen pornography. If I didn't, I would be like I don't know what the hell to do.

In this case pornography provided Shane with very specific and useful information—it gave him both a sexual script (cultural scenario) that focused on men's sexual gratification and women's desire to please and, thus, an interpersonal script that he could follow. As he says, without it he would have been at a loss. All the men we interviewed who were born in Asia and then moved to the United States or were first-generation East Asian/South Asian mentioned the critical influence of pornography in learning about sex and, consequently, performing masculinity. What they were learning, however, was a very specific and narrow performance of sex and one that portrays women as easy to please, voracious sexual partners.[12] This performance of masculinity is one that relies on men's domination and women's subordination and shows that sex is an act that reinforces gender hierarchies.

Men noted pornography as a substantial influence on their sexuality in multiple ways. But it was perhaps most significant as a point of entry to "getting" sex. As men use pornography to "get it" they become entrenched in a culture that teaches them to view women as objects for sexual gratification and conquest. Although their interaction with women here is indirect, knowledge about women's bodies as objects to act on still serves as capital that they can use to signify their masculinity with boys and other men.

Peers

Peers were critical sources of information about sex, though their influence was usually more indirect than direct.[13] As with the situation Craig described when studying *Playboy* and other explicit material, interviewees talked of looking at pornography as a social experience or opportunity for "fraternal bonding."[14] Boys perused images or videos with friends and discussed what they saw. This was a way they could show their articulation of hegemonic masculinity as they understood it. Talking about girls' bodies or sexual acts they'd seen confirmed their heterosexuality, which confirmed their "manliness." When boys contributed to conversations with information that other boys did not know, this helped boost their status as more mature and masculine.[15]

Peers were particularly crucial sources of information for men who grew up in places where premarital sex was taboo, like India or China. Akshay (41, married, researcher, South Asian) explained:

> I was growing up in a small town of India. . . . That society was very closed. . . . [My peers] were very curious about sex. They loved to talk. But they all talk . . . very secretly, without knowing someone is listening to them. They used to go to movie very secretly and also watch porn movie or blue film by VHS. . . . You need to go very secretly because in India you cannot ask openly to the shopkeeper to give you the porn movie. It was illegal, too. There was some secret code. We need to say like, "We need to watch Mickey Mouse movie."

For Akshay, there was no sex education or sex talk with parents. Sex was top secret, so friends were his resource for information and they relied on each other to get or understand sex and to access pornography, and doing so was a collective endeavor.

Overhearing peer conversations also helped men "get" sex. Peter (48, married, works in higher education, white) commented on the indirect nature of peer socialization regarding sex. If he did not know something he was unlikely to openly ask a friend (or anyone) for that information. He explained, "I didn't have intercourse until like the weekend before high school graduation, which for some was kind of late. But even [then] I never talked with anybody. Some guys would say they did this that or the other, but I never took notes from anybody. I think it's . . . some of it's playfulness, some of it's instinctual. And I guess, yeah, trial and error."

Such reluctance to admit they did not know something (or anything) about sex was very common. Most of the men we spoke with did not ask anyone direct questions about sex for most of their lives. So, much of men's discussion about sexuality focused on accomplishment and demonstration of manhood by talking with authority about female bodies or sexual conquest or experiences. Asking questions represents a failure of masculinity because boys are expected to know about sex—even before they participate in it.[16] Peter's comment, "I never took notes from anybody," and his description of sex as "instinctual" are ways of avoiding a mention of not knowing. In private, in experimentation with a partner, he could figure it out without his peers knowing what he did not know.

When men gained knowledge *indirectly* by listening to peers, they acquired useful information *and* preserved their manhood. When asked how he learned about sex, Devar (42, married, researcher, Black), born and raised in the Caribbean, noted frequent conversation about sex among his peers at his all-boys school. He said, "Basically from about 13 up, sex was a big thing. . . . I just think that's what teenage boys talk about. . . . I mean you had some older guys who did it, they had sex. So you learned vicariously from these older guys in the school, in my class." Devar thus learned most from what he overheard, rather than from asking. In retrospect, men sometimes challenged peers' stories or dismissed them when they learned that sex happened differently from the way friends suggested it did. However, when young and inexperienced and reliant on peers for information, most took in what they heard as pieces of a puzzle that they put together in private.

Even some of the men who'd had many sexual experiences when they were younger admitted that they learned about other aspects of sex by listening to peers. Issac (30, married, a case worker, Black), for instance, learned about sex by having it when he was in a gang as an adolescent. But that did not teach him everything he needed to know. He learned about masturbation in college by paying attention to peer conversations. He said, "It was my roommate—they were talking about jerking it off. And I think . . . I was like, 'Ohhhhh!' you know, *in my head. I didn't say this out loud*. . . . 'Oh is that what guys do?' I was like, 'Oh, is that what that is?' I thought that was just a transition into putting it into the vagina. 'You mean you do that whole thing on your own?'"

As sexually experienced as Issac was, it was only through hearing these friends talk that he understood masturbation as a solo act. His emphasis on keeping his dawning realization private ("*in my head. I didn't say this out loud*") highlights the ways that possessing sexual knowledge is an important means of signifying a masculine self. Privately, Issac was curious and did not understand some of the mechanics of sex. Like Peter, he had questions, but did not want to ask his friends. Indirect conversation or hearing stories from more experienced or knowledgeable peers was a way men "got" sex. But by staying quiet and paying attention, they could pass as experienced, gain information, and avoid emasculation. Peer influence was significant for many of the men we spoke with as they learned about sex from friends, but often in an incidental way.

Parents

Parents also had an indirect influence on interviewees' learning about sex, though not in the same way as peers. As is generally the way in U.S. culture, across generations, parents rarely talked openly about sex.[17] Rather, they made it clear sex was not to be discussed, which prompted men to seek out information through other sources. Mario (23, single, student, Latino) explained the code of silence around sex in his home. He said, "As a kid I wasn't—my parents never talked about it or like did anything, like it was never talked about. Like they never sat me down and talked to me about it. I pretty much just grew up like learning about it with other kids, I guess, and other people. But yeah, sexuality was, I guess, not a big topic, not important . . . in our family."

A few parents provided books or other information, sometimes with a directive to ask questions (which rarely happened) if they did not understand what they read. Only a couple of men benefited from having open parents, some of whom worked in the medical field, similar to women I interviewed for *Deserving Desire* who had informative parents.[18] Samuel (30, married, counselor, white) explained, "My mom was a nurse and she had all these books and I read them and I started asking questions. . . . Probably in the 2nd or 3rd grade, I started asking questions about these things. I was slowly introduced and then through the—maybe a talk with the parents but not a very in-depth talk with the parents, it was more 'We're going to tell you a little bit' and then, 'Here, read this.' They would just give me things to look at."

Others noted their parents were not direct, but did try to foster an open environment and provide information about sex. Cameron (32, dating, graduate student, white) recalled, "I learned about sex sort of gradually. We had a few books lying around the house for kids about the reproductive system, and how sex works. It wasn't anything that was really hidden from me. It was something out in the world. It wasn't overtly present—it was something that happens, not something restricted. Usually if I had a question, my parents answered it for me. Not in a pornographic way, but sort of a way kids could understand, and in a way that was more or less accurate." Men like Cameron and Samuel were more fortunate than most of the men we spoke with as they had the benefit of at least understanding sex as they went through puberty. This allowed them to make sense of what was happening with their bodies.

Randy (35, engaged, trader, white) recalled that though sex was not discussed, there was some degree of openness about it in his household. However, he was not receptive to conversation about sex with his father. He said, "[Sex] wasn't [talked about]—it was just—there was none of that talk. There was never the birds and the bees. My dad always subscribed to *Playboy* magazine. It wasn't a big deal. It wasn't hidden. . . . It was just there. (Jon: But you said there was no talk?) No, no. I mean you had friends for that. It would be a little awkward. Obviously I'd be like, 'Dad, you should shut up.'"

Randy partly saw sex as normal because his father was open about his own desire, though the *Playboy* magazines lying around his house likely sent particular messages about manhood and sexuality. But he did not want to talk about it and, like most of the men we spoke with, saw this as conversation to have only with friends. This may be due to cultural scenarios surrounding teenage sexuality in American culture. Sociologist Amy Schalet noted that American parents tend to "dramatize" teen sexuality—focusing on risk and crises, rather than approaching it in a pragmatic way.[19] For most of the men we spoke with, parents were not a major influence in "getting" sex. Although some provided resources, most men said that as boys (and even older), they did not feel comfortable asking their mothers or fathers about it.

Keep Calm and Think of Grapefruit: Becoming Sexually Aware

Learning how sex worked was usually the first step in "getting it." But feeling desire and understanding *personal* capacity for sexual pleasure served as another important phase in sexual development and the development of manhood. Some learned about sex before they had any sexual feelings, yet most men (55 percent, $n = 52$,) noted they felt aware of their sexuality when they first became attracted to girls, which happened almost overnight for some. Hector (55, divorced, truck driver, biracial) recalled when, at 12 and beginning a new school year, all of a sudden he found himself looking at girls differently. He said, "I still remember to this day I'd seen this girl and I was like, 'Wow, she's really pretty, I like her' (laughter). To this day! . . . I had never looked at a girl like that before. So that's when I knew. That's when it must have hit me about sex. That was the first girl I was scared to talk to."

Hector felt aroused before he understood what it was all about. Seeing girls triggered fear and stimulation—and through those emotions and physical reactions boys and young men like Hector started to think about girls and their own bodies differently. This is another way girls and women functioned as objects of affirmation. Many participants connected their sexual awareness with developing an attraction to girls, rather than a maturity or general feeling of arousal. Being attracted to and stimulated by girls could confirm both heterosexuality and manhood.

Some men (16 percent, $n = 15$) said they first became aware of their sexuality when they saw *Playboy* magazine or a pornographic image, sharing stories similar to those in the previous section. But, in these cases, instead of just using pornography to understand anatomy or the mechanics of sex, they *connected* arousal and the desire to see those images to their own sexuality.[20] For other men, awareness happened when they experienced an erection or a "wet dream" for the first time—or the first time that they associated it with being turned on. About one-third of men (30) said it was these physical responses that triggered awareness of their sexuality. For instance, Troy (39, single, printer, white) said that for him this happened around the age of 8. He said, "I remember I was in the bathtub and I got a boner for the first time and I was freaked out. I didn't know how it did that and I thought it was pretty cool. (John: Did you ask anybody about it?) No. I didn't want to be the one guy that had something weird about him. So, no, I didn't ask anybody."

Mario (23, single, student, Latino) felt both arousal and desire at a young age. He soon realized this was not always a good thing because, at times, having an erection was embarrassing or inappropriate. He explained:

> I guess at a very young age I knew I was, you know, I liked females. I mean, I liked their bodies, you know?
>
> JON: So you remember having your first sexual feelings, so what was that like . . . what made you feel those sexual feelings?
>
> MARIO: I guess it was the female. I guess her body, the way she was dressed and stuff like that made me want to do it. . . . When I thought about it, like, I would definitely get an erection, like a boner and stuff like that. And I would definitely just think about other stuff. I remember like thinking about grapefruits, you know? Like stuff like that, like just to get away from that mindset. Like just to calm me down, I guess, so nobody can see, you know?

Mario was embarrassed by the thought of having his desire apparent to other people. Like other interviewees, he did not want his private sexual feelings made public by surprise erections. In this way, private thoughts are informed and regulated by public scripts. Errant erections signaled not being in control of their bodies. Boys recognized that as "manly" as it was to be knowledgeable about and interested in sex, being visibly aroused in public was not a good thing. In other words, as teens and even young men, the men we spoke with often felt out of control in their bodies and struggled to make sense of their feelings. Most confessed they felt as if there was no one to talk to who could help them understand what was happening. They did not want to be embarrassed or emasculated by admitting that they did not know what was going on with their bodies. They had internalized sexual scripts from peers, parents, and media that inhibited their asking about what was going on with their bodies, seemingly because as boys they were supposed to know.

Eleven men shared that they became cognizant of their sexuality through molestation. National studies find that as many as one in twenty American boys are victims of childhood sexual assault; self-report data indicate approximately 5–10 percent of adult men convey that they were sexually assaulted or abused as children.[21] The eleven men in my study who were sexually abused were not involved in "fooling around" or "playing doctor." All their experiences were described as nonconsensual or as sexual abuse. Men recounted being molested or sexually assaulted by family members, neighbors, or friends of the family who had been trusted to care for them, most of whom were men. In these cases, as with women I interviewed who had similar experiences, sexual awakening preceded "getting" it—meaning they were sexualized before they really understood how sex worked.[22]

Minjun (39, married, instructor, East Asian), for example, was plagued by his early sexual experiences as a child. He said, "My start was kind of distorted because I learned how to [ejaculate] . . . or masturbate [from] a man who was living, who was kind of a tenant in my grandmother's house. He was divorced and he kind of invited me and then give me a few dollars for coming into his room. And then showed me how to masturbate and showed me the porno videos. I was in 7th grade. . . . So that's how I learned. . . . I was abused. Later I realized, I was paid for childhood sex."

Minjun hadn't thought much about sex prior to this encounter. He was a kid without sexual cognizance or desire. But in these experiences, his body responded. And, as time went on, he found himself becoming obsessed with sex and pornography. Although he felt shame, he was also aroused and then preoccupied with sex, even after the molestation stopped. He explained:

> When I was an adolescent, I was really active. I couldn't control my desire and—of course I did not go out and have sex with other people. But watching porno videos and [fantasizing] and masturbat[ing], I think I masturbated many times, sometimes 10 times a day. And so those kind of, I think I just could not stop that kind of energy. . . . I never received a proper sex education and my exposure was not normal, I guess. So that relationship (with the molester) lasted about 6 months and . . . he pretty much taught me that sex is everything.

Without a chance to cultivate his own desire, he connected sex with pornography. Frequent contact with this molester also stimulated his yearning for sexual release on a consistent basis. His obsession with pornography and masturbation continued into his adult life. As we talked, he reflected on this. He said, "I think I kind of struggled to resist sexual desire, [with] wanting to sleep with [every woman I met]."

In his early twenties, Minjun converted to Christianity and wanted to be celibate as part of his religious practice. He said he did his best to abstain and had no sexual activity—not even masturbation—for about two years. Then he started to feel desire and questioned whether or not having sex was right for him. Yet he also felt confused about having sex with a partner, because his "bad start" and fixation on pornography made it difficult for him to think about a partner's pleasure or desires. He could only focus on his own.

Because Minjun went so far in the direction of becoming obsessed with arousal and ejaculation, in his twenties and even in his marriage, he has felt as if sexual desire was something to be resisted and controlled.

Although Minjun got the message that sex was "everything," he also internalized the idea that he should be able to control his urges, similar to the way boys spoke of the importance of concealing erections. Like other men who were molested, these early experiences resulted in cumulative disadvantage for Minjun throughout his life.[23] Minjun has found it hard to free himself from guilt or shame he associates with this early and stigmatized start.

In recent years, Minjun and his wife have struggled with infertility and he wonders whether he is being castigated for what he did when he was younger. He confessed, "I often think I was punished . . . for my sexual sins before marriage. I—it just comes back, continues to come back. I guess by having a baby—if I have a baby I guess it would be the confirmation to—to say in Christian terms [I'm okay]. I think when I accepted Jesus Christ and repented [for] my sin—I think my sin was forgiven by God. But it looks like something was not forgiven. Like just from the fact that we don't have baby after trying several years." Getting sex by means of someone else's control and direction created a perpetually conflicted sexual self for Minjun. He experienced high levels of interest in sex, but also shame and the fear that his early experiences had consequences for his fertility.

Other men expressed similar feelings of confusion when nonconsensual sexual events (or events not fully understood as sexual) instigated their awareness of sex. Eli (64, divorced, consultant, white) shared that he "got" sex as a result of sexual coercion from an older man when he was a teenager. Eli had a difficult, abusive childhood and sought any opportunity to be out of the house. In high school, he eagerly took a part-time job working as a caddy. To save energy for walking the golf course, he hitchhiked from school to work. As he said:

> One day this guy picked me up and—you know where this is gonna go. So he starts asking me questions about sex and my experience, I mean really graphic stuff. And, of course, I am completely—I have never had an experience! I didn't even know half the words he was—I didn't know

> his vocabulary, I didn't understand it. He was not a—he was an older guy, probably in his 50s, 60s. . . . I was scared. So he got me as far as I had to go and I got out, and I didn't think anything of it. I remember having an erection when I got home and thinking about all the things he had said, but didn't know what to do with it. . . . About a week later I met the guy again. He picked me up and the guy talked to me about it and he asked me if I'd be interested in going for a ride. I'm trying to think, he said, "I won't do anything to you" and dah, dah, dah, dah, dah. And so I—you know, going home was always a trauma. I lived in the basement. I didn't really want to go home so I said, "Sure." So he takes me around, takes me around, goes around in circles and I'm still very scared. So he decided not to do anything and takes me back. Now this happens a third time, but this time he's a little bit more insistent and he said to me, "You know, you might as well get your rocks off. You should learn how to do that. I won't hurt you." And so he takes me into the woods, not that far from the golf course and where my bike was, and he says to me, "What I'm gonna do is gonna be wonderful, there's no pain," et cetera, and of course, he goes down on me. And that was my first sexual experience of my life. And it was my first orgasm, it was my first—I never actually—you know what? I never did masturbate before that. I didn't know what to do, I never did. But from that moment on I never let him come by me again. I never pursued him after that. . . . But that changed—that had an effect in that I knew what an orgasm was and I knew what masturbation was, and from that moment on I was masturbating two, three times a day.

Like Minjun, Eli recalled feelings of fear, of going along with something that he did not really understand but felt was not right. Yet he also felt aroused and that led him to feel both captivated with and confused about sex. He liked the feeling of stimulation and orgasm, but didn't think he should be feeling that way with another man, nor did he really "get" what was happening with his body.

Both Eli and Minjun described these experiences as particularly formative, a "bad start" that could never be corrected. Other researchers have made similar discoveries, finding, for instance, that those who've experienced sexual abuse as children are more likely to have unstable relationships in adulthood.[24] In this way, the nonconsensual experiences of their youth influenced their later interactions with women partners, where these men described feeling unsure, inept, or self-focused. They, like other men we spoke with who were assaulted or molested as children, had difficulty with accepting their desire and finding sexually compatible partners.

The men who described this as how they really "got" sex stood in stark contrast to most of the other men. Other men noted that although they may not have felt sure about what they were doing and were concerned about embarrassment and rejection, their confidence increased with sexual experiences and relationships with women. But for men like Minjun and Eli, who had sexual experiences before they desired them, feeling at ease with their sexual urges and wants was complicated and showed how these early experiences could lead to cumulative disadvantage.

Most of the men we spoke with who were sexually abused were abused by other men. In cultures like Korea and the United States where Minjun and Eli grew up, heterosexuality is a key element of masculinity. Identifying as straight as teens and adults, Minjun, Eli, and the other men we spoke with who had similar experiences, likely also had trouble reconciling these homosexual encounters with their sexual identities. Having sexual encounters with men and sexual encounters in which they were not in control was inconsistent with masculine norms. So, they had to work out what this said about them as men. The stories of Minjun and Eli reveal how men can feel about themselves when they have the "wrong" type of sex and how not all sex constitutes a manhood act. Men must comply with norms associated with heterosexuality and power in order for sexual experiences to signify masculinity.

"You're a Monkey on a Space Shuttle": Getting It by Doing It

Most of the men we interviewed understood sex in three stages: first, by making sense of the mechanics of sex and the realities of female anatomy; second, by feeling desire or arousal; and third, they really got it when they masturbated or had sex with a partner for the first time. Most of the men had stories of sexual self-discovery that, at the core, were like Craig's (31, dating, project manager, East Asian) depiction of driving without a manual:

> You are kind of—it's like joy-riding (laughs). You know? You don't know what the hell you're doing. You just got control of a really powerful car and you're just going down the road and you don't exactly know anything. . . . Not knowing street signs, the traffic signs, not knowing the controls of the car. What does this button do? You know? What does this do? How fast am I going? What does RPM stand for? . . . You're a monkey on a space shuttle. But you enjoy it. It's a joy ride. You're like, "Hell yeah I want to do this!" You know? You don't know what you're doing, you just know it's fun.

Solo Learning

For some men, learning by doing started by experimenting without a partner. Almost all of the men who did so expressed little understanding of how to masturbate or that it was even a thing people did. Issac, who, earlier in the chapter, was quoted telling of learning about masturbation by listening to college friends' conversation, recalled: "I instinctively had the need to hump. . . . So I used to masturbate by humping the mattress and it would give you hell of a dick burn. Hurt like ass. But I remember that was probably the first time I got off. And that's how I masturbated for years. I didn't actually know about pulling it out and wanking it until I went off to college."

Justin (28, dating, medical assistant, white) also remembered his earliest experiences with masturbation as "learning by doing," after he came across an arousing image. He recalled:

> It had to have been a 1970s catalog that was sitting in a box. It was like a comic book—but an adult naughty comic book. At the end, at the back there was like advertisements for lingerie or more risqué adult magazines. There was a woman in a nightie and you could see her breasts through the nightie. That was probably—I felt like I needed to take care of this thing. And this is kind of embarrassing to admit but I didn't even know how to do it when I was that age. I didn't even realize like the normal motion guys use. That didn't come to me first. What came to me first—I'm sure you've seen in movies and cartoons and stuff and someone's trying to make a fire and they have a stick and they're rubbing it between the palms of their hands and trying to make a fire—that's what my first thought was with that. So that's embarrassing, but that's the honest truth (laughs). It works! Haven't done it that way for 10 years.

Both Justin and Issac constructed a right way and a wrong way to masturbate. In their early days, they simply responded to their arousal in whatever way they could figure out that would lead to the feeling they wanted. They described these experimental times with embarrassment, indicating, in retrospect, their awareness of sexual scripts for masturbation. Although both noted that they did it the "wrong" way initially, they also recognized they had no idea.

None of the men we spoke with suggested that anyone told them directly about how to masturbate. This reflects the lack of information and discussion about masturbation as a sexual practice, despite cultural rhetoric, at least in contemporary society, that it is normal and expected for boys.[25] The men described *not* discussing this with their peers or anyone else. They didn't ask about it. They didn't read about it. And for most it was not until later that they heard about it or saw men masturbating in pornography that it dawned on them that they were doing it "wrong."

The idea of talking about masturbation also embarrassed our interviewees because, when they were young, they did not have a sense that it was a normal thing to do—or that people they knew were actually doing it.

Gary (68, widowed, photographer, white) expressed feeling awkward talking about it during his interview. He said:

> I feel funny bringing that up. Even now I feel funny talking about it. [Because] it's a personal thing. Sexuality is a personal thing. . . . See, back then I felt like I was the only one doing it. And I know I wasn't. Obviously, I wasn't. I knew my friends were doing it. So I'm doing it, they're doing it, too. . . . I certainly didn't want it to get around back then. . . . But then I found out [my friend] was doing it and this other [friend] was doing it, and . . . he went into the navy. Human reaction. What human beings do.

Despite cultural scenarios depicting men being open about sex and free to talk about it, men rarely spoke about it directly and certainly did not discuss questions or confusion about masturbation.[26] Gary felt self-conscious about masturbating and clearly he hadn't had discussions with friends or found out it was normal until years after he'd been doing it. Hearing that peers were self-gratifying made him feel better about it, though he still didn't talk about it. It was interesting that in particular he mentioned that knowing his peer in the navy was doing it was reassuring. He seemed to be saying anyone who joins the navy is a "manly man" and so if that friend was doing it, it must be okay. Knowing *this* friend was doing it allowed him to redefine masturbation as a manhood act. And when Gary says masturbation is a "personal thing," he differentiates between solo sex and partnered sex—with partnered sex prioritized. Partnered sex is not embarrassing since it is an act of affirmation because men can say that they got it or that they achieved the masculine feat of finding a woman to be with them. So it was not just sex or gratification that men talked about—but sex *with* girls and women. Girls and women act here, too, as objects of affirmation because they allow men to show they are having the right kind of sex.

In addition, talking about personal sexual behavior or insecurities reveals vulnerability and could thus be perceived as more feminine, so men seemed to avoid it. This has two consequences. First, it perpetuates the idea that men do not and should not talk about their feelings or reveal weaknesses (i.e., not knowing something). Second, it furthers the likelihood that boys do not share information about their own sexuality and struggle with anxiety, nervousness, and confusion regarding their own bodies. Though some research finds boys and men do a lot of talking about girls' and women's bodies and what they would do to them, this is a very different type of sex talk.[27] In this way, silence around masturbation compromises the development of sexual self-confidence for boys in early experiences.

When combined with lack of direct discussion with parents, teens and young men have few resources for understanding their own sexuality. Sexual scripts from popular culture films or television shows usually start with a man who wants sex and either gets it because he knows how to charm women or with an immature boy/teen/man who wants sex, but doesn't know how to get it because he lacks the necessary erotic capital or "game." The former is masculine, the latter is not. And even though there is no shortage of images of sex in pornography, most pornography marketed to straight men avoids focus on men's bodies, short of the "money shot" of men's ejaculation.[28] Pornography does not teach boys and men much about, or provide scripts for, understanding their own bodies. So, despite the cultural rhetoric and sexual scripts about boys' sexual self-confidence and feelings of mastery and desire, this does not hold true when looking at interview data like mine or that of other scholars who have looked at adolescent and teen boys' sexualities.[29]

Learning with Partners

Many of the men we spoke with—particularly those born before 1985—said that they only truly understood sex when they had it. The majority of these men described feeling a lack of preparedness at the time of their first sexual experience. This is unsurprising, given what they said about the ways they learned about how sex worked, in the abstract.

Jamie (56, married, engineer, white) described what happened during his first sexual encounter, which occurred when his sister's friend slept over at their house and came into his room during the night. He recalled that she kissed his neck and said, "'Ohhh, you're getting hard.' And I would be like, 'What's that? What's that mean?' [She said] 'it means you want to have sex.' That's when I realized, 'Oh, ok! That means you're ready to have sex, when you get aroused.' She was the first girl that started getting me that way." Reflecting on this, Jamie continued, "You didn't know what to expect. . . . I think [the girl I was with] was probably more experienced than I was or should've been. . . . You're just kind of ignorant. You're not well versed. You just don't know what you're doing. Frankly, you're kind of inept."

Inept, ignorant, inexperienced—these words represented most interviewees' reflections or descriptions of their first sexual encounters. And many, like Jamie, felt embarrassed as much by the sexual situation as by the idea that they "should have" known what to do. Boys are expected to have sexual agency from the time they hit puberty and to perform masculinity by demonstrating sexual aptitude.[30] Jamie's recollection—both that the girl he was with was more experienced and that he *should* have been—reflects sexual scripts about how boys and men are supposed to act in sexual situations. Most of the men did not want their partners to know about their inexperience. Jamie assumed his partner knew more and had done more than he had, but he didn't ask her. In fact, men in this study, as other scholars have also found, were reluctant to initiate sex in first or early encounters in large part because they felt that if they did it "wrong" it would reveal their lack of knowledge.[31] Sociologist Laura Carpenter found this among the men she interviewed in her study of virginity loss as well. Some hid inexperience from first sexual partners because they felt they would be badgered or chastened for it.[32] Women can act as agents of denial of manhood when they tell of men's ineptitude, as sex only affirms manhood when men do it with proficiency, not when they are emasculated by a more experienced woman or by their own incompetence.[33]

Glenn (58, divorced/dating, retired carpenter, biracial) noted the lack of resources available to boys when he was a teenager back in the late 1970s. He said, "How did I learn about sex? Spur of the moment. Didn't actually learn how you do [it]—I mean when I was comin' up that's how we learned. We ain't have nobody teachin' us, we just learned ourself. . . . We ain't have no video, no DVD, no books. . . . Learned in the backseat, you know?"

Juan (55, married, manager, Latino) also remembered figuring out sex through "trial and error." Like a number of men, connecting the dots between physical intimacy and pregnancy took a while, too. He explained:

> You're always, just as a guy, and this is me when I grew up, your number one fear was getting a girl pregnant. And that was a big deterrent for a long, long time. . . . As I said, I never had a class. I don't know how that works, you know? If that's one time and you're going to get pregnant? 'Cause no one's really said anything. And I do remember things like you can get pregnant on the first time you have intercourse. But there wasn't an internet at the time. Does that happen all the time? Or is it once? You don't know that, so to me, that was my number one fear and concern because it's like I don't want to ruin my life.

One might think that men of Jamie, Glenn, or Juan's generation should have had more information about sex. They came of age in the era of "free love" after all. Yet the uncoupled sex that was happening at the time and progressive attitudes about sex were mostly confined to small subcultures and not happening among the general population of teenagers or young adults. And, even an abundance of images of sex or living in a time where sex was everywhere didn't necessarily help men "get" it.

The stories of Jamie, Juan, and Glenn are representative of what we heard from most men, across generations. Even the youngest interviewees' stories bore similarities to those of older men. For example, Marcus (20, single, student, Black) noted he had no idea about sex until he had it. He said, "Before I even had an idea of what it was, I always thought, like when I seen a new woman, I ain't know what to do with her or nothin' like that." And his first time being intimate with a girl, he recalled, "I guess I would say I was nervous. Like how would this go? How would this work?"

The digital divide kept live action pornography inaccessible to working class Marcus as he shared, "With the absence of internet, I didn't have access to a whole lot of pornographic videos, it's just images. So you kind of understand the mechanics of it, but you don't know what do when you're there. Until you start doing it. Like okay, yeah, this feel natural, like okay, yeah. So I would say 16. That was kind of my first real lesson about sex."

Although most men knew something about sex from peers, parents, or pornography prior to having it, they did not feel a sense of confidence or really "get" it until they had it. Doing it for the first time yielded all sorts of surprises and new information. But once they gained some experience, for most, their sexual self-assurance was affirmed and they were ready to "have it," with focus shifting to performance.

Men "got" sex in a series of steps. First, they had to understand it intellectually. They had to make sense of the mechanics and what body parts go where. At times, some of this phase of discovery involved hunting for images of female anatomy to study. As boys, the men we spoke with used *Playboy*, *Hustler*, and pornographic videos to construct a visual idea of what they heard in the abstract.

In so doing, they also "got" the importance of girls and women's bodies in helping them understand sex. They needed to know what female genitals looked like in order to make sense of how to actually have sex. Through pornography, women became objects of desire, and looking at naked women in *Playboy* or pornographic videos with friends was a way men, in their formative years, not only learned about sex but also cultivated status with peers. In addition to working out the process of sex, they had to start to see themselves as sexual—to recognize their own desire and capacity for arousal. Women mattered in this stage of getting it, primarily as objects of desire and vehicles for figuring out the mechanics of sex. Seeing women as objects of affirmation then helped men confirm manhood. This benefited men and reinforced the notion that female bodies are useful in this way.

Knowing and understanding sex is an important aspect of straight manhood, particularly for boys as they go through puberty and are expected to be able to hold their own in discussions about girls and sex.[34] So getting it was not just intellectually significant but also vital for boys and young men as they jockeyed for position in the hierarchy of men. Being able to present an informed public masculine sexual self is something that grants boys status, in the same way that not being well-versed in this subject embarrassed and emasculated boys.[35] Men's reluctance and discomfort about not understanding sex at early ages, coupled with the fact that they just didn't talk about it or ask questions when they had them, indicates that sexual knowledge was of chief importance in constructions of masculinity and in the process of proving manhood.

CHAPTER 3

Getting *It*

GAINING ACCESS TO SEX

In 2005, author Neil Strauss published an exposé on men who pursue sexual conquest using stealthy techniques. In his book, *The Game: Penetrating the Secret Society of Pickup Artists*, Strauss described his time living among these men and trying out their methods to "get" women.[1] *The Game* started a profitable industry. Coupled with technological advances like internet marketing and accessible platforms like YouTube for sharing "pickup" strategies, the business of "getting girls" has expanded dramatically into a multimillion dollar "seduction" enterprise in the twenty-first century.[2] Sociologist Rachel O'Neill studied the seduction trade in Britain aimed at straight men. She attended boot camps and seminars, and studied online tutorials created to teach men how to get women. O'Neill found that this approach appealed to men, in part, due to its rationality and formulaic nature. If men followed the steps in the seduction seminars, they felt they could expect results.

The popularity of *The Game* and the ventures O'Neill and others have documented reveal men's anxieties about how to go about getting sexual attention from women and how imperative it is to do so.[3] "Getting it" was a crucial manhood act for my research participants as well. It established them not only as mature, but as men. So, after they understood how sex worked, they focused on getting "*it*"; *it* being sexual access to girls and women.

Men link rejection from women with emasculation.[4] When it comes to sex, boys and men are generally socialized to see women as objects (and sometimes agents) that have the potential to affirm or deny their manhood. Affiliation and intimacy with girls and women solidifies their status as heterosexual and as men.[5] Men desire certain women—women recognized for their looks—because they know that those women impart more status to the men they are with than do less attractive women. That is, they make their men partners look better as they show that these men could "get" those high status women.[6] Though men may seek women sexual partners for a variety of reasons, when men focus on getting certain women due to their beauty and what that beauty signifies for the men, women function quite clearly as objects of affirmation. Getting it is about sex, certainly, but it's also about position, prestige, and power.

The men we interviewed repeated this narrative of garnering women's attention and framed it as quite important in enhancing their status among peers. Walker (39, married, works in information technology, biracial), for instance, remembered a friend teaching him how to get the attention of girls, in a way reminiscent of steps in *The Game*. He explained, laughing: "We'd go to the mall and he'd try to help me with my swagger. How to walk, how to talk, what to wear." When asked what that involved, he said, "All the things you had to show. Definitely don't talk about your hobbies with the prospect. Keep eye contact, you know. Turn it on. Don't look away. Don't look down at your shoes. Um, you know, try to keep a very low-key profile. Get the phone number in the first couple of minutes."

Walker learned from this friend not only how he should approach women but also the importance of getting their attention. Although he doesn't mention this explicitly, he also learned to see girls as something to be conquered or coerced (note the use of the word "prospect" in his "training"), following a predatory sexual script.[7] Getting phone numbers was a way of verifying desirability, of proving himself to other men as well as himself, all of which were part of the process of conveying manhood.

Marcus (20, single, student, Black) also got this message from his peers. He explained:

> Like high school, middle school you should be having girlfriends. And if you wanna show your sexuality you should be very outgoing towards girls, you should be accepting towards girls. You should be like, "Oh, damn, look at her, bro! You see that chick right there? She's like super hot!" Or something like that. Like you should be giving off signs that you're sexual—a certain way—heterosexual—in my stance. If people don't pick up on that then they start to question like what is your sexuality, like what are you? . . . So as a teenager . . . I seen tons of men brag about the girls they been with and the people they talk about. . . . The messages they sent about how much women you should have, like stuff like that, that made me think like, once again, like I should be the macho man and having sex with all these women again. . . . The big man in high school, the most popular guy . . . he's having all the beautiful women and stuff like that. That's the guy everybody wants to be 'cause he's having tons of sex and stuff like that. So stuff like that, those kind of messages, they sink into you as an individual, like it makes you think like, "Yeah, my sexuality, I should be like him."

Marcus's comments reveal a great deal about his experiences with masculinity, sexuality, and teen culture. First, he shows awareness of the ways boys police other boys for heterosexuality and masculine behavior via high school sexual scripts. Teenage boys must posture and actively show interest in girls to live up to the standards set in their peer culture.[8] In this way, he shows how manhood acts are collective undertakings. Boys and men need an audience for this presentation of manhood. Similarly, labeling girls or talking about girls/women with other boys/men is a means by which boys show belonging with other boys and, critically, substantiate or demonstrate their heterosexuality.[9]

This shows how the objectification of girls and women (e.g., "Look at that girl—she's hot!" and "pursue sex as aggressively as possible") functions for boys and men. Studies looking at the sexual objectification of girls and women have mostly focused on what it does *to* them. Marcus's comments, and the whole idea of "getting girls" or using women as a prop or vehicle, shed light on what sexual objectification does for boys and men.[10] Boys "brag about the girls they've been with" or go after them as a status display for other boys (or men). Doing so affirms that they were desirable enough, man enough to get those girls and that they are sexually knowledgeable. This is an example of a discursive performance of sexuality, which, as sociologists Tristan Bridges and C. J. Pascoe emphasize, along with physical practice, is a critical expression of sexuality. Boys and men talk about sex to show what they know.[11] Objectification also connotes power—the power to look at or watch. Marcus's framing of girls as objects of affirmation underscores boys' power over girls.[12]

Living the Game: Getting Sex as Getting Power

Many of the men we interviewed described "getting" sex as work. They felt this way both early on when they were inexperienced and throughout their lives when not in relationships. Randy (35, engaged, trader, white) declared, "It's tough. It's like—I know how hard it is for me to go to a bar, a relatively good [looking guy]—I'm not a mongoloid, I'm not some crazy, my eyes not sagging off of my face—for me to go to a bar and pick up a woman. The amount of work that goes into that is crazy. Like how many drinks, money, this that and the other thing. If all the stars align, I might be able to take a woman home."

Randy suggests that there is a hierarchy of desirability (and a racially specific hierarchy—given his stigmatization of "mongoloids") that influences who is more likely to get girls.[13] Although he sees himself as reasonably attractive, he remarked that that alone was not enough to get a woman. Randy describes a calculated effort involving spending money, loosening up his potential partner with alcohol, and looking good. Here again is a description of the sexual scripts men associate with "getting" women and with manhood. These scripts position women as reluctant partners who need to be coaxed and conquered. In Randy's mind, doing this is work and he implies that there is a specific strategy that needs to be followed in order for that work to pay off.

Some men spoke directly about feeling that they had figured out "the game." Barry (44, engaged, postal worker, Black) boasted that he could hook up with or date multiple women simultaneously without the others knowing. He could do this "because [women] liked the way I look and the way I perceive myself. . . . [One woman] it took one day. I had sex with her the same day I met her. I mean the game basically was just listening and reciprocating what they said. . . . I didn't have to go off the deep end and tell a whole bunch of lies. It was pretty much listening, listening to what they were talking about."

A few men talked of aggressively pursuing sex and "wearing down" partners to give in, consistent with gendered cultural scripts about how men get sex.[14] Like most other interviewees, Kirk (54, married, self-employed, white) felt nervous about initiating sex his first time having it.[15] He explained, "It was very awkward. I didn't know what I was doing. I was just sort of figuring it out as I went along, no muscle memory involved 'cause it was all like, well, 'What do I do now and how do I act?'"

But, Kirk, then a teenager, was determined to have sex, so he pursued it doggedly. Although he recalls it as a positive experience for him because he actually had sex, it doesn't seem as if it was for his girlfriend. He continued, "We dated awhile. She was very resistant to anything for a long time and I had to *wear her down*. . . . She was very uptight about the whole thing so that put a damper on the positiveness. But I was, you know, I was being an aggressive male. . . . And she wanted to keep me happy, so she gave in (emphasis added)."

Kirk saw his first sexual experience as about *his* gratification and pleasure, about his wanting to feel like a man. He seemed to not feel any remorse or wrongdoing associated with pressuring his girlfriend to do something she wasn't ready for, despite his recollection that she was "uptight." He framed her demeanor as an obstacle to his enjoyment. Kirk followed the "push and resist" sexual script, thinking that getting sex was about "wearing down" his girlfriend's resistance, even explicitly noting that she did it not because she wanted to but because she wanted to "keep [him] happy."

Kirk, Barry, and Randy recognized the importance of women in their sexual development—they wanted to have sex with women so, obviously, they needed women to comply. However, these men talked about women as objects to use for personal benefit. There was no discussion of women's pleasure, desire, or gratification. Manhood acts are about exerting power, demonstrated by another person yielding.[16] In this way, women played a significant role in men's sexualities because they were viewed as obstacles or conduits to what men wanted or felt entitled to. Succeeding at not only getting their attention but *getting* them to have sex with them positioned the women as pawns in this display of masculinity.

Such scripts are pervasive in heterosexual sexual encounters.[17] Women have sex when they do not really want to because they believe that men's sexual needs are more important than their own or that they should gratify men if they have turned them on.[18] In a recent study of teenage girls' dilemmas about responding to requests from boys for revealing photos—aka sexting—girls reported being pressured to send these images. Boys used "push and resist" scripts where they pressured reluctant girls, sometimes with grave consequences.[19] Men learn this language of coercion both implicitly and explicitly, through popular culture and peer dialogue as well as from a culture that systematically devalues girls and women.[20] In the seduction industry, this was labeled as "LMR—last minute resistance," which is "the idea that women offer 'token' resistance prior to having sex as a way to protect their reputation."[21] Seduction professionals offered "a range of techniques and tactics by which these objections can be managed."[22]

In the #MeToo era, identifying and recognizing the commonality of these scripts that show men that this is how to "get it" is very important.

The implication is that men deserve access to women's bodies and that getting it is a "game" and challenge.[23] Pressuring girls or figuring out "how many drinks" it will take to lower women's inhibitions or pretending to care about what women are saying are all examples of the devaluation of women's subjectivity. Following sexual scripts such as these enables *and encourages* boys and men to assert dominance over girls and women and to view them as things used in the process of asserting manhood.[24] And although this was not the dominant *interpersonal* script for most of the men we interviewed in their first sexual experiences, it was a common *cultural* scenario throughout many interviewees' sexual histories.[25] In other words, it shaped men's ideas about how sex is supposed to go, even if they didn't necessarily pursue it that way.

How to Get It: Navigating Early Experiences

Many interviewees recollected that as boys or teens, they *really* wanted to have sex. Zack (34, married, lecturer, white), for instance, shared, "For the first part of my adolescence, [it was] something that I wanted desperately. Once I got it, [it was] something I wanted to keep on getting desperately, I suppose. I think it was like every party, every weekend was the attempt or trying to. Hopefully, this is going to be a weekend I'm going to sleep with some beautiful girl of my dreams. It would happen very rarely."

Despite the prevalence of coercive sexual scripts (primarily discussed in terms of cultural messages or recollections of sexual encounters when they were teens or young men), most of the men we talked to described themselves as ill at ease most of the time around new girls or women they desired, feeling as if they did not know what to say or do to "get girls." Some interviewees explained they were worried that girls or women might think all men wanted was sex. These men had trouble following conventional sexual scripts encouraging assertion or aggression. They couldn't picture themselves doing what they saw men in movies do. They felt awkward and insecure and just didn't believe they could flirt effectively. These men were unlikely to push girls or women who resisted initial advances. For the most part, these were men with less erotic capital—younger men, men who did not have money or career status to buttress their displays of masculinity, men who described themselves as less attractive or as socially awkward, and men from conservative cultures or religions who received mixed messages about sex. Unlike Randy, Barry, or Kirk, they hadn't learned how to employ seduction techniques, nor did they believe girls would be interested in them.

Men who called themselves "geeks" or "slow starters" felt particularly stymied by the challenge of "getting it." Casey (29, engaged, works in media, white), who described himself as a "late bloomer," felt awkward about sex and the idea of himself in sexual situations. Although he was very interested in girls and pornography before becoming sexually active with a partner, he felt that he had no clue about how to move from thinking about sex or masturbation to actually being with a girl. He explained, "I had a lot of social anxiety especially in high school and stuff. So I hadn't—I had like zero idea how to talk to (girls). I had a girlfriend in the 6th grade but I wouldn't really call it sexual. We never even kissed because I was so nervous about having a girlfriend and stuff at the time. . . . So there was never really an opportunity to have a sexual experience or anything."

Although Casey had no luck with girls, he became preoccupied with sex in his teenage years. However, like a few other men we spoke with who were raised in Christian households, Casey felt ashamed of his sexual desire.[26] Because of this, in his late teen years he decided not only to try to curb his fixation with masturbation and pornography but also to stop thinking about sex altogether. He wanted to control and resist his desire, to feel good rather than guilty. But, this was unsuccessful. After a while, he realized that he still really wanted to have sex so he actively sought out information about how to talk to and flirt with women. He scrutinized *The Game*, as well as movies and TV shows, looking for interpersonal sexual scripts or techniques he could put into action. He said:

> I'd say TV and movies to a degree [influenced my sexuality]. You have all of the college movies like the—*American Pie* is the first one that comes to mind as an example, like a lot of kids out trying to lose their virginity. . . . In college I started reading the pickup artist books, like *The Game* . . . and so that kind of changed my attitudes about sex a little bit. I found it very helpful in a way, too—not that I went out and tried to be a pickup artist but it had a lot of good advice about being more confident in social situations.

Even after getting tips about how to flirt and pick up women, Casey was still reluctant to try out these techniques on women he knew. He was worried he would embarrass himself or be rebuffed. Ultimately, he decided to seek out a professional for his first sexual experience. At 19, he hired an escort with the intention of addressing his sexual frustration, losing his virginity, and gaining experience and self-assurance in a situation where the outcome was foreseeable. He explained:

> It just kind of like—even though I was 19 and pretty old to be doing it for the first time . . . I was really starting to get to the point where I'm not meeting anyone. I really felt like I needed to like do this to kind of build my confidence up and [then] eventually do it with somebody I did care about it. . . . It was a frustrating experience. Let's just say I didn't finish. But afterwards I felt exhilarated because it was kind of like "I did it!" And I think that's why I did it that way, saw an escort, because it's kind of like I just needed to do it. Because I needed that confidence to be able to meet someone on my own.

Casey's story shows how fraught and important getting it is for young men like him. At 19, Casey felt too old to still be a virgin. Like other men, he saw it as a "stigma," which made him feel less manly than his peers.[27] He was unfulfilled and believed it was never going to happen in the way he wanted (with someone "special, somebody I was in a relationship with") particularly since he could barely imagine even talking to girls, let alone finding someone who would have sex with him. Even though he'd been studying pickup techniques and looking for sexual scripts to follow, his lack of confidence and knowledge regarding flirting, coupled with his insecurity in being able to carry out these scripts made him wary of going about things in a more casual way. So he went about getting it almost clinically, as if checking that first time off a task list.

Having sex with the escort, though frustrating since he did not ejaculate, made him feel more confident because at least he knew how to have sex and could say that he had done it. Although most men in Casey's position don't hire escorts, one study found that, for inexperienced men, having sex with a more mature or more knowledgeable woman was an effective face-saving strategy that allowed them to preserve their masculinity by both learning from and "getting" an older woman.[28] In Casey's case, experience provided knowledge that helped build confidence. As he explained:

> Right around that time, internet dating was getting bigger. It was still kind of a weird thing at the time. I started doing a lot of online dating and that kind of made it easier for me to meet women. . . . I'm a strong writer, so it was really easy for me to communicate with women in words. And so once I already had that rapport with women online, it was a lot easier to meet them in person. So that's—having that first encounter out of the way—there was definitely shame associated with that—especially the manner in which it happened, but there was also, it was really just twin feelings. Like really exhilarating feelings afterwards.

Casey's story illustrates the importance of getting sex to establish manhood and the difficulty some men have getting it. He wanted to lose his virginity for the sake of losing it, to both remove stigma and as a rite of passage (at 19, he felt it was time).[29] Until he gained experience he would not feel confident, but he was not confident enough to gain experience. Being with the escort helped him work up the nerve to pursue other women. This newfound self-assurance led him to chat up women online, where he could use his strength as a writer to flirt in a more careful and rehearsed manner. And eventually he took some of those relationships offline, too.

The business of prostitution, though not always or even primarily patronized by men who don't have access to sex through other means, provides evidence of the complexity associated with getting sex.[30] This, like the modern seduction trade, would not be such a profitable industry if getting and having sex were simple pursuits. Take Henry (59, married, consultant, white), also a self-described late bloomer, who had trouble finding women who were interested in him when he was starting out sexually. He, too, turned to a professional at the age of 30 because he felt this was the most efficient and productive way for him to have sex, since he had never done so at that point. Talking about his first time, he said, "That was in [another country], that was a prostitute, a very nice . . . girl. And I explained to her, 'I'm 30, I've never done this.' She explained, 'Yeah, that's fine.' [I felt] a little bit [nervous], but again, by 30, you know, I just figured, well, [I should have sex]."

Like Casey, Henry supposed since he was not meeting anyone he might as well get it out of the way with someone who wouldn't say no. Both men turned to professionals to affirm their status as men. Although Casey's and Henry's narratives may seem atypical, their lack of access to women, insecurities and fears of rejection were similar to most of the men in this study. Even Barry, the confident man quoted earlier who said he has figured out "the game," had a "pay to play" relationship for many months. He felt having sex with this woman for money or favors was easier than the work associated with a romantic relationship.

Getting sex, particularly when inexperienced, was a tricky endeavor and the men we spoke with did not want to fail. Many chose not to try to initiate sex or physical intimacy with women until or unless they received clear signs that their partner was receptive. They did this because they did not want to be perceived as unskilled or be rebuffed and, consequently, emasculated.[31] Soliciting sex from a professional mitigated some of the fears men had about rejection and failed expressions of masculinity. Paying put them in a position of control, too.

Who Gets the Girls: Identity Politics and Feelings of Desirability

There is no level playing field in the world of sex and dating, where the arena for finding partners has been described as an "erotic marketplace." Qualities like appearance, wealth, race, and social class work as capital that people either have or lack and can subsequently trade on.[32] The result: some people have more value than others and can be more selective in choosing sexual partners and for some men it is thus easier to prove themselves or signify masculine sexual selves. The men we interviewed not only had a lot to say about which women were more desirable, they also had strong feelings about who "gets the girls." Most men believed women had a preference for good-looking, athletic, tall, financially well-off, able-bodied, white or Black men sexual partners. When they themselves did not fall into these categories, they felt less able to attract women, particularly the ones more men wanted.

Appearance and Ability

Men said that being physically attractive and able-bodied were the most important things in the erotic marketplace. Strapping, fit men who resembled Ryan Gosling or Taye Diggs or James Bond (with the exalted actor/character depending on the generation and sometimes race of the interviewee) held the most erotic capital. Those men, interviewees thought, could get whichever girls they wanted. Many men came to this awareness early in their lives. Vlad (20, single, student, white), a first-generation Russian immigrant, noted that having acne as a teenager inhibited his chances with girls. He said he "felt like crap. I felt like I couldn't pick up a girl because of my face."

Minjun (39, married, educator, East Asian) felt his smaller frame and lack of masculine looks made him less desirable. He said, "A person like me, those kind of stereotypes was contributing to my—I think I was not very proud, as a man. I'm not tall, I'm not muscular, I'm not very handsome. . . . And I don't talk like, like manly person. . . . So I always thought maybe I'm not manly enough." Both Minjun and Vlad felt that girls and women would not be interested in them because they did not fit with conventional scripts of desirability. Vlad knew from cultural scripts in movies and on television that the guys who got the girls did not have pimples. Minjun's comment that he was "not very proud, as a man" due his appearance shows how much he connected looks to manhood. He knew he had to work harder than other men to convey masculinity.

Eli (64, divorced, consultant, white) also recalled that when he was a teenager his looks made it difficult to get the attention of coveted girls. Unlike Vlad or Minjun, however, at first Eli didn't understand why. He explained:

> I think that I was naive, overwhelmingly naive, because I didn't understand what I think a lot of my peers did and what it took to get a woman interested. I had no clue. I thought the only way to get a woman was to be funny, so that's what I did. I would be funny. I was a plump, husky little Jewish kid and so the only skill I had was my sense of humor and my intellect, so those are what I used. And the only women that seemed interested were Jewish, plump women who were not what I was looking for. So I was frustrated. . . . When I was 16, 17, I knew . . . for me that sexuality was a major interest. When I was in college I thought, well, that must be just every guy. But I was also not having it. My roommate as a freshman in college had this gorgeous girlfriend and every so often the two of them would sleep in the same room as me, because I had no place to go. And it used to kill me.

Eli's comments show not only the hierarchy of men but also women's roles as trophies.[33] The least desirable girls and women, in his estimation, were those available to men like him. But he wanted the girls he'd been socialized to want, and knew being with them would boost his status. His jealousy of his college roommate and his "gorgeous girlfriend" (not just girlfriend, but *gorgeous* girlfriend) shows how he saw himself in comparison. Women confer status and that status can enhance feelings about approximation of hegemonic masculinity.

For other men, being athletic or good looking (either by self-perception or by virtue of others' opinions) served as an advantage in the erotic marketplace, consistent with other sociological research.[34] Attractive men believed (and other men believe this of them as well) that they had their pick of women and could thus "get" the women who garnered them the most status. Brett (42, divorced, works in sales, white) commented on this. He said, "I think that luckily I'm pretty confident. I'm pretty attractive. So that helps when it comes to . . . finding a girl or . . . having a girl like you. So I'd say I've got that going on."

Knowing that women found him good-looking made Brett feel good—and his attractiveness was likely enhanced by his upper-middle class status. Although he didn't use terms like "erotic marketplace" or "hierarchy of men," he knew that his looks and wealth advantaged him throughout his life. As he explained, it was great knowing that girls were interested in him because "part of it was like—made you feel like a man at age 15, 16, 17 if you were having sex . . . even more than just the pleasure it gave you. Also like an ego thing."

Brett's comment, that feeling desired was better than the actual sexual activity, is quite telling. It shows that getting sex is not just about the physical experience. His friends could see that girls liked him and his popularity affirmed his manliness. For men like Brett, confirmation was easy and public and made him feel more confident and self-assured from an earlier age than was the case for men who were less attractive or less stereotypically masculine in appearance.

Bradley (49, married, health-care administrator, white) also said as much when he talked about the attention he received in high school. He said:

> I've had a great, I'm probably in the top 5 percent of what—other than rock stars and sports stars and just like super smoking Adonis's that could have another girl every night—I think I was in that category down where I thought that it was easy for me to get pretty girls. Not that I had sex with all of them but, you know. There were the football quarterbacks, I mean there was that whole group that—I wasn't in that one category but I was in the next category down. And some of my friends were with me, but a lot of them were in the lower categories that didn't have my experiences. So they lived through me and my friends.

Bradley very explicitly details a hierarchy of desirability and shows not only awareness of it, but the importance of it. He seems affirmed knowing he was near the top of the pack and that this meant he could relatively easily get not just girls, but "pretty girls." He had erotic capital to trade on, which granted him status among his peers. Less attractive peers had to settle with living vicariously through his stories and sexual experiences. Here again, the erotic capital of both men and women matter in defining men's sexual self-worth.

Peter (48, married, works in higher education, white) also commented on how his appearance has made it easier for him to get the attention of women and girls—even when he didn't necessarily want it. During the interview, he told John that he saw a text from one of his teenage children's friends that said he was "hot," about which he felt both complimented and embarrassed. When asked if he felt his sexuality was related to his feelings about his appearance, he replied: "I think for me there is some direct correlation. I told you about the text on the phone that I read. Not that I'm going to be on the cover of *GQ* or ever would have been, but I've been blessed . . . with enough physical traits that since I was young I've been complimented as far as the physical appearance goes." When asked if that made him feel better about his sexuality, he said, "Yeah, because it makes you feel more desired. I think that's part of it."

It's notable that all three of these were well-off or solidly middle class white men. Although there were Black men who described their race as a sexual advantage (which I discuss later in this chapter), they did not speak of their appearance or good looks in general as what helped them to get girls. The intersection of race and class privileged some men in the erotic marketplace.[35]

On the other side of the spectrum were men who felt their social status, appearance, or ability impeded their chances to have sex and their ability to convey masculinity as a key aspect of identity. Perhaps the man whose sexual self was most defined by his inability to get sex was Wesley, the never-married 68-year-old man introduced in Chapter 1. As noted, Wesley was born legally blind and throughout his adolescent, teen, and young adult years, he never had any intimate contact with girls or women. But, he learned to want the same women other men wanted. Initially, in his early days of pursuing women, he thought he might be able to get one of those coveted women. He said:

> What I learned in *Playboy* is that all women are beautiful. They're only too willing to take off their clothes. And they are oh so friendly and approachable—all you have to do is talk to them. Well, gosh! I can do that. So in my adulthood, when I thought I should go meet a woman, there was a radio show in my area . . . [and] the guy who ran the show also sponsored dances at these big banquet facilities. And a thousand people would show up at these dances. . . . That's where the girls are—you gotta go there! So I put on my best suit and aftershave and I go there and I look around the room and I picked out the women that I thought came out of the pages of *Playboy*. These were the tall, stacked blondes and I would approach them. And they were completely dismissive toward me, actually they were downright rude. How dare I even think I could speak to them? I wasn't on their level at all. It was a very heartbreaking experience to be treated that way. That's what I thought I was supposed to pursue!

Wesley went for the women he'd learned were the most prized and was surprised by their lack of interest in him. He knew that getting the attention of a woman like that would boost his status and make him feel like man. And his popular culture education made him believe they would be approachable and receptive. He describes the experience as "heartbreaking" but it also seems emasculating, as this was when he started to learn about power differences among men. He recognized that some men were always more likely to get the girl and he was not one of them.

As noted in Chapter 1, Wesley first had sex at the age of 35. This happened after he developed a friendship with his neighbor, a medical student. Knowing her busy schedule and trying to earn her favor, Wesley would cook her dinner and over time they grew closer. Because he had not been sexually intimate with a woman before, he had no expectations that anything physical would happen between them. He spoke of how he truly enjoyed her companionship—just having someone to share a meal with was exceptionally pleasurable to him. One day, however, things changed: "She invited me into her bed. And she was so fast! She could turn off the lights and be in the bed before the room got dark. If I had more time to think about it, I'm sure I would have chickened out. Because I did not know what I was doing." When asked if he thought the woman knew he was a virgin, Wesley said:

> At that moment in time, no. She just assumed me being older than her I must have had experience. But it turns out in her life I was number one-one, 11. I'm thinking, "You're 26 years old and you've had sex with 11 people?" I didn't know 11 people on the face of the earth! But she was very experienced. She knew what she wanted. She was the boss in bed and I was very happy to let her be the boss in bed. I was just happy—I was happy to be anywhere. It didn't—the relationship didn't last very long, unfortunately. . . . After 6 weeks, she got bored. And I had to watch a succession of men go out of her apartment.

Finally getting sex and a woman's interest felt affirming. Having someone pursue him allowed Wesley to feel seen and appreciated, which was something he had not felt much of in his life.[36] Before he had sex, he knew there was a part of his life that felt incomplete. He craved physical touch. After having sex, Wesley felt awakened as a man with sexual desires and as a person with a desire for *recognition*. He now understood the feeling of closeness and affection and, most important, attention from a woman. When the fling ended, being tuned into these feelings created a deeper sense of the loss of intimacy in his life—not to mention that he had to watch himself being displaced by other men with whom she subsequently hooked up. Sorrowfully, he said, "For the first time, I understood what I'm missing. So, yes, I wanted the approval. But I had an opinion based on experience rather than an opinion not based on experience, which I think changes your perspective quite a bit. So it became very important for me that a woman would want me in her bed."

Unfortunately, little changed for him after this. Very few women were interested in him during his life. And from his stories, most seemed interested in him for his money rather than because of feelings of warmth toward him. He told stories of multiple failed pursuits and empty, quid pro quo relationships in which women granted him limited access to their bodies in exchange for his taking care of them financially. Over time, he realized he would not have luck with women he felt were conventionally desirable. So he pursued women he thought others might not want in order to increase his odds of success in the erotic marketplace. In fact, he described the women he dated in rather pejorative and objectifying ways, saying:

> What kind of women did I have access to? Not the tall, stacked blondes—they wouldn't even talk to me. You can't drive, which means you can't go just anywhere that you want to go. So the kind of women I met were basically the kind of women who couldn't run fast enough to get away from me. Basically I dated women that other men would not date, for one reason or another. 'Cause they didn't put out, they weren't sexual enough.

> I dated women who were overweight, who had no boobs because they put on so much excess weight their boobs disappeared. But those were women that would tolerate me because they didn't have a lot of other choices. And they saw—I tried to be nice. They at least saw I was making the effort to make them feel pretty and appreciated and desired even if they weren't a 10. So they gave me a little, you know? That was my sex life. I always got a little but never too much. . . . I really don't know a woman until after I've touched her—and after I've touched her I've dated her for 6 months already. If she turns out to be grossly obese what are you going to do about it? Stop dating her after 6 months?

This strategy was one of practicality, not of respect or appreciation for women beyond their appearance, showing Wesley's internalization of trophyism ideologies.[37] He frames his actions as almost charitable—these were women who couldn't do any better—while at the same time acknowledging his clear understanding of his place in the hierarchy of men. Physical intimacy and getting it still affirmed his manhood, but less so than it did for men who knew they "scored the hot girl."

Most of Wesley's stories focused on his failures with women, which seemed to translate, for him, into his failure as a man. His only relationship characterized as one of mutual affection was with a woman with a mental illness who lived in a group home. Their relationship was challenging, however, because she was limited in the time she could see him and because neither could drive. The relationship ended when she stayed out with him one night past her curfew. Her family found out and took her out of state. Soon after, he learned she had passed away. This was a crushing blow to Wesley, as he had loved her and believed she also had strong feelings for him. Since that time, he has not had a relationship or felt desired by anyone. This tragedy, coupled with his lifetime of failed relationships and sexual pursuits, left him feeling depressed and hopeless about his sexuality. He pondered, as did most of the unpartnered men in their fifties and sixties with whom we spoke, whether he would ever have sex again.

If he *could* ever get it again. Still, when asked if sexuality was an important part of his identity, Wesley replied:

> It's very important for me to have a physical connection with a woman. I haven't touched a woman in the past 10 years. So that's very, very missing and it's a single source of sadness in my life that I don't know what specific steps I can take to bring it about. There's no plan as to how to go—[to] have it. I don't know what nightclubs I need to go to. I don't know what clothes I need to wear. I don't know what words I need to say. I'm 68 years old. My sex life may be over already without my even realizing it.

Wesley's declaration of defeat illustrates how men of all ages struggle with getting it and how getting it remains important as a measure of a man. Even at 68, he is still pondering clothing and word choices and how to present himself so he stands out among men. Although not all are as physically limited as Wesley or feel that way, many of the single men said similar things about feeling as if they did not know the "specific steps" necessary to help them get women's attention, even when they wanted it desperately.

Despite scripts that frame men as generally sexually self-assured and knowledgeable, few of the men interviewed for this study came across or described themselves as such. The ones who did were men who knew they were attractive and had consistently been in relationships and had sexual partners. They were also often men with class privilege. So, when getting it was not a challenge due to their appearance or other erotic capital, they were more self-possessed.

Race, Class, and Sexual Desirability

Many of the men we spoke with described race as salient in their sexuality and in the hierarchy of men, consistent with popular culture scripts about desirability.[38] Asian men, in particular, felt not as attractive compared with men of other races.[39] Greg (20, single, student, South Asian), explained how he feels his race impacts his ability to "get girls." He said:

> I feel like if I were to try to go out and date a girl my chances are limited because, minus Asians, the majority of girls don't want to date an Asian man. You never usually see that, you never see a Black girl with an Asian guy, a white girl with an Asian guy. And I'm not really that tall and I don't really look like manly or anything. I look like a kid. So that's—my pool of girls that I can choose from is like severely limited. . . . I [am] more attracted to like the darker skinned Asians and stuff like that, and more tanned white girls. But like I just felt like I never had a chance to look at white girls or Black girls 'cause, you know, my appearance just like they don't—I don't think anyone wants someone as short, like young, super young looking [and] Asian. That's like a "No," like Tinder swipe (laughs).

Similar to most of the Asian men in this study, Greg recognized stereotypes about Asian men's desirability. Most Asian interviewees also noted their tendency to be physically smaller, both in terms of body and genital size, which they felt made them seem less sexual or masculine. Clearly, their sexual self-images were influenced by cultural scenarios. Greg's comment that women would "swipe no" on Tinder because of his race is indicative of his internalization of these ideologies about Asian men's sexualities (and masculinities) and about women's perceived role in affirming standards of desirability.

In contrast, some men saw race as a marker of their desirability that made it easier for them to attract women and have sex. Although Glenn (58, single, retired), who is biracial with white and Pacific Islander roots, sometimes felt burdened by the attention he got from women, he also noted the advantages associated with looking different. He told me, "I got very, very—I got a lot of confidence in me, in my looks, too. Even for my age I still look good—that's what they tell me (laughter). I don't have no problem catchin' no female, put it like that."

I asked, if he felt like women have been drawn to him due to his being biracial. He replied, "Yes . . . I got the eyes, the hair, the build, I got everything they want. More nationality. So I see myself more—I guess I could say international. . . . Wherever I go, wherever I went somebody chose me . . . wherever I go all with a buzz, you know?"

Notably all of the men who commented on their race as an asset, like Glenn (who lived in a West Coast city), lived or grew up in urban areas in the Northeast or on the West Coast where interracial dating or hooking up were more socially accepted and where there was more racial diversity. Other than Glenn, most of the men who said their race could be an advantage were Black. White men rarely mentioned race as playing a part of their own sexual self, probably because white men are likely to have lower racial identification.[40] But, about one-third of the Black men mentioned that their race sometimes helped in "getting it," particularly from white women who expressed curiosity about stereotypes related to Black men's sexual virility. For example, Jack (32, dating, works in media, Black) said:

> I'm sure my race has absolutely played a part in some of my younger getting laid days. 'Cause I was absolutely, on a few occasions, the rebellious "He's a black guy that my parents will like" blah blah blah. I definitely got into a couple of situations over and over again where my race definitely got me laid. I can't say it played a part in the way I behave towards sexuality, but I know that it has affected the way other people have behaved towards me. . . . I know more often than not it has been because of me, the charm and the humor and just all of that in general. But there have definitely been times where someone was just basically trying to "Try out Black." I've heard once or twice "I wanna see if what they say about Black guys is true."

Curtis (55, engaged/previously divorced, retired military, Black) said he once was with a white woman who admitted she wanted to be with him because of his race. He said, "After we had sex . . . she told me that she never had sex with a Black guy before and she was hearing these thoughts or whatever. You know? I told her that stuff is not true. You know—Black guys—not all Black guys are dogs but not all Black guys are good. Stuff like that. It just depends on the guy and the chemistry you have.... She said, 'I wanted to have sex with a Black guy and I wanted to do it with you.'"

For both of these men, as well as several others, feeling desired because of their race elicited mixed feelings. They were happy to have sex but not as happy about the idea that what was appealing was serving as an object in a white woman's experiment, fantasy, or rebellion. Like most other men we interviewed (in many circumstances), they wanted to be wanted for who they were not what they represented to others. This reveals the complexity of sex as an affirmation of manhood. When men were objectified or othered due to their race and when women shifted from affirming manhood to affirming racial desirability, men of color seemed conflicted about how these sexual encounters signified manhood.

Class was a major factor in men's assessment of the hierarchy of desirability and their perception of value in the erotic marketplace. Being financially successful or at least stable is a key measure of manhood.[41] Most men mentioned the importance of money or wealth in getting girls or women, and thus, sex. When asked about the relationship between class and sexuality, many said that if they had more money they probably would have had more sex or at least an easier time getting sex.

Ruben (35, single, customer service representative, Black) mentioned that cultural images about the importance of money in men's desirability fuel connections between class and sexuality. He said, "It's all about—it's not even about your looks anymore. If you have—it's about your possessions that get you sex.... You can be the most ignorant person, but as long as you got the most drop top, reddest, nice looking car, your bank account's fat, and they see some jewelry, you can be as stupid as you want to be. Somebody gonna want you."

Several men noted that it was not just class but the intersection of class with race, as well as ability and appearance, which created advantage for certain men. Craig (31, dating, project manager, East Asian) was especially passionate about this. He harangued:

> Women love to say "I like a sweet sensitive guy." . . . I've heard it from every girl I've dated. "I like a guy with a good sense of humor." . . . They like certain things but in reality . . . they want someone who is stable. Who has a good job, ok? . . . Women say a lot of things they don't mean at all. "I would never—I don't care what kind of car a guy drives." I'm like, "Would you go out with a guy that takes you on a bus? Probably not right? But if he comes rolling up to you in a Beemer you're going to say yeah." . . . I've been on a date where these girls actually say bold-faced, out loud, "I will not date a guy that owns a car more than 3 years old." They said this to my face, ok? In mixed company. They're not shy now.

Craig's embittered association of money and sexual allure as signifying masculine desirability—as well as his sexist classification of women as overwhelmingly shallow and superficial—highlight sexual scripts that shape his thinking about "getting" women. Although Craig was more vocal than most, many men made the connection between class and desirability—which the women I interviewed for *Deserving Desire* never mentioned in terms of their own "value." Having money was recognized by about half of the interviewees as significant in being desirable or being perceived as masculine. This shows how men in this study constructed sexual scripts that position men as providers and women as dependents, reinforcing gender hierarchies.

Accomplishment, Experience, and Acceptance: What "Getting It" Means to Men

Having sex, particularly in early experiences, was meaningful as both achievement and affirmation for the majority of men in this study. Jack (32, dating, works in media, Black) said, "I feel that even if it's a girl I don't want to sleep with . . . knowing that she wants to sleep with me comes off as a positive regardless." Being wanted made Jack feel good, likely because he knew this was a measure of manhood.

Unlike other cultures, secular American society lacks formal rites of passage to adulthood.[42] So, in Western societies, sexual experience, particularly virginity loss, serves as a tacit initiation into manhood.[43] I found that men spoke of "getting it" this way. Telling of his first sexual experiences, Peter (48, married, works in higher education, white) explained, "It makes you feel like more of a man. . . . You feel like you're in a club. . . . You feel a little more complete." Many interviewees echoed this idea of being in a "club" or feeling like a man. Having sex legitimated their maturity and masculinity and made them feel they belonged among other men. In this way, getting sex or a girl or woman to have sex with them increased their status in the hierarchy of men. So "getting it" was more than a rite of passage. It was a way of confirming manhood and being able to feel that they were "normal" or "like everyone else."

Donny (20, single, student, East Asian), born and raised outside of the United States, said he felt a sense of relief when he lost his virginity because it meant he could join conversations and not be embarrassed or emasculated by inexperience. He said that after having sex, he felt "finally I tried it, and I know what this is. And when I was 18, before the sex, there was shame—shame, to me. So at that time, people would ask you, 'Are you still a virgin?' I kept saying no because they will laugh at you if they know you don't have experience. After now, after I attend college, uh I think it's different. I can say, 'Yes, I have experience.'"

In this way, the experience was not *just* about knowing what to do (which it was partly) or knowing that a girl liked him (which it partly was also) but also about knowing he could join conversations with other people (presumably other men) and truthfully say that he had sex. The shame or stigma of being a virgin was no longer something Donny had to carry or mask. Men like Donny felt the need to try to "pass" as more sexually experienced in conversation.[44] Here again, this shows how sexual discourse is a critical aspect of the collective performance of masculinity and the importance of women in enabling men to participate in the conversation.[45]

Although Walker (39, married, works in information technology, biracial) had his first sexual experience at a younger age than Donny, he basically communicated the same idea. He said having sex for the first time "gave me some credibility as a guy, in the neighborhood. Definitely gave me something worthwhile to talk about at that time, I felt. I could call somebody and say, 'Hey, hey! Today was the day!' . . . I made my first 3-pointer. Now I'm not in the same pool as the other lowly lot." Both Donny and Walker differentiate between experienced and inexperienced men, with the status hierarchy clearly identified. Being able to truthfully say they'd "gotten it" made Donny and Walker feel they had something on less-experienced peers. This is all critical in signifying a masculine self.

When asked what getting sex the first time meant to him, Warren (40, engaged, surveyor, Latino) replied, "It meant an accomplishment. Like she was my girlfriend and having sex was not guaranteed, it was something I had to work for. And like a good ol' American boy *if I got it, then I accomplished something*" (emphasis added). Warren's memory of this relationship contains some reluctance on the part of his girlfriend. He *worked* at getting her to say yes, so it felt like a triumph when it happened. He proved himself in his ability to be powerful, to have his will realized, consistent with ideals of manhood.

Warren, born in Central America, noted that in his case this meant achievement not only as a man but also as an *American* man. He emphasized that the first girl he was with was white and in that way he saw her as a badge of assimilation. He explained, "I mean with the white woman, you know, it feels like an accomplishment. Like, 'Yeah, I got a blonde, blue-eyed woman.' In terms of sex, just the whole dynamic of difference makes it more interesting." Warren's objectification of this woman shows how he viewed her as a tool in enhancing not only his feelings of accomplishment in being able to "get" a woman like her but also his status as a man and position in the hierarchy of men. In her study of seduction training, sociologist Jane Ward noted the ways in which "coaches invite and normalize the fetishization of white women's bodies. They all but promise white women to male trainees, men for whom sexual access to 'hot blondes' symbolizes not only heteromasculine success but also successful assimilation as an immigrant."[46] Among men attending these seduction trainings, white, blonde women were highly coveted for these reasons. Like Warren, such men recognized either implicitly or explicitly what being with or getting women like that meant for them.

Repeatedly, the idea of getting specific types of girls—those who, because of their appearance, possessed more erotic capital than others—was important to men. Being with "hot girls" resulted in a qualitatively different assessment of getting it than when men "got" less desirable women. Men's talk of women in this manner was the clearest articulation of the idea of women as objects of affirmation. Most of the men we spoke with reinforced the notion that the most beautiful women were prizes for the best men.

Curtis (55, engaged, retired military, Black), for instance, said he felt excited about his first time because, "The girl was hot. And I wanted her. And all the guys thought she was hot and I was like, 'Hey man.' . . . I was the man then. I was a man now." Curtis proves himself as "the man," by getting some*thing* that other men coveted. Curtis likely felt more powerful, more desirable than other guys—because he "got" this hot girl and other men did not. It was like he won in an imagined competition with other men. Sociologists Douglas Schrock and Michael Schwalbe argue that "successful manhood acts elicit deference from others in concrete situations."[47] When Curtis gets the woman that other men want, he can feel a sense of victory and esteem.

Although generally ancillary to their stories, many of the men in this study emphasized how attractive past or present sexual partners were, seemingly as a means of conveying their own desirability. The implication of their choice to share that detail was to confirm they could attract and "get" women that other men wanted, thus demonstrating their place in the hierarchy of men as well as the objectification of women as "trophies" representing that position.[48] I italicize comments about women's appearance to underscore the commonality of this.

Barry (44, engaged, postal worker, Black) reflected on women he'd been with before he met his fiancé, saying, "Through all the years that I been [having] sex. . . . I had my hand on *some of the most finest women* all around. Almost all across [this city] and I could say I had my hands on all of them. On every last one of them."

Luke (42, married, financial professional, white) told a story about dating after his divorce during which he described the appearance of women he'd dated. He said:

> The first person I had sex with after I was divorced, she was younger than me, *very attractive, had done some modeling*. She was Black, and I was a white guy, and that was different for me. And the sex was good, particularly from her point [of view]. . . . I had a few more relationships. . . . One of them, she was probably the #1 news anchor in [Western city] and *she was incredibly attractive*. . . . I remember seeing this woman, going, that's an amazing woman . . . [and] all of a sudden she wanted to have sex one night. I was like, really? Ok.

The details in Luke's story highlight the physical and stereotypical qualities associated with his sexual partners. Models and anchorwomen are generally known for needing to be exceptionally attractive to be in those jobs. His emphasis on the physical attributes of his sexual partners and his inclusion of these details in his response to questions about sexual experiences after his divorce show how much this mattered to him.

Bradley (49, married, health-care administrator, white) also honed in on the appearance of his sexual partners as key detail in his stories of sexual conquests.

- "When I graduated high school this *beautiful girl* came up to me at a bar and said, 'You're Bradley?' And I said, 'Yeah.' I had no clue who she was. And she said, 'You know, my name is so and so,' I forget her name, and said, 'I had the biggest crush on you.' . . . We ended up like messing around in my car that night, like just—only because *she was really good looking* and I blew it 'cause I could have had her in high school."

- "There was a girl I liked . . . [she] kind of had a crush on me . . . *she was so developed—D cups, beautiful body, blue eyes, blonde hair*, and I saw her again and was like wow. And we just started swimming in the pool for a few days and then all of a sudden we were kissing."
- On a woman he dated for two and a half years: "*She was in the high school homecoming court, absolutely beautiful girl*. . . . And my friend said, 'You'll never get a girl like that, you know? I couldn't even get her.' I took her to the prom, all we did was like kiss twice and that was it, you know, I was fixated . . . I loved being with her, I loved having sex with her. *I loved just that every guy just puts me on a pedestal when they see me with her, like wow, he's with that girl.*"
- "And after about a year of dating her, [this] *beautiful Italian girl*, she asked me to marry her one Sunday."
- On a woman he dated secretly, because she was married, "Thursday night was set for this *beautiful girl*. And it was a thing where she needed it and I needed it."
- "She was *the hottest little 5'1", little Spanish chick, and every guy was checking her out, and I liked that*. I had no problems going out and a guy was like checking her out because like I knew that she felt it and I knew that hey, guys liked her, I got points."

In every example of every relationship or sexual encounter, Bradley, like many other men, detailed the appearance of the woman he was with. He mentions this as a way of telling about himself. When he was in his prime, he could garner the attention of women whom other men wanted—he "got points" for being with these women. He got them, which means other men did not. It is not just that he could "get girls," but these *beautiful* women who raised his status by being with him.[49] He mentions that he liked when other people stared or were jealous because it allowed him a feeling of superiority that those women chose him. At the time of the interview, Bradley had been married for about twenty years. It may be that reflecting on those experiences allowed him to feel a sense of pride and identification with his younger sexual self, one who had the freedom and opportunity to validate his desirability and show off a masculine self through relationships with "hot" women.[50]

In these stories, men who emphasized partners' appearance could have focused on what a kind or nice or loving person their partner was. They could have talked about other personality traits or about the quality of their sexual experiences (which some did, though not as frequently) or women's sexual skills. However, such characteristics say less about a man's manhood and status in the erotic marketplace. The accomplishment of getting—*even more than having*, made them feel powerful. In interviews, they may have been more interested in or concerned with presenting a masculine self, since the interview focused on heterosexual sexual identities—and perhaps more so with men interviewers than with me (all of the men quoted above were interviewed by Jonathan or John). Hot women were trophies or symbols of men's status.[51]

Like the men Rachel O'Neill interviewed or those Jane Ward observed in studies of the seduction industry, the men we spoke with were not at all hesitant to present a list of aesthetic qualities that objectified women and reduced them to their physicality.[52] Women I interviewed for my study on women's sexuality seldom mentioned a man's "hotness" or their own wealth or lack thereof as a contributing factor in their dating lives or their sexual selves. They rarely commented on men's looks and never as an indication of their own status or femininity. But it was clear that for the men we interviewed, getting it—sex and sex with particularly desirable women—was important in their performance of masculinity because they defined it as central in proving themselves as men. In these stories, women's chief role was as an object that affirmed manhood and status.

Getting sex meant proving manhood. When getting it, both in the form of understanding sex and its mechanics and in gaining access to it in early experiences, girls and women functioned as objects of affirmation, whose presence or absence influenced men's status and relative power among men. Women mattered—and attractive women more so than those deemed less attractive—because they were markers of manhood. Boys could say they had experience, could contribute capably to conversations about sex when they had been with girls. This is not to say that as boys, teens, or young men the interviewees only thought of girls and women as objects. Some talked with affection and tenderness about their early sexual partners or first loves; yet these women generally still came off as means to manhood or prizes for their position in the hierarchy of men.

PART II

Having It

CHAPTER 4

Having It

PROFICIENCY, PRESSURE, AND PERFORMANCE

[In my early 30s] I started learning about [women] and how their feelings are and how my feelings are towards them. And then it was all about them. As I said, there's times I don't ejaculate and they [climax]. . . . I would always ask afterwards if they did. I mean, I think it's important they do. . . . My satisfaction is that they're satisfied. I'm not worried about me, I'm worried about them. It's always been that way since my 30s. . . . The meaning [of sex] for me is that they enjoy being with me and having sex with me and that, in their eyes, I am going to perform. And not only I perform but hopefully I have—that they think I perform the way they want me to perform. . . . I'm not happy if they're not. If there is a problem with my performance, I like to know so I can work on it.

—Barry, 44

Barry, an engaged Black postal worker living in the mid-Atlantic region of the United States, worried about sex. He didn't worry about getting it, he worried about doing it well and pleasing partners. As he entered into relationships he wanted to be sure that he performed capably. Barry sought out "reviews" from partners so he could take those suggestions and improve for the next time. He wanted to exceed expectations and be better than other men. This focus on partners' satisfaction was a newer thing for Barry. In his younger years, he didn't think much about the women he was with. It was all about him and his gratification. For a long time, that was how he thought sex should go.

Barry learned about sex in his teenage years by watching pornographic videos with his father. It was his dad who told stories about his own proficiency, describing, for example, how one time he had "sex with women 10 times in one day." Pornography taught Barry "how to talk to some women, when to talk to them. . . . It taught me as far as physical things. . . . What they like the most and what's better for them and what's better for myself." These images and scripts stayed with him and he's used pornography as a basis for comparison in thinking about his own sexual performance. Learning about sex in this way likely provided cumulative disadvantage. He's tried to live up to a fictive standard of performance that does not typically bear success in real life.[1] He equated pleasure and satisfaction with the routinized sex he saw in pornography and seemed to believe that doing it this way would prove something about him as a man.

Barry didn't actually start having sex until he was 21 when, while in the military, friends set him up with "this chunky girl [who] wanted to have sex with me." Given this, he thought of himself as somewhat of a late bloomer, not feeling confident during his teen years. But, his first experience taught him he "was good at it. And I am good at it till this day. I had no complaints," he shared, laughing. He has enjoyed having sex with many partners, more often choosing multiple partners over monogamy, even when in relationships. For him, getting sex was not a problem. But having it—despite his statement about being good at it—was more complex. A bad experience in his twenties led him to doubt himself.

> [I met this woman] who was married to a cop. I worked at [an auto parts store] back in the '90s. There was [a] woman I helped put a headlight on for. She gave me her number and uh, you know, she told [me] she was married and I didn't care. And she wanted to have sex. And we had sex out in her car somewhere and she, uh, she said, "I thought it would be bigger." And I said, damn. . . . That was the only complaint I ever had. . . . I was shocked and surprised. Rejected 'cause I never got with

> her again. Obviously she must have had some big dude. . . . Obviously I didn't satisfy her or something.

This one "complaint" stayed with Barry. His narrative around "working on it" and improving his technique to ensure satisfaction was likely influenced by this experience. He remembered and chose to share this as a negative experience, one in which racial stereotypes about the size of Black men's genitals were held up as an expectation that he did not meet.

Barry, like a few other men we interviewed, described racially specific scripts related to sexual performance, which provide some context for his emasculation in the above-described experience. He said, "I believe that Black men have to perform better than white men sexually. Definitely. I can't say really how. I guess it depends on how the women feel. I don't know exactly how they feel about it. I just know they expect Black men to perform a lot better than white men." Barry thus felt another layer of pressure or expectation for how he was supposed to show up in sexual encounters; his intersectional identity influenced the way he thought he needed to have sex.

Barry's concerns about sexual performance were echoed in the stories of the majority of men in this study. In addition to uneasiness about getting sex, they felt apprehensive about *how* they had sex. Were they doing it "right?" Were they satisfying women? Were they lasting long enough? Were they big enough? Were they as good as, if not better than, other men their partners had been with? These questions dogged men when they reflected on their past sexual experiences. Like Barry, men wanted to feel that their partners saw them as "performing how they want[ed them] to perform" and felt like failures as men if they failed to please women. Sex only affirmed manhood for Barry, like other men in this study, when he felt that he did it well.

Barry's emphasis on his partner's pleasure (although for many men pleasure seemed to be defined as orgasm—which was something men frame as their responsibility to provide) and on getting it "right" show the performance pressures that dominate sexual scripts in contemporary culture.[2] From movies, music videos, and pornography, women are shown as desirous and men as responsible for their pleasure.[3] Sex is not defined in these images primarily by men's ejaculation, despite discourses around the male sex drive.[4] Instead, pornography and popular culture depictions of sex geared toward straight men teach men about sexual mastery, domination, and providing women with sexual gratification.[5] These scripts guide men's ideas about sexual performance.

And as much as men like Barry wanted to satisfy women, concern for a partner's pleasure was also about men's ego and sexual self-image.[6] Psychologist Gary Brooks suggests that masculinity is "elusive," such that "men are never really sure manhood is established, since any failure can be cause for re-evaluation of manliness."[7] Masculinity is thus tenuous, and men ascertain that they must consistently work to prove it, throughout their lives.[8] Men learn that women's "bodies and sexual responsiveness are direct avenues to feelings of virility."[9] In this way, women validate manhood with their reactions to men's sexual performance. Straight U.S. men learn that women should affirm a good performance and if women complain then men have failed as men.[10]

Here, women serve simultaneously as objects and agents of affirmation. Men looked to scripts from pornography and popular culture for what they believed made for a strong performance—and for what types of reactions from women signaled it. In this way, women were fungible objects, unilateral in their expected response, which was interpreted as a reaction to men's behavior—rather than to women's own actions during sex. Yet they are also agents of affirmation because their reactions, reviews, or rebuffs are seen as instrumental in guiding men's performance. In having sex, men *perceive* women as having power to reinforce or refute their enactment of masculinity.[11] In this way, sex is a performance of gender.[12] Men "do" or fail to do masculinity in having sex. In the remaining chapters of the book, I share examples of how men framed and thought of sex in this way—both in how they had it and in their fears about not being able to have it.

The Proficient Man: Doing It (or Not Doing It) Right

"If you can't perform like a sexual dynamo then society tells you you're less of a male, less of a man. It's not just that women throw themselves at men because they look like men, it's because they're satisfied."—Patrick (25, dating, educator and graduate student, white)

"It was a lot of the 'Am I doing this right?' in the back of my head. Not necessarily is this good or satisfying. More like driving a car. 'Am I braking far enough from the stop sign? Am I putting my turn signal on soon enough before I turn?' The mechanics [not enjoyment]—it was more don't screw this up."—Scott (37, married, educator, white).

As I listened to men interviewed for this study talk about having sex, it was clear that most believed there was a right and wrong way to do it. Sexual scripts, particularly those informed by pornography and popular culture, generally feature a "Proficient Man" image. The Proficient Man is sexually self-assured and skilled; his manhood is affirmed by his sexual performance. He is thus rewarded with attention from desirable women and recognition from other men.[13] This is a man who can maintain an erection for hours (and has a partner who sees this as a good thing)—who is always ready and always satisfies. He is James Bond. He is Joey from *Friends*. He is Ryan Gosling in *Crazy, Stupid, Love*. He is the lead singer of a rock band. He is Cristiano Ronaldo and Derek Jeter. He is Tony Stark and Don Draper and a host of other fictional characters and celebrity men. This is a script men know well and support—a recent study found that both men and women believed men should be strong sexual performers who are able to gratify their partners.[14] And this is true even when it doesn't match their own experiences or desires.[15]

The image of the Proficient Man influenced men in this study—both in the way they thought about sex and in the way they actually had it. This was especially true in early encounters when men had little else to go on.

Kent (47, married, sales manager, white), for instance, felt disadvantaged by his relatively late start and few sexual experiences. Going into his first experience at the age of 23, he recalled thinking, "I heard a million times about sex not taking long enough for the female to be satisfied and that definitely was on my mind." Because he was in his 20s, Kent felt apprehensive, as he had fewer years to practice and get it "right." He said, "I think the majority of it is a psychological issue and, you know, anxiety, not just performance anxiety, but anxiety in general. I honestly do believe that there is some measure of a physical experience there that was lacking and [it] inhibited my performance."

While there are sexualized bumbling or awkward men characters in popular culture that men we interviewed referenced (such as Jim Levenstein in *American Pie*), those characters do not come off as masculine in an idealized way.[16] They are men to laugh along with or at, not to aspire to be like. Dominant cultural scenarios weighed heavily on the men in this study during their early sexual experiences. As noted in Chapter 2, many men felt they did not fully understand sex until they had it. But they felt pressure to successfully do something they did not really know how to do. Because they didn't fully understand how to control their bodies, men told stories of premature ejaculations or inability to sustain erections as long as they felt they were supposed to.

Dennis (67, married, retired, white) recalled feeling concerned about how he performed his first time. He said, "I remember like the first time I had sex—that's exactly what I thought—is she going to laugh at me? Was I any good? Did she enjoy it? But of course you don't want to ask because if you're asking then, you know, you're not confident in yourself." Brett (42, divorced, works in sales, white) spoke of similar concerns going into his first sexual experience, "I mean you just want to make sure you can get it up. I don't think even back then—like I didn't know anything about trying to give a girl an orgasm or anything like that. I just wanted . . . [to] make sure I wasn't a total failure."

Brett and Dennis, like many other interviewees, had the same concerns—would they do it right? Would they get an erection and maintain it long enough to pull off a solid performance? Or would they be embarrassed and emasculated by doing something wrong? In all these situations feelings of pressure were implicit if not explicit. Men used language of success and failure and their narratives revealed the ways in which their first sexual experiences were proving grounds for manhood. They knew cultural scripts identified high-status men as ones who satisfied women and did not suffer from erectile malfunctions. And they wanted to be in that category. Early on, pleasure was not the main concern—it was getting through the experience without being embarrassed in front of women partners. As sociologist Scott Melzer noted in his research on members of an online support group for men who were concerned about their penis size and functionality, this "pressure to impress alienates men from their own bodies, as well as potential and actual sexual partners."[17] Men see their bodies as tools for performance and women as agents of affirmation or denial of the quality of that performance.

Pornography: Learning and Unlearning Sexual Scripts

Australian political theorist Ian Cook, who has studied pornography and masculinity, notes that men use pornography to acquire knowledge about sex. They see that men in web pornography are dynamic, virile, and skilled.[18] Men in pornography are confident and do not have performance issues.[19] Thus, according to Cook, "men are anxious to prove themselves and become more anxious as more needs to be done to prove themselves."[20] In contrast to the still images of women contained in the often covertly acquired *Playboy* magazines viewed by older men we interviewed (in their forties to sixties), live-action, omnipresent web pornography constructs a masculine sexuality that is powerful, well-endowed, and able to please (and often conquer) hypersexualized women partners. It provides interpersonal scripts and cultural scenarios for what having sex looks like.

For participants, this hindered more than it helped. Pornography aimed at straight men added pressure on men to try to emulate this hypermasculine style of having sex, much of which casts women as sexual things, devoid of emotion or humanity.[21] These images—which tend to focus on expending women to physical depletion—reinforce the devaluation of women more broadly as well as activating the script that women love to be used, often violently, as sexual objects.[22] When men take these fictional interpersonal scripts into real situations, it rarely yields good results for anyone.[23] So, in addition to using pornography to understand or "get" the mechanics of sex, men in this study watched it to learn how to "have" it—that is, to learn sexual techniques or positions or skills. Men's language and pride associated with wearing out women to the point of exhaustion show their internalization of these scripts and their understanding of sex as a manhood act. For younger men (those born after about 1975), it is not just about "doing it," but "doing it well." Where many older men in this study felt affirmed by having sex, many of the younger men focused more on being viewed as sexual dynamos known for their prowess.

Viewing pornography is normalized in American society for boys and men.[24] Studies find that approximately 90 percent of men have viewed pornography at some point and that nearly half of men are weekly users.[25] It's not too surprising then that many men we spoke with had a story about how pornography affected their sexuality. Take, for instance, Casey (29, engaged, works in media, white), who said:

> I started watching pornography as a teenager, like on the internet. . . . I think there is an addictive nature to pornography and masturbation and stuff and I think—I think viewing that kind of thing over and over again I think that does kind of alter your perception—maybe perceiving women as objects and stuff. But more than that, I think it just kind of warps your perceptions of how sex works in real life. Kind of, I think, I've heard people make jokes like ordering a pizza . . . if you were the delivery guy that every call you get you were going to be invited in to have sex with somebody.

> And that's not how it really works. I think more than what they say about men viewing women as objects from pornography, I think what's the bigger danger than that is that it—what I've experienced in my life is that it warps your perception of how sexual situations occur in real life.

Casey describes a variety of sexual scripts he gleaned from watching porn. Even though he realized they were not realistic, on one level he also felt as if he couldn't help but imagine their possibility. When he had sex and it wasn't like this, it took some adjusting to figure out how to have it. There is research to support Casey's claim that viewing pornography, particularly heavy viewing of it, can impact men's attitudes about women, such as causing them to see sex as an arena for domination of women.[26]

Minjun (39, married, instructor, East Asian) internalized scripts of patriarchal dominance from watching pornography, but later concluded that this did not serve him well. He grew up in Asia and watched a lot of Japanese pornography—which he said depicted submissive women who rarely displayed sexual needs or desires. These videos provided interpersonal scripts that encouraged him to objectify his partners. He said:

> I think [sex is] a man dominating a woman and . . . touching certain parts of the body to please. And so it's just certain part, I was focusing on certain part. And it wasn't—a relationship is never intended. . . . Japanese version had ladies . . . and they make noises a lot. And they make noises as if they really liked it. So, as a person who likes to help and things like that, I feel like I always have burden to please. But also in a violently dominating sex that I see from the Western pornography made me think I can do something like that.

In Minjun's first sexual experiences with women, he approached them as objects to be controlled because that's what he learned from pornography. Having been coerced and abused by an older man in his first sexual experiences (see Chapter 2), he had no real-life experiences with women/consensual partners and so did not know of sex as anything else. Sex was about power and he took what he saw in pornography as instruction that he be the one who controlled the situation. He saw heterosexual sex as a gendered act with both dominant and subordinate roles.

This is not an uncommon way of viewing heterosexual sex and women's role in it. In rape cultures like the United States, men are taught to think of women as conquests and of sex as a means of establishing manhood through aggressive performance.[27] There is contradiction here in that while most men do not sexually assault or force themselves on women, men learn that aggressive sexual behavior will be well received by women partners. So, men who focus on pleasing their partners in this way may be following scripts that objectify women, even if objectification is not their aim. Rather, they think this is what makes a good performance and confers manhood.

Through experience, some men "unlearn" these scripts. For Minjun, this happened after college when he met a woman who told him that the way he was having sex was not at all pleasing to her. He explained:

> So the girl I met before my wife, we dated for a year and we were sexually fairly active. And we really enjoyed it. I think she kind of helped me realize that I am doing this with someone who has personality and who has [the] right to feel, to be respected and things like that. Because a lot of things that I—a lot of information about sexuality I had was from pornography. So a lot of Japanese pornography I watched conceptualized the woman as kind of servant . . . and not a person I need to be very attentive [to]. She expressed—my ex-girlfriend expressed—that [I was] not very attentive to the person [I was] doing sex with. So that kind of helped me understand it's a relationship. . . . I think I began to perceive women as human being and not as an object.

It took a real relationship with his former girlfriend (and later his wife) to change the way he had sex. Different from the scripts he'd picked up both from pornography and his own abuse as a child, Minjun had to learn a new script centered on mutual gratification. With his wife, he said, "It's something we do together and we enjoy together. And I don't have to work hard to please her and like to give orgasms to her." As he changed the way he had sex, sex became better for his partners and for him as well.

Dean (33, married, property manager, biracial) also recognized the downsides of using pornography as a guide to having sex. His story reveals the ease with which what he learned from pornography filtered into his thoughts and created pressures to do it "right." He explained:

> Pornography puts a lot of unrealistic expectations into one's mind. Especially dudes. If she doesn't moan a certain way, you're failing. If she doesn't shake a certain way, you're failing. It puts incredible stupid unrealistic expectations 'cause not everybody reacts the same way. Obviously some people are quiet. Some people are loud. It's actually kind of damaging. . . . I feel . . . a lot more free and a lot less pressure when it comes to sex when I'm not looking at pornography. Like I said, I don't do it very often. I really don't. But when I do, I do feel intense pressure all of a sudden. Like I get nervous if my wife says she wants to have sex. Why do I feel nervous? She's my wife . . . I really, really love her. . . . . There's a societal opinion that if you don't constantly satisfy your wife she will lose interest in you and she will go somewhere else. And so the moment you don't perform, the moment you have a night where it doesn't happen, or the moment something goes awry, it just builds and it builds and it builds and it builds. And it sucks, it's a horrible feeling, because all it is, it's just pressure. It's just . . . your own mind, what society tells you. It's not like anything's actually going on. My wife is not going to leave me. She loves me. But in my head when something goes wrong, I cannot shut it up.

Dean's worries about his performance reveal a great deal about how he sees himself as a man. His narrative shows that, even in a loving and committed relationship, the specter of "better men" out there does not go away. If he wasn't turned on instantaneously or didn't last long enough or couldn't bring his wife to orgasm, he seemed to imagine there were was a man who could and why wouldn't she go to him? Even though, rationally, he knew this was not likely to happen, he couldn't ignore the script he'd internalized from pornography. His comments show how consequential he felt sexual skill was and how much pressure he put on himself to prove his manhood.

Like Minjun, Dean also learned from pornography about the noises women are supposed to make and seemed to believe that Proficient Men should make their real life partners do the same. Men read women's reactions as gauges of their performance. This is an example of women acting as agents of affirmation—in these intimate situations strong performances were thought of as measures of manhood. Women could also be agents of denial when they didn't moan or writhe like women in pornography—their behavior an indication of men's failure. Masculinity is not just something men do for or in front of other men. Expectations for gendered performances are internalized and influence the way men act in intimate situations.[28]

Performance and Manhood

As with getting sex, when talking about having it, men showed awareness of hierarchies among men. Those who saw themselves as late bloomers felt as if their social status and identity made it unlikely that even if they got it, they were going to be good at having it. Such men observed that dominant scripts were not very helpful because there were few details on what led to success or failure, beyond a man's social identity or status. In other words the hypermasculine "studs" were most often the winners in sexual situations, and the geeky men were the losers. Cultural scripts showed that men who have it the wrong way are laughed at, teased, and emasculated. This was a major concern for the majority of men we interviewed, which endured throughout their sexual lives.[29]

Even those who felt really eager for sex worried about performance. Mick (56, married, retail manager, white) described the scenarios playing out in his head around the time he lost his virginity at the age of 17. He said:

> It was with my first real girlfriend. . . . We'd probably been together for a while, though. It was obviously my first time and it was allegedly her

> first time as well. And so we talked about it and how that, you know, of course, I was ready at any time. I would have been ready to do it the first week we were together. . . . But this one night we were watching movies and I'm sure we were making out on the couch and . . . I probably asked her, "Is it time? Are you ready to do this?" And she agreed. . . . I had all these ideas in my head. One, that it was going to hurt her, which I was deeply terrified about hurting her. I had no interest in hurting her at all. I also had heard a lot—like a lot of teenage guys do—that it lasts like 4 seconds. Like when you're with a girl the first time, don't expect it to last very long and she's going to be like—I was afraid she was going to be bleeding. I was afraid she was going to cry. I was terrified of this kind of stuff happening. It luckily lasted longer than 4 seconds, probably not a lot longer than that. There was no tears. So that was, it was very—it was good.

This is not the tale of a confident teenager ready for anything. Although eager, Mick felt pressure to have sex in a way where he both performed well and was careful with his girlfriend. Mick's assessment of his first time as "good" seems to be due to his *not* failing by lasting longer than those other guys who lasted "4 seconds" and that his then girlfriend did not cry. This is a pretty low bar for a "good" experience. Also, notably, pleasure did not even seem to be a factor.

When I asked whether he had expectations for his performance going into it, his reply revealed even more apprehensions:

> I think most young guys do. It's always a concern. You want to make sure you don't peter out. Whatever—you're trying, getting all hot and heavy. Use the condom. "Do you have protection? Are you taking the pill? Do you have an IUD?" That was always the stumbling block with us because once I realized to be smart. . . . Damn condom got in the way. Not just that it was a barrier, but it slowed things down, got in the way, or made things not happen. . . . And it caused a stumbling block in performance.

Contraception was thus another variable that played into performance, and it was one men felt they had to manage. Condoms not only could lessen sensation but also could draw things out and some men spoke of qualms about keeping up their erections during the process of putting on protection. What struck me about Mick's story, like that of many of the other men in this study, was how concerned he was with how he came off to his girlfriend. He needed to show that he knew how to have sex and that he had mastery over his own body. Contraception got in the way only because it might interfere with his ability to be and *appear* aroused during those moments before intercourse.

Most men developed confidence in their sexual performance over time, particularly when they made it through several encounters without failing. Given that masculinity is something that must be consistently demonstrated, it makes sense that the more men had sex, the more self-assured they became. Patrick, the 25-year-old quoted at the beginning of this section, described his progress. In his early experiences he was reluctant to initiate sex because he "was very awkward and unsure of what was supposed to happen." Although he understood sex on a basic level, actually following through made him quite anxious. As he said, "there was a lot of concern at the time. I think it's the same for a lot of people. Their first kiss, their first anything they're worried they're screwing it up. With a lot more practice I felt like I wasn't receiving any bad reviews so I was probably doing something right."

Men like Patrick implied that if partners were not complaining then this meant they were doing at least okay, if not well. While some directly sought out feedback from partners, more relied on their own perception of how partners were receiving their performance. This is not necessarily a good measure of a partner's satisfaction as women are not encouraged to speak up about their sexual needs, desires, or preferences. Studies have shown that women go along with sex when they don't want to because they feel that they should, particularly when men are already aroused.[30] Furthermore, studies have shown that women fake orgasms as a means of sparing men's egos.[31] In this discussion of having sex, men rarely mentioned pleasure as part of the equation. Men were much more concerned with avoiding the emasculation they associated with doing it "wrong."

Lifelong Learning and Measuring Up

Although most men in this study became more confident with experience, new partners brought new concerns about performance. And even within long-term relationships, men questioned their sexual abilities at times. What men discovered through experience is that being a Proficient Man, though critical in their early experiences, was not always enough. In this section, I focus on the continuous learning curve associated with having sex and how this reinforced men's insecurities about measuring up.

I met Kurt (48, divorced, educator, white) at my campus office for our interview. At that time he had been in an on-again/off-again long-distance relationship for several years. Even with having been married and having had a good deal of sexual experience, he still dealt with performance issues in new situations. In between these two relationships, he had a sexual encounter that stayed with him, mostly because of how emasculated he felt by it. He explained, "There was no emotional connection. . . . She was exactly my physical type—if I could design a physical type, it would be her. And it was just one of those things where the stars aligned and I had this opportunity with no expectation and it was horrible. Horrible to the point for the first time in my life, I actually had performance issues, which was like, 'Are you fucking kidding me?!' You read the word lesbian in the dictionary and it snaps to attention, but I actually had performance issues."

This experience was hard for Kurt because he was used to easy arousal—to responding as a man "should." Not being able to perform in this one experience made him doubt himself as a man. I wondered whether or not this was something that he commiserated about with friends afterward. When asked, he responded, "No. As a matter of fact, it was just so bad I just kept it to myself. In fact you're literally the only person I told. Mainly because it was just a horrifyingly bad experience. And I don't judge myself but others might and it's kinda like I don't wanna have to deal with that shit." Clearly, this lackluster performance really mattered to Kurt—not just in that situation but for how he felt about himself. Even though he knew he didn't feel anything emotionally for this woman, the fact that he was very attracted to her should have been enough, in his mind, to ensure proficiency.

The fact that he has *never* talked about this is also striking. Men talk a great deal about sex, with stories of sexual expertise and knowledge peppering conversations from adolescence onward.[32] This type of talk establishes manhood. Not talking about this bad experience—because it involved a "failure" on his part—shows that for as much as men may talk about sex, this is one thing that was avoided. Although he said he didn't judge himself, it seems he did. And he seemed fairly sure other men would as well. He imagined he'd be viewed as less of a man if his peers or anyone knew about his inability to have sex in this situation. Here, too, the way women function as objects of affirmation is made visible. The attractiveness of this woman was a meter for performance expectations. The woman as object did her part in being appealing—Kurt failed in not responding.

Kirk (54, married, self-employed, white) said he likes to be in control of sexual encounters for this very reason. Even though he's been married for twenty years, he likes to take the lead because if he doesn't and isn't ready, he doesn't want to be embarrassed by not being able to perform, even with his long-term partner. He said:

> I'm pretty uncomfortable with women being the initiator . . . because like, I want to make sure my train is ready to leave the station before I get on it. Otherwise, I could step on an empty track, you know? Just to use a silly metaphor. Like if she initiates it all of a sudden [and] if I'm not really into it, I'm not gonna be able to, you know, have sex with her and then I'll look like an idiot. . . . It's like if I know that rocket is ready to go it's like

> cool, and I know all the countdown stages, that's great. But if she starts to count down, it's like, well, I'm not really. . . . It's gonna work if I control it.

Kirk's fear of looking "like an idiot" and his belief that men should be aggressors in sexual situations show his concerns about emasculation. He, too, seems to have internalized the script that men should be ready to have sex at any chance.[33] And Kirk's train and rocket metaphors frame sexual performance as mechanical. He is one of many men in this study who used a machine metaphor for sex. As Susan Bordo notes, there is a cultural association of men's penises with power tools.[34] Being able to perform is equated to turning on a switch, having the ability to get "hard" at any time. These automated metaphors also imply that if there is a problem, there should be a straightforward fix and that men should have control over their bodies.[35]

Size Matters

Another part of the hierarchy among men that came through in discussions of "having it" was the importance of penis size. Men connected penis size with masculinity—with bigger penises seen as more emblematic of hegemonic masculinity.[36] Penises have become more public in our culture—with emphases on size and performance highlighted in the mass-marketing and advertising of enlargement and erectile dysfunction drugs—and are read as measures of manhood.[37]

A recent review of research on penis size, which covered over three hundred articles from 1995 through 2014, with samples of a total of more than 37,000 men, found that in most studies about half to two-thirds of men (both heterosexual and homosexual) were dissatisfied with the size of their penis, with the majority wishing it was larger. Most men saw themselves as average in size, though more men estimated penises as smaller than they actually were.[38] Some studies find that pornography viewing influenced men's thoughts about "ideal" penis size and sometimes fueled sexual insecurities, with a negative correlation between pornography viewing and sexual self-esteem.[39]

Many of the men we interviewed shared these concerns. Chad (33, married, educator, white), for instance, talked about how he felt slighted when his ex-girlfriend told him he did not measure up to her new partner. He shared:

> There's always been like the penis size thing. And almost every guy would say am I adding up? . . . When [my ex-girlfriend and I] broke up she started dating another guy right away. And that was her thing, "Oh, he's got a much bigger dick than you do." I don't think I took it that much to heart but it planted some insecurity or wonder in me. It has never held up or been a determining factor but, you know, I guess I never felt it from their side. . . . I have never entered a sexual situation where the woman was expecting a certain anything. If anything, it was in my own head . . . I wonder what they have had before.

Chad's experience is revelatory. He details the intrapsychic script—his fantasies about how sex should go—that shows he felt pressure not from his partners, but from within. Although he says he did not take his ex's comments to heart—it seems he did. Those comments stayed with him and caused him to question whether he is big enough, which seems to translate into feelings of being man enough.

Kenneth (26, engaged, warehouse worker, Black) also linked size and performance. He explained, "I'm very confident in what I have because I know I could use it right. . . . Sometimes if you see a girl that's really hot, you think about your size. Like they usually like guys that are bigger, but you won't know until you talk to her. Your first look is just like, 'I don't know man, am I going to be satisfying her enough that she's going to stay for a little while?'"

Kenneth starts by saying that he's confident in his size but as he continues he shows how easily this confidence is tested and how much he believes that size is a determining factor in maintaining a woman's interest. And it's quite interesting that he thinks the more attractive the woman, the more concerned she will be with penis size. Just seeing an attractive woman is enough to make him question if he will make a good enough sexual partner. There is little research corroborating that size matters to women in the way men seem to think it does.[40] A study with a national sample of over 52,000 heterosexual men and women found that most women were satisfied with their partner's penis size.[41] Other research finds that size matters more to men than to women. Men's internalization of the idea that size matters can impact men's sexual performance and sexual self-esteem.[42]

In spite of this, competition with actual well-endowed past or imagined future lovers of women partners was not uncommon. Part of the way we think about manhood in American culture involves hierarchies and being more than other men.[43] Men are encouraged to be tougher, stronger, better looking, more successful with women, and bigger than other men. Women are used as leverage in men's power games with other men.[44] So it makes sense that men are thinking about other men and expressing concerns about their imagined competitors when having sex.

When men are firmly entrenched in this stage of having it, they are less likely to be in homosocial environments in which they experience daily posturing contests to prove themselves to other boys or men. For men who are rarely in situations where they see other men naked (such as in school locker rooms and showers) and could observe the range of penis sizes and shapes, women become especially important as assessors of manhood. As agents of affirmation, women's reactions to men's size can confer confidence or induce insecurity.

These narratives about size and competitive performance also reveal the idea of an imaginary "insatiable woman" who requires a man with a very large penis. This is yet another way that women—even in the abstract—influence men's sexual selves. Perhaps prompted by pornography, men spoke of women as having high standards for sexual gratification and little patience with men who did not measure up. Many of the men we spoke with believed that women would seek out other partners if a man failed to deliver a command, gratifying performance.[45] This is in contrast to what much research finds about heterosexual interactions, which shows that some women fake orgasms, perform desire, and use sex as a means to express intimacy.[46] Although there is certainly evidence that women are disappointed by men partners in sexual interactions, many of women's complaints are about men's lack of attention to them as sexual partners or men's lack of concern with women's orgasm.[47]

In a similar vein, frequently, men spoke of women's orgasms as something they "gave" or provided. A part of the script of proficiency is being able to "make" women climax. A sampling of the language men have used in this chapter so far includes: "I didn't know anything about trying to *give* a girl an orgasm or anything like that"; "I don't have to work hard to please her and like to *give* orgasms to her"; "definitely had expectations to *make* her orgasm." Rather than being something that women had or that came from women's bodies, women's orgasms were constructed as a measure of men's ability to perform.[48] This holds up in research on women's perceptions of their orgasms. Based on in-depth interviews, Breanne Fahs, a professor of gender studies, found that women often used a "gifting paradigm," where they framed their orgasms as something they received from their partners.[49] So it makes sense that men's view of women's perception of men's performance influences their sexual self-image.

Men's performance successes made them feel great, as if they had achieved something. Justin (28, single, medical assistant, white) communicated this when discussing the fun of sex. He said, "Getting her where she needs to be is probably the fun part. You know, the ending for the guy is fun, too. But there's kind of a challenge in getting a woman to climax. They're not—guys are like tic, tac, toe and women are like a Rubix cube kind of thing. So that can be pretty fun. And then once you achieve your goal—that sometimes feels like quite an accomplishment."

Lance (45, separated, works in real estate, white) recalled that the first time he experienced a woman orgasm during sexual activity was a "peak" in his sexual experience that made him feel "kind of God-like, actually. There's just no other word for it." Men's responses hinted at satisfaction related to an ego-enhancing experience in which they felt good because they were the source or vehicle of pleasure. Many men spoke of how they derived pleasure from seeing their partner's face while climaxing or after climaxing and felt good because they made it happen. Women's responses gratified men because they served as tangible affirmations that they had succeeded at this manhood-defining act.

Women as Agents of Affirmation: The Importance of "Good Reviews"

Clearly, men in this study felt pressure to perform and to have sex in a way that showed they were masculine, strong, and proficient. Because of the scripts around performance, being told that they were doing a good job or satisfying their lovers (i.e., getting "good reviews") was particularly meaningful and affirming of both their manhood and self-worth. What was interesting was how often, during the course of interviews and unrelated to a direct question, men noted that partners had "no complaints." As noted earlier, not getting bad reviews was a sign they were doing okay. But getting good reviews or compliments on their sexual prowess was even better. Psychologist Gary Brooks's assertion that men are taught to think about women and sex as validators of masculinity is particularly relevant here. Brooks has suggested that men are "programmed" to think about women as sexual objects and measure their sexual successes by women's reactions.[50]

Neil, a retired, white, twice-married 47-year-old, remembered how relieved and pleased he was after his first experience when his girlfriend expressed her satisfaction. He said, "I had all those feelings and thoughts of falling on your face or not being able to perform or whatever. You know, I came off really well. She was really, really happy with it. She told me how much better I was than her boyfriend and everything and really made me feel good about myself." Neil's concerns were assuaged with her positive feedback. Her comments made him feel good not just because of his own performance, but because his girlfriend affirmed that he was more skilled and thus more of a man than her previous partner.

Jack (32, dating, works in media, Black) said that his self-assurance increased when women "came back for more." He boasted:

> The confidence definitely grew. I didn't come out of it thinking that I was the best around.... But, yeah, it was just a confidence builder because as time went on, even though she was enjoying it in the beginning, I could definitely tell that repeat performances were getting better reviews.... I like the reaction—I'm a very big fan of, if you haven't noticed from the other answers, when I can tell [how] I'm actually doing. Like with or without words, just physical reactions and responses also. When I can tell I am doing a great job that is actually a gigantic... a further turn on. I absolutely enjoy that.

Why is getting "good reviews" such a turn on for Jack? It's not just because he knows he is satisfying his partners and they are feeling pleasure. Being told he is sexually proficient validates his manhood. He can feel better about himself as a man when he gets confirmation that he is doing well at something that high-status men are supposed to be good at. He's also probably watched the same pornography other men have watched, which taught him that women's noisemaking during sex is a barometer of women's pleasure and men's skill.

Ruben (35, single, customer service representative, Black) said he was sexually self-confident in general but *hearing* that he is having sex the "right" way is still important to him. Of his performance, he said, "It's good man, because they come back satisfied. You know, they let me know how it was for confirmation. I know I put it down, but once they confirm it and let you know what it is, then you ain't even got to pat yourself on the back. You can just go continuing doing what you're doing. You know you did it right." Once again Ruben conveys the idea that there is a "right" way to have sex and that success can be determined by the reaction or confirmation of a partner. Being skilled at having sex and doing it "right" were important concerns for the men in this study. In most cases women, as sexual partners, were the only ones who could provide men with feedback to know that they were at least proficient and, at best, better than other men.

One thing that struck me about this was how very different this was from the women I interviewed for my book *Deserving Desire*. Most women never mentioned their own sexual performance. How they had sex was not something that most thought about—though it was also not something I asked about in the same way I did with men. In addition, being good at sex was not something that most women aspired to, which makes sense given that it violates cultural norms about the idea of being a "good" girl or woman. Although a few younger women mentioned sexual skill, it was never a major concern. Women sought validation that men wanted to be with them in relationships—but having sex did not provide assurance for them the way it did for the men we interviewed. For women it was more about getting and keeping the attention of men—not as much getting or having sex. For men, having sex was a way to keep their partners, but also an important way to be a man.[51]

Studying to Be the Best

Some men felt that if they were better lovers, most relationship problems would be solved. Like Barry, quoted at the start of the chapter, who was on a quest to be the best lover and actively sought feedback, or Issac, whose story (in Chapter 1) focused on his desire to figure out the puzzle of women's pleasure, a number of men talked about how they regularly sought information to improve or enhance their sexual performances. Whether through reading or experience—they wanted to learn how to best satisfy women.

As I mentioned earlier, this is likely partly about interest in making partners feel good but also partly, if not mostly, ego driven. Feeling and being able to see one's self as a skilled sexual performer was a means of demonstrating manhood and perhaps masculine superiority.[52] Like the men who worried over girlfriends' previous partners and how their genitals measured up, these perpetual sex-ed students wanted to be better than other men. So they asked questions of their partners. They scoured the internet for good advice. They hung out at Barnes and Noble reading sex advice books as a way of preparing to satisfy an imagined community of ravenous women.[53]

One of the men in the study who has been on this quest is Darren (37, single, government worker, Black). Darren lost his virginity when he was 19, which he considered late, both compared to his peers and to when he thought guys were supposed to have sex. He said he had few expectations about his performance during his first sexual experience other than feeling "happy to be there" and wanting to "get through it." But as the relationship progressed, he set higher standards for himself. It was no longer about getting through it. Instead, he "definitely had expectations to make her orgasm. Make it the best experience for her. Be better than her previous guy." When asked if these thoughts helped or harmed his performance, Darren replied, "I think the first few experiences it didn't harm my experience, because I was inexperienced, especially [because I started late]. I always felt nervous about not being experienced enough. Not really knowing what I'm doing. Sort of being at a disadvantage because I was late to it. You know, if we were both teens and we were both finding out at the same time [it would have been different]."

Darren compared himself to other men and felt perpetually behind in developing skills, bolstering the perception that boys should be knowledgeable about how to have sex. This insecurity led to "reading books, reading *Men's Health* magazine. The section on sexual performance." When asked which books he said, "I think it might have been *What Women Want*. [That] was one. I read parts of the Kama Sutra. Recently, I read this book called *She Comes First*." From what he says, Darren's focus was on women's pleasure and he was surely interested in being as good as if not better than "the previous guy."

The imagined and fictitious "Proficient Man" that Darren compared himself to added a level of pressure about being "man enough" to satisfy most women. It also maintained focus on social comparisons. Men not only thought about how they had sex but about how other men had sex. They wanted to be better at sex than other men because that meant they were better *men*. This is hegemonic masculinity at its finest.[54] Take an unattainable ideal of what it means to be a man and encourage men to try to attain it. This is not to say men can't be skilled at sex or learn new tricks from books or websites. But the idea that men are in both direct and indirect sexual competition with one another sustains hierarchies among straight men.[55] It also reinforces the idea that masculinity is tied to dominance not just over femininity but also over subordinated masculinities.[56]

Even older men who were not currently sexually active sought to improve how they had sex. Eli (64, divorced, consultant, white) explained that although he has had a good amount of sex, he feels that there is much to learn about how to please women. So, he has sought and accumulated knowledge about sex as a lifelong fascination.

Eli married a woman he described as generally uninterested in sex. This was unfortunate because he was very interested. This unhappy relationship was relatively short-lived. They were married only five years, and divorced soon after their second child was born. He believed their lack of sexual compatibility led to the demise of their relationship. In retrospect, he questioned whether or not he was skilled enough to satisfy her and if things might have been different if he knew more about pleasing women. He recalled that he never saw his wife have an orgasm and that she never seemed to enjoy sex.

Eli didn't have a loving and mutually sexually satisfying relationship until he was in his fifties. In that relationship, he felt more understood and cared for by his girlfriend than by his wife. But when his girlfriend developed a serious illness and told him she could not handle a relationship with him at that time, he was devastated. In the aftermath, Eli wondered if things might have been different if he were a better lover. So, in the months and years after that breakup, he felt determined to maximize his sexual performance. He shared:

> Up until about a year ago I stopped engaging women. I completely shut down. But it didn't stop my interest and my drive so I turned to pornography. And I turned to, you know, reading about it. And that's when I became aware that there was so much more that I didn't know! And that *I should have known and that it would have been better had I known it*, you know? You sort of, well, I sort of resented the fact that I didn't know what I had learned subsequently in terms of skill and performance and what makes a woman respond, and all those things that you think you know (emphasis added).

Eli felt he "should have known" or that his sex life and relationships "would have been better" if he had known more about how to have sex. Maybe he would have been happy with his ex-wife. Maybe his ex-girlfriend would not so easily have ended their relationship. If only he'd had these skills, maybe things would have been different. Although there were multiple factors that could have contributed to the demise of these relationships, Eli connected these failures with his flawed sexual performance. As a man, he should have known how to satisfy women, he should have been a more proficient lover. Although he does not say so explicitly, the idea of being better here, too, implies that women will go to other men if their current partners are not good enough.[57] Eli, like many of the men in this study, puts a great deal of stock in sexual performance as critical in making relationships work.

As we talked through this, I asked Eli what he did to cultivate greater understanding about sexual performance. He explained that in addition to watching and studying pornography, he read articles online:

> I would catch it by the title and I would, you know—there's a plethora of this stuff out there. . . . I was reading what I thought was women writing about women. Women writing about what they wanted from men

> sexually. That's what fascinated me because I looked at it and I said, "You know, the woman that's writing it isn't any different than my ex-wife or the women I was sleeping with in my 20s or 30s and 40s. They were all the same women. They looked the same way." It's just—one thing I came away with from reading these articles is that women today in their 20s and 30s they would not tolerate a man not knowing what you do for them and with them. . . . I think the woman that I met when I was 50, she was wonderful in her willingness to say, this is what I need from you. And I subsequently said the same thing to her, and she did it. I have never known anybody to do that, I mean that was amazing to me.

Learning from women writers, whom Eli considered experts, really changed his perspective on having sex. The idea that a woman might say what would please her was a novelty. So the relationship with his former girlfriend was like an awakening, ephemeral though it was. From then on he focused on acquiring as much information as he could about having sex from women's standpoints. Yet his conclusion that all women are "the same women" implies an overly simplistic and reductionist approach to women's sexual satisfaction and pleasure. From what Eli said, his ex-wife was nothing like his most recent ex-girlfriend, and there may have been partner-specific techniques or acts that would have gratified them differently.

When speaking with Eli, one of the last men interviewed for this study, I wondered how much of his interest in pornography and reading these articles was for learning and how much was for titillation—to satisfy unsatisfied desires. When I asked, he said, "It was both. It certainly was both a release as well as, you know, deep interest [in] . . . if I could, how to be better." I was struck by the almost desperation with which Eli sought out information about pleasing women, particularly given that he didn't currently have a partner or chance to put this knowledge into practice. So I asked him if this quest to be the best sexual performer was about really trying to understand new sexual positions or how to use his body in ways that derive pleasure or if it was more of an intellectual exploration. In other words, was he interested in learning how to have it so he could put it into action given the opportunity? Or was he just curious how other people do it in ways he didn't know about? He said:

> So it's about the mechanics. So one of the things, and I can only say for myself, for my age—and I'm 64 years old—so from my sexual development, my knowledge development, I, for whatever reason, was never fully educated by anyone on what really good performance is in the bedroom, what a good sexual partnership is, with the mechanics. I'm not talking about the emotional aspects—we're not talking about that. We're talking about all of the things that make a woman say, "Yes, I want to be with him again" kind of thing. . . . So what I'm looking for when I watch this stuff is that. It's not about emotion, it's not about intimacy and it's the recognition that, you know, I don't know how to put in an electrical outlet, I'm gonna watch a video on how to do that. And I don't know how to do this for a woman, and I've got to figure that out.

Like the men quoted earlier who used mechanical metaphors and analogies for having sex, Eli, too, seemed to believe that he just needed to study hard enough, to find the right instruction manual, and that is what would make a sizable difference in his imagined future sexual encounters. He seemed to suggest that he had missed important information in his sexual socialization and that if he fixed this, he'd be ready to maintain a satisfying intimate relationship. Some men, like Eli, felt they were studying how to have sex throughout their entire lives—even when it may have been an intellectual exercise as they may not have sex again. A part of Eli's identity as a man involves knowing how to have sex, knowing how to please women. The knowledge itself has currency, even if it is never put into practice. Being ready, willing, and able is a marker of manhood. For inactive men, talking about desire and interest in sex, particularly for older men, is a means of showing that they are still men.[58] Eli's continuous search for information on how to have it is also a good example of the tenuousness of manhood. As manhood must be consistently proved and more is needed to prove it as men get older, it seems likely that Eli's days of study are not coming to an end anytime soon.

In some ways, this quest for information about how to please partners is encouraging in thinking about gender equality in the era of the "orgasm gap."[59] Wanting to satisfy women and looking for material about how to do so can yield better sex for women (and men)—provided the sources men consult truly have useful information about what some women actually want. It's also good because it shows that men are recognizing women's sexual desire and interest in sexual pleasure. Many of the women I interviewed for *Deserving Desire*, particularly women born before 1970, said their men partners did not show such concerns.[60]

Yet blanket sex tips and use of pornography as an instruction manual complicate the situation because doing so reinforces the idea that most or all women want the same things (and that these things can be learned from pornography). Women, like men, are diverse, and while some sexual suggestions might work for some women—others may not. What's also discouraging about this perpetual focus on sexual performance is that it limits men's sexualities to sexual skill and reifies the "power tool" metaphor.[61] Men who focus on improving techniques can miss what their partners may want instead—intimacy, physical closeness, connection (which I turn to in Chapter 5). And, the fixation on sexual performance binds sexual prowess and masculinity, rather than pleasure.[62] To be a "real man" one has to be a Proficient Man, leaving those who don't feel sexually skilled or who are less interested in sex to view themselves as failed men.

Not Having It or Having It with Guilt

A handful of men in this study had minimal to no sexual experience. These men were in their twenties, Asian, either first-generation or recent immigrants, who had come to the United States within the previous ten to fifteen years. Why didn't they have sex? Although they lived in the United

States, their values were aligned with those of their home countries. In other words, the cultural scenarios and scripts they learned were different from those of American teens. For many, their families or religions strongly discouraged or prohibited sex before marriage. Arjun (20, single, student, South Asian), for instance, has not engaged in any sexual activity. He sees premarital sex as wrong, though he tries not to judge his peers who have sex. He said:

> It depends on who you grew up with . . .'cause like if I did that, people would not respect me. . . . That's what I think. I still think you should wait until marriage. But I've seen—like a lot of my close friends do it now. I guess it's like, "Aw dang, I wish they would wait." But it's their personal—I'm not like a person who goes "You have to stop! Because I believe this!" It's like their personal—I'm not going to force my beliefs on anybody else. I'll still respect them and let them do what they want.

Raised by Indian parents and with a strong Catholic upbringing, Arjun believed sex was not something to have casually. Still he described mixed feelings about having it, given pressure from his friends and overwhelming American cultural messages connecting sexual experience with masculinity. He explained, "A lot of my close friends are starting to, which is fine. But it's like, damn—it's like one of those where I feel like maybe I should. Then I realize I shouldn't—like [the] following one second. Like if your best friend—like my best friend did a lot of stuff and it makes me feel like, 'Am I doing the right thing?'"

Akshay (41, married, researcher, South Asian) who had been living in the United States for one year at the time of his interview was raised as and is a practicing Hindu. He explained cultural influences on having sex this way:

> In India, or in Asia, you need sort of guts to express anything to your girlfriend about sex. It is considered highly taboo or not very common in society. . . . It is difficult for women to get married, because it's still, in India, most of marriage is arranged marriage. So it is not allowed. . . .

> There, it is arranged marriage most of the time because between the families and you're married and then you started doing sex. . . . Still in Asian society, marriage is very formal there, very less potential of divorce. Most of the sexual life is limited to only one lady, or maybe more. If you're lucky enough you're going to have two or three.

For both Akshay and Arjun, cultural values about sex were strong motivators for their behavior. Even when living in the United States, they had (or did not have) sex the way they learned South Asian men were supposed to.

Religion was a barrier to having sex for other men, too. Although these men were a small minority of interviewees, a few talked about dealing with guilt when they had premarital sex because it went against how they were raised. Darren (37), the self-described late bloomer mentioned earlier who didn't have sex until he was 19, was born and raised in the Caribbean. He explained that into his twenties he felt conflicted about having sex due to his upbringing:

> I was raised in a very religious household. I was extremely shy. I didn't lose my virginity till my mid—I was almost 20. So like the summer of my 19th year. My early 20s I was still, you know, still really experiencing it for the first time. It was really nerve-wracking for me, because I was not as experienced as the other . . . or I met women who were way more experienced than me. . . . And I still had some guilt . . . just because of my religious upbringing. There was a youth congregation at my church. The main topic was "Thou shall not have sex." Just beat into your head. And all these negative things would happen if you have sex. So that was always like prominently . . . like immediately after the act I would be thinking about "Did I get her pregnant? Did I catch an STD? Am I going to hell?" [This] overall was not a good experience just because of how I grew up.

Seventy-two percent of the men in the sample identified with a religion. And most of the men who did not consider themselves religious as adults were raised with a strong religious influence. Yet religion was rarely a factor in men's feelings about having sex, particularly after their first sexual experience. This was in strong contrast to the women I interviewed for *Deserving Desire* who dealt with both cultural pressures and sexual double standards about "good" and "bad" girls, as well as religious taboos discouraging sexual desire and sexual activity.[63] Men like Akshay, Arjun, and Darren, in contrast, had to grapple with religious and family values that were incompatible with American sexual scripts that encouraged sexual activity as a defining act in demonstrating heterosexual masculinity.

By looking at how men "have it" we can again see how sex is an act that can affirm manhood—but only when it is done right. Men internalized the image of the Proficient Man, to whom they felt they needed to live up as sexual performers. Men were concerned about penis size, about pleasing women, and about getting "good reviews." Sex was something that men believed they were judged on as gauges of manhood and when they were having it, women were the ones doing the judging. In some cases, women were necessary for this only as objects. This was true when men felt they could measure their success by women's reactions, often comparing their responses to those from women in pornography.

However, women needed to act in order to affirm that men were better or bigger than other men. In addition to and sometimes instead of men peers, women become arbiters of manhood because they are perceived as having the power to judge a man's sexual skill—and because they are the other party in the sexual encounter. They are typically the only other person in the room and thus the lone one who can provide affirmation of proficiency or prowess.

CHAPTER 5

Having It

DESIRE, RELATIONSHIPS, AND SEX

In the wake of the #MeToo movement, there has been a lot of talk about the concept of toxic masculinity. Toxic masculinity, defined as "strategic enactments of masculinities that are harmful both to the men who enact them and to the people around them," can manifest in sexual harassment, rape culture, substance abuse, and violence.[1] One of the roots of toxic masculinity is the discouragement of emotional expression and intimacy among men. In compliance with hegemonic masculinity, men are supposed to conceal feelings of vulnerability, sadness, and even love.[2] As the journalist Melanie Hamlett wrote, "American men—with their puffed up chests, fist bumps, and awkward side hugs—grow up believing that they should not only behave like stoic robots in front of other men, but that women are the only people they are allowed to turn to for emotional support—if anyone at all."[3]

Yet research shows that American boys and teenagers crave close relationships with friends in whom they can confide and on whom they can count as sources of support.[4] These boys lament gender norms that inhibit emotionally intimate friendships with other boys and wish they could freely talk about their feelings of vulnerability.[5] They also long for "genuine friendships in which they are free to be themselves rather than conform to rigid masculine stereotypes."[6]

So, in their adolescent and teen years, straight boys seek out relationships with girls not just for physical intimacy or sexual conquest.[7] In some studies teenage boys talked specifically about the importance of dating because girlfriends were a source of comfort and allowed for the emotional intimacy they yearned for but felt was no longer socially acceptable to pursue with male peers.[8] In her research on teenage sexuality, sociologist Amy Schalet reported that although American teenage boys were well aware of sexual scripts that suggested they were ruled by "raging hormones," some of the boys she interviewed characterized themselves as romantic, as wanting to fall in love, and some thought of marriage as an ideal (and sometimes as *the* ideal) context for sex.[9]

These studies show how heterosexual intimate relationships can provide men with a space for emotional expression. Here, where others are rarely watching, they can enact "private masculinity," which, as I've classified elsewhere, is "the way men demonstrate masculinity in intimate situations, where they are less likely to be policed."[10] The closeness associated with sexual contact allows men a respite from expectations of emotional silence. However, because of the pressures associated with performance, as detailed in Chapter 4, men are not completely free of expectations to demonstrate conventional masculinity—nor are they expected to demonstrate femininity. Private masculinity is still a "front stage" performance, where men imagine how their partners might perceive them and how their appearance and manner convey what's expected of them as men.[11] Women, then, play a complex role in being seen as emotional support and as imagined judges of men's approximation of manhood. Women also bear the burden of being the receptor for men's vulnerability, which positions them in the subordinate role of emotional care-keepers, that is, the ones in relationships who do the care work to support, encourage, and reassure their men partners that they are man enough.[12]

In this chapter, I look beyond performance to shed light on how men have sex in relationships. In intimate relationships, women allow and even encourage the expression of feminized emotions in men. I note how sexual intimacy enhances closeness among partners and discuss the role love plays in men's sexuality and men's expressions of masculinity. I also look at how Western culture affirms manhood through heterosexual sexual behavior and relationships, even when men's concerns shift from self to partner as they mature.

Becoming Emotional: Shifting Definitions of the Meaning of Having Sex

Although men discussed sexual encounters of all kinds—casual, friends with benefits, dating, one-night stands—the majority of the men we interviewed said they preferred sex in relationships. Having sex provided men with physical sexual pleasure, to be sure, but it also made them feel good emotionally and psychologically when they felt validated as men and loved as partners or people. As Devar (42, married, researcher, Black) said, "For me as I've gotten older the need to prove and the need to do what I have to do has declined. It does, it does change. . . . In my younger days it was a message, I'd say, of quantity over quality. I would say at this age it's more—I wouldn't say only quality, but I'm more inclined to focus more on companionship and somebody who is dear."

As Devar suggests, sexual scripts can shift over time and with different sexual experiences.[13] Sociologists Chiara Bertone and Raffaella Camoletto interviewed Italian men in their fifties to seventies and noted changes in sexual scripts over the course of their lives.[14] In some cases, men who used to approach sex and women following "predatory" scripts replaced these with "respectability" scripts as they matured and entered into relationships and learned to respect specific women. These findings parallel what I found in this sample of American (and American immigrant) men. As men entered into and cultivated lasting relationships, they described interpersonal sexual scripts focused on mutual gratification and the importance of sexual activity as an expression of intimacy. Bertone and Camoletto pointed to men spending less time in homosocial contexts and more in heterosexual relationships as the chief means of learning about sex and reconstructing sexual scripts. Like these scholars, I underscore the salience of heterosexual relationships and see women as playing a crucial role in guiding men to develop new scripts or ways of thinking about and, more critically, of having sex.

A major shift in how men had sex happened when the way they thought about women as sexual partners changed. Most of the men in this study felt they went through a time in which they "matured" and started to think about sex as a cooperative experience of mutual satisfaction and enjoyment. When younger, the emphasis was on the number of partners and the feeling of power that came from executing sex as a manhood act. It was about *getting* women to have sex with them, rather than about *having* sex with those women.

Likewise, as the men I spoke with gained experience and entered into relationships, the way they had sex changed. Zack (34, married, educator, white) described the shift like this:

> I think there's expectations through Hollywood and media to be very virile and be able to go forever, 5 times a night. I definitely felt I think that lasted for a long time too, that expectation. . . . I guess I'd say that it kind of stopped when I got married. Didn't necessarily feel the pressure, or it became—maybe not when I got married, I should say, one of my first longer lasting relationships where again the change from being a casual, recreational thing, to more an expression of deeper feelings and things like that. And then also learning more about sex and understanding that there's more, far more, to giving your partner pleasure than the stereotype of male sexuality.

For Zack, like many other men in their thirties and older with whom we spoke, this change was not just in terms of wanting to perform better to satisfy their partners or because they feared the competition of other men, as noted in Chapter 4. Often, they spoke of wanting to make their partners feel good for the partner's benefit and as an enhancement of the overall experience and relationship. Marriage—or, for some, being in a long-term committed relationship—made a difference in how men viewed their sexual partners, and how they viewed their sexual partners made a difference in how they had sex.

Men asserted that in these relationships they wanted to please their partners because they cared about them, as an expression of love, *in addition to* an expression of masculinity. Barry, a 44-year-old engaged Black postal worker, described how this happened for him:

> I really didn't become [sexually] aware until I was in my 30s.... All I was worried about when I did have sex from 21 to my 30s is that I was having sex and [that] I liked it and they liked it. But I really wasn't aware of what was going on, how they felt about it, and how I really felt about it till I was in my 30s.... [Becoming aware of women's feelings] changed how I would do it, too. It changed to different positions. Because by that time I knew the position they liked. How—what positions they liked the most and where and how much they wanted it and how much I wanted it. Before that it was like a military march "left, left, left right, left." It was like that before, where I didn't care. I didn't care, I was just having it.... It wasn't until I was in my 30s that I became aware and cared about their feelings.

Barry described his earliest experiences with sex as a "military march," going through the motions with a focus on performance, rather than on anyone's pleasure. Although he said that in his twenties he cared whether both he and his partners "liked it," his other comments indicate that he cared that they didn't *dis*like it or have concerns about his performance (see the beginning of Chapter 4 for more about Barry's performance concerns). Once he started to realize that sex was not just imitating what he saw in pornography and he actually sought information about what his partners preferred, the way he had sex changed. And it changed not just practically, as he noted, when he used different positions that he believed were more likely to result in orgasm for his partner, but also emotionally when he started to care about his partner's feelings. Although, like other men, he was still concerned with doing it right and following instructions that he seemed to think would yield a particular positive result, he emphasized the importance of caring about his partner as an instigator of change.

Other men were more reflexive in their discussion of how the way they had sex changed during their lives. When asked if he'd had any negative sexual experiences, Chad (33, married, educator, white), recalled, "There was one where I broke up with a girl after we had sex. . . . She was in high school and I was in first year of college. And I think [I] really hurt her. And I was her first and it was nothing for me and a lot for her. And like I said I have always been attuned to that—I have always tried to not hurt people. . . . I think that sticks with me as something that I'm not proud of. . . . Like did I leave a scar on her sexuality?"

Chad's regret came from his shifting definition of the meaning of having sex and of his sexual partners. For him, that experience had been about conquest and he acknowledged that he really didn't think or care about her feelings at the time. He realized in retrospect that she had a very different conception of that encounter and it eventually made him think more about who he had sex with. Sex became something to share with a partner. In this situation, similar to those shared by other interviewees, it was a relationship with a specific woman he cared about that inspired the shift to how he thought about women as sexual partners in general. When he recognized women as subjects, he could then think back on his objectification of this past partner. Although he did not frame the past experience as one in which he had sex as a means of demonstrating masculinity, when he said the experience "meant nothing to him" at the time, the idea of sexual conquest is there.

Many men indicated that when the way they had sex shifted from thinking of their own satisfaction, they learned to derive pleasure from their partner's pleasure. Lance (45, separated, works in real estate, white), for example, explained that as much as he enjoys feeling sexually gratified, it is also very pleasing to him to see his partner satisfied, even when he is not directly involved. Lance's current partner, whose libido complements his, allowed him to realize the extent to which he can derive pleasure from sharing such passions with her, as he had felt repressed from doing so with his ex-wife who participated only grudgingly in sex a couple of times a year.

For Lance, watching his partner masturbate brings sexual satisfaction, which he would not have imagined in his younger years. He said: "My definition of pleasure is so broad. Like there is, if there is a thing that my partner really enjoyed doing but I didn't, it doesn't matter. It's intimacy. Like she has an orgasm . . . I'm getting off just watching, how could I not enjoy this? How I could watch, you know, sit across the room, drink a glass of wine, watch you masturbate with a wand and not be pleasured? I'm not actually getting stimulated but I am enjoying it because it's glorious."

Is Lance affirmed by his partner's satisfaction if he is not directly involved? Is this still a manhood act? Absolutely. Being in the room and watching his partner is consistent with pornographic scripts where women perform for men's voyeuristic pleasure.[15] So, even when Lance speaks of feeling gratified by his partners' pleasure and the intimacy being there brings, there is also a hedonistic and masculine performative aspect of this interaction.

Other men also commented that maturity brought changes in how they had sex. Juan (55, married for twenty-five years, manager, Latino), explained that when he was younger, "I'm not even thinking about the other person, not very much. And as I get older, I'm starting to think about, okay, I need to be worried about—and it's probably totally wrong—but you get to be more concerned with how is the other person feeling? Are you satisfying the other person? And when you're younger, that's like hardly even on the radar."

Juan's thoughts here seem similar to those of the men described in Chapter 4, whose focus was on performance. Yet, as he continued, he made it clear that this is not just about his performance as an act of affirmation, but also about the result it brings and how it solidifies in his relationship with his wife. He shared:

> I know how to satisfy the person more or I'm more comfortable with how to satisfy the person. And I'm not—I guess the other part is I'm not hung up or I'm not—I guess I'm not trying to—I'm not worried [that] each single occurrence has to be perfect. That's the only good way to put it. So the longer I was with somebody, first of all, I was more comfortable because I thought I knew how to satisfy the other person. But, the other thing is that when you're with someone at the beginning, for me, you're very self-conscious—maybe that's not the right word—but you're thinking that I'm only gonna get one chance or two chances to impress this person. So I have to really, really try hard. As you're with someone longer, you are not—you don't think that way.

JOHN: Sounds like you kind of relax the pressure on yourself.

JUAN: Exactly. And I don't think it's from the other side. I never—I'll have to think about it—but I don't think I had anyone ever say, "Well that was lousy" or something. But in your mind you're thinking, "Well, I really gotta be on my absolute best because I need to impress this person each time." But as you go along you start to let your guard down, you feel more comfortable, and it's not as nerve wracking.

Juan, like some of the men quoted in Chapter 4, noted the internalization of sexual performance pressure. He did not remember ever having a partner who critiqued his skills but, in his mind, he'd absorbed messages about how men are supposed to have sex. So he felt the need to follow dominant sexual scripts, even when he had no such confirmation from his women partners that they were judging him that way. Even in these intimate situations, the need to perform private masculinity prevailed. It was only after he really felt he trusted a partner that things started to change.

In their study of hookup culture on college campuses, Paula England, Elizabeth Armstrong, and Allison Fogarty wrote about the sexual "learning curve" that happens in relationships and explains why the "orgasm gap" decreases in relationships compared to causal encounters.[16] As partners know one another's proclivities and sources of pleasure, they become more confident in their ability to please. And that's part of what Juan was talking about here. The longer he was with someone, the more he felt he knew how to make that person feel good.

But Juan also suggests that in a committed relationship he feels a greater sense of security that his partner will stick around, even if he has an off night. The security of the relationship means that he doesn't have to feel the same performance pressures he felt in his earlier days. There is more than just sex bonding them. In their role as wives or girlfriends, women act as *objects* of affirmation. But in their responses, commitment, and stability they act as *agents* of affirmation; women's behavior as relationship partners increases men's sexual self-assurance.

Like Juan, Luke (42, recently remarried, financial professional, white) said that having sex in relationships has allowed him to be more at ease and enjoy sex more. He said, "I'm with someone that I don't feel massive anxiety if I don't please them all the time. . . . There's a longer term commitment and understanding. I think she knows that she's going to be satisfied pretty much all the time. Like if I were to have an orgasm first, which happens plenty, it's not very often that she won't have an orgasm based on me doing some other things. . . . I don't think she feels like she's going to be left out in the cold."

In Luke's case the pressure to perform and please is lessened because he knows they, as a couple, have other opportunities if sex doesn't yield mutual or multiple climaxes each time (although he still implies there is an orgasm gap in his favor). In both Luke's and Juan's cases, although they do care about pleasing their partners, the lessened pressure to perform comes from knowing they are accepted for who they are. They can focus on their partners not just because they've learned to care more about partners' sexual needs and desires or their specific ways of being pleasured, but also because their masculine selves are shored up by a committed relationship. So men in long-term relationships were better able to construct new sexual scripts for having sex. Wives and long-term girlfriends were often described as trusted sexual partners who provided a feeling of closeness, comfort, and security. This helped men like Juan assuage their worries about imagined competitors. When men viewed women as subjects, rather than objects, they started to view them differently as sexual partners, too. As agents of affirmation, women's commitment, actions, and emotional openness assured them they were "man enough," and helped men "do" masculinity.

Love Makes Sex Better

Sex and love are linked in American culture. Research finds that the connection between love and sex is gendered; girls and women are expected to connect the two, while boys and men are expected to be able to dissociate sex and love.[17] In my research on women's sexuality, I found that love was important in women's sexual lives and most would not have sex if they did not feel love for a partner.[18] Although dominant scripts suggest that sex is physical rather than emotional for men, more and more studies provide evidence that contradicts this.[19] For instance, sociologist Louisa Allen interviewed 17- to 19-year-old New Zealander boys/men and found that romance, though often displayed alongside "hard masculinity," was an important aspect of their relationships and "one of the pleasures of intimacy." Feeling loved by partners positively impacted men's self-esteem.[20] So it was not just being in a long-term relationship that made a difference in how men had sex and viewed women partners, it was feeling loved by and love for a partner that allowed this shift to happen.

Like the women I interviewed for *Deserving Desire*, most men said they either could not separate love and sex—that is, they would not have sex when they did not love or deeply care for their partner—or that they would not want to. Love enhanced the sexual experience and was their preferred situation. Greg (20, single, student, South Asian) put it succinctly: "It's like you don't have to love each other to have sex but the happiest you'll be when you have sex is when you love each other."

Vishan (24, single, student, South Asian) also said that feeling love changed the way he felt about having sex. He opined:

> Sex is an important part of a healthy relationship, I would say. . . . It's fun but it should be—it should be with someone you love, not just someone you want to have sex with. When I was younger sometimes I did have those thoughts like it would great if I could have sex with random people. But, I don't know, I feel like when I was with my girlfriends, there's something different having sex in that environment compared to just having sex with someone just to have sex with and then just leaving right after that. . . . From my experience hooking up with my girlfriend who I was close with is great 'cause—it's like expressing your love or whatever. You're intimate. It means something, I guess, when there's feeling behind your sex. It just feels much more better.

Like Vishan, most interviewees noted that much of the enjoyment of sex was as an expression of their relationships and love for partners. When men feel loved, they are less likely to feel that they have something to prove to their partners and less likely to worry about performance reviews. Men seemed to appreciate being in loving relationships for that very reason—sex was needed less to affirm manhood.

Jack (32, dating, works in media, Black), said that he came to this realization after having sex with someone he cared about: "I learned . . . that actually hooking up with someone that you had an emotional connection with just seemed better in general than just the random hook up." Jack prefaced his preference for emotionally connected sex by saying, "I find that [my feeling about sex] is a little closer to that of women I've spoken to on similar things than a lot of guys . . . it's the sensuality that they attach, the emotionality which I attach to a relationship rather than just the sex." Jack explicitly feminizes the idea of linking emotion and sex. It's interesting that Jack assumes he is not like other men—something common among men when it comes to the idea of emotionality. This is an example of how much hegemonic masculinity (which calls for emotional stoicism and detachment) is something men are encouraged to follow, but not what they necessarily do much of the time.[21]

More of the men who talked about the role of love in having sex were in their forties to sixties. Tyrone (61, separated, entrepreneur, Black) also made it clear that sex is better with a strong connection. He explained, "For me I think love is, if you're in a sexual relationship and you love that person, it's more of a meaningful thing, the sex. So, like I say, I'm a guy but I'm more of an emotional dude, so I need to know the person I'm with sexually for it to have more meaning." When I asked if he can separate love and sex he said, "I think you can but for me it would be pointless because I need—I prefer to have love with my sex, you know what I mean?"

Like other interviewees, Tyrone noted that meeting his wife and getting married changed things for him. Before that, "it was about me sexually. But over time, I realized I got more pleasure from making sure she reached her climax before I did or whatever. Just making her satisfied. Knowing she was looking forward to spending the night with me when the kids went over to my mother and father's house or my sibling's house or something like that."

Several themes come through in Tyrone's comments. First, he maintains the "men *give* women pleasure" script. Part of his sexual satisfaction seemed to be knowing that he was the one providing his wife with sexual gratification (rather than her pleasure coming from her body). In this way, he signifies his masculine self. He can be sexually vulnerable; he can express love and still link it with his virility and sexual prowess. Yet sexual vulnerability is more likely to be confined to intimate moments and contexts, as well as more likely when men are older and less liable to have their manhood policed by peers.

Tyrone's words also reveal how much affirmation from his partner meant to him. When he says, "knowing that she was looking forward to spending the night with me," he suggests that it made him feel valued and loved for who he was (as well as how he performed) as a person. And when he said, "I'm a guy, but I'm more of an emotional dude," he, like Jack, seemed to see himself as different from other men. Yet many of the participants in this study expressed these same sentiments about the importance of love and emotional connection in sexual encounters and relationships.

Nick (52, never married/dating his girlfriend for six years, unemployed, Black), for instance, described how love enriched his sexual experiences:

> When you first start, you don't feel no closeness, no bonding, you just feel happy to have sex. Satisfaction now is a little bit different. When you're with your main lady . . . you feel satisfied 'cause you satisfied your loved one and she satisfied you. And you know there's gonna be more times of satisfaction together. So there is a difference from youngness to oldness and being with someone you love. . . . Sex is totally different when you're young . . . you ain't thinking about her, you thinking about you.

For Nick, as well as for Tyrone, Jack, and many other interviewees, commitment and love were the catalysts for their changing perspective on sex. Maturity also made a difference. In this way, masculinity can be framed as having a "life course," during which men go through stages of how it's performed. As they've had several decades to have their manhood affirmed in different contexts, including by the presence of a committed partner and sometimes by fatherhood, men who are more secure in their manhood feel less need to prove it or seek validation as frequently as they might have during their youth.

However, because men in their forties, fifties, and sixties may have fewer opportunities to display masculinity in ways that fit with hegemonic masculine sexual scripts, this may be a time when they shift their narratives in ways that accommodate these changes.[22] As Linn Sandberg argues, framing intimacy as focal in sexual encounters may "be a part of the process of adaptation to the changes of the aging body."[23] I suggest that this is about adjusting not just to embodied changes but also to alterations in one's ability to be and be seen as masculine in a youth-oriented society. It may very well be that love and sex are separated by *masculinity* and that this thus explains why the shift occurs for men in their forties and older and more often for men in committed relationships.[24] Men who can let their guards down, who have had their masculinity affirmed by loyal women partners, can worry less about each sexual performance. Feeling loved is feeling affirmed and it may be that a broader sense of affirmation changes men's perception of sex solely as a manhood act—particularly in midlife when they are having it regularly and with few performance issues.

The Importance of Being Intimate: Closeness and Affirmation

The stories and quotes above show how important sexual relationships are to the men interviewed in this study. As noted at the start of the chapter, straight men are discouraged from seeking emotional intimacy with other men because doing so challenges their manhood. That straight men sometimes qualify feelings of love or affection for friends with hashtags like "no homo" shows the power of gender rules about who should and shouldn't communicate homosocial feelings.[25]

Though few said so directly, when men talked of how much they liked the intimacy associated with having sex, they seemed to suggest that they appreciated the confirmation of their desirability as men as much (if not, often, more so) as the physical enjoyment of sex. Dylan (21, single, student, white), for example, commented, "Well, there's the obvious physical pleasure part, but I mean I love the connection mentally about it. It's—you're opening yourself up to somebody completely and I love that—just being with somebody, knowing that somebody cares about you and loves you and like is happy to be with you. That's what I like the most."

Even at 21, Dylan focused on emotional connection. I was struck by what he said he likes most: "knowing somebody cares about you and loves you and is happy to be with you." Dylan is describing the importance of confirmation of his worth, of knowing that he matters to someone. Even though most men in their twenties did not express such sentiments, I think it's important to note that quite a few did. These young men appreciated feeling loved and saw sex as an act of affirmation not just of manhood but of worth as a person in general.

Expanding on Sigmund Freud, the psychoanalytic feminist Nancy Chodorow wrote about how, as infants, boys suffer from an Oedipus complex, which causes them to distance themselves from close relationships with other men. They learn that they can seek and receive comfort from their mothers but not their fathers, as they are in competition with their fathers for their mother's affection.[26] Chodorow suggests this teaches boys to connect with their fathers as a means of masculine identification in which they learn that a "sense of secure masculine self [is] achieved through superego formation and disparagement of women."[27] According to psychoanalytic theorists, this is what men are up against going into heterosexual relationships and it is what encourages nonrelational sexuality.[28]

But as we see in this book, relationships are important in providing affective connection as well as authentication of men's self-worth. If men consistently imagine themselves in competition with other men, then it is women partners, as agents of affirmation, who can provide needed emotional support and reassurance, in addition to bolstering men's status by their mere presence.[29] Sexual intimacy is important then because it affords much more than physical gratification.

Justin (28, dating, medical assistant, white) said this explicitly. At 28, he'd had several relationships, few of them serious, by his classification. He noted that one-night stands and casual dating were not fulfilling to him. He said: "Closeness and intimacy with these women is something that I—I probably was more interested in than even the climax of the whole thing. Because that, it's pretty easy for guys to take care of that whenever they feel the need to. But that intimacy isn't something that you can logon to Pornhub and take care of." And when asked what he likes most about sex, Justin replied, "Having no barriers between you and this other person is something you don't really—there's really nowhere else you can experience anything quite like that. That's pretty much the only place you can experience this like literally skin to skin, can't be physically any closer to someone kind of a thing. In a society where we keep our distance from people a lot . . . having all those barriers removed and this person accepting you, *just you*, and them being comfortable, being that close to you is really great."

Justin's apparent yearning for affirmation comes through in his narrative. Sex is not just an opportunity for carnal pleasure but for deep intimacy and acceptance. His comments also serve as an indication of how profoundly men can internalize messages about toughness and emotional distance. He sees sex as *the only place* where he can feel this longed for deep closeness to another person. Although the pressure to perform masculinity does not go away entirely in these situations, it seems that it is mitigated by acceptance from a committed partner.

Repeatedly, the men we interviewed emphasized that sexual satisfaction comes from closeness, in addition to (or sometimes instead of) climax. Although some of the younger men (men in their twenties and thirties) who were or had been in committed relationships communicated this, older, partnered men were most likely to say so. Among the women I interviewed for *Deserving Desire*, trust and vulnerability were major themes. And though this theme has appeared in research on adolescent and teenage boys, I was surprised to see it come up among men, of all ages, in the same context with such frequency.[30] Many men did not trust easily and sought out sex as a chance to be vulnerable and accepted by loving partners.

These are prime examples of how men constructed having sex as an act of affirmation and how women played the critical role of agents who, in words and behavior, conveyed sentiments of men's worth. By having sex with emotionally connected partners, men were able to see themselves through someone else's eyes. As with the cultural validation that came from having a trusted mentor teach that sexual desire was normal, men described feeling affirmed by a partner's willingness or eagerness to have sex with them. When men trusted their partners enough to be vulnerable with them, they also revealed their desires, and felt validated when they were not rejected or rebuffed in turn. However, this arrangement of women bearing the responsibility of being emotional care-keepers in relationships reinforces existing gender hierarchies.[31] Both women and men sustain the idea that emotional expression is women's domain.

PART III

Keeping It Up

CHAPTER 6

Keeping It Up

SEXUAL AND RELATIONSHIP PROBLEMS

The catchy Train song "50 Ways to Say Goodbye" is about a man trying to save face when talking to friends after his girlfriend breaks up with him. When she gives him the "It's not you, it's me" line, he goes on to make up elaborate lies about her tragic demise, which include: dying in a plane crash, being electrocuted by a tanning bed, shark attack, drowning, and dying in a mudslide. Though the song is obvious hyperbole, it is a good example of the emasculation associated with rejection by women.[1] In this case, the message is: better to lie grandly and say a girlfriend died than admit she no longer wants you. The refrain of the song about has the singer having this dialogue with friends, which echoes the ways in which manhood is a collective action—shaped by and with men peers.[2]

Gender studies scholar Linn Sandberg, who has studied men's sexuality in later life, noted that even men in their seventies and eighties "seemed to think of sexual desire as something natural that was worth keeping up."[3] Being able to get and have sex is not just the pursuit of younger men. Indeed, keeping up with sexual activity can make men feel youthful and valuable, as sex and intimacy can "enhance or reinstate one's feeling of being valued as an individual."[4]

Participants' stories showed that once men figured out sex and gained experience, then they became concerned with continuing to have it. There was pressure to "keep it up"—that is, to carry on having it as a measure of manhood.[5] Doing so was a means of demonstrating control and mastery over one's body.[6] And to do so, men needed women to be and stay interested in them, sexually. Being rejected or broken up with by women left men in a position of vulnerable masculinity and the risk of being seen as or feeling like "failed men." As much as men wanted to be the Proficient Man described in Chapter 4, they did not want to be the "failed man" who could not keep it up.

Keeping it up is similar to getting it—though it is about getting it on an ongoing basis and throughout men's lives. Keeping it up was an issue for interviewees of all ages, though, to be sure, physiological changes associated with aging and diminishing erectile function were particularly acute for men in their fifties and sixties. For younger men and those with no physical concerns, keeping it up was also a challenge due to breakups, feelings of habituation, parenthood, loss of affection or intimacy within a relationship, sexual incompatibility, or dissolution of marriages.

In this chapter, I share stories of men's struggles to maintain an active sex life with women partners, which was important not just for the pleasure, satisfaction, and health benefits associated with sexual release but also for interviewees' sense of themselves as men and their performance of gender.[7] Not being sexually active—whether by choice, chance, or circumstance—weighed heavily on men and caused many to question their desirability and worth as both sexual partners and as men more broadly. Women mattered in shaping manhood here because men could not keep it up without them. Women partners functioned primarily as agents of affirmation (or agents of denial) in all aspects of keeping it up. In this chapter, I focus on relationship issues and transitions before taking up (in Chapter 7) physiological troubles that made it difficult for some men to keep it up.

Does Monogamy Mean Monotony? Habituation and Keeping Up Desire

Marriage did not influence the sexual selves of most of the men we interviewed (unlike many of the women I spoke with for *Deserving Desire*, who found it a major transition). Because there are few cultural taboos or restrictions for men about having sex before marriage and because sex is often encouraged as a demonstration of masculinity, getting married did not provide a sense of freedom or an alleviation of guilt or shame for the majority of men in the way it did for many women.[8] Basically, most of the men did not feel remorseful about having sex before marriage, so marriage didn't really change much for them.

Yet the vast majority of men interviewees believed that sexual desire and ability to perform decreased over the course of men's lives. In response to questions about how sexual activity changes with age, many talked about sexuality within a frame of "stages." These stages echoed stereotypical notions of straight masculinity in popular culture. For teenagers and young men, the common narrative was copious sexual experimentation and thinking about sex in terms of personal gratification and, often, conquest. During this time, women functioned mostly as objects, which signified men's status and sexual appeal. This is followed by a period of seeking out a partner with whom to settle down. The "settled" phase is when the man marries or commits. And then, many interviewees thought, comes the phase of decline—when there is a lot less sexual activity, and men have or worry about having problems with erectile dysfunction.

I saw this trajectory frequently in analyzing interview transcripts, even those of younger interviewees who expected their sex lives to follow this pattern. Greg (20, single, student, East Asian), for instance, commented:

> When we're young we tend to have high sexual desires. Not everyone, but some men, and as they grow older they eventually find, like they settle for someone, they settle down with someone and they just, I guess their sexual desire goes down because they can't just like keep switching [partners]. And I guess they're just used to having—like they already had that spark in their life early on when they had a lot of sex. . . . When people get older they stop caring about their image as much, and . . .

they might gain weight or stop caring about their appearance. So that might factor into why they're not as attracted to each other anymore.

Greg seemed to view this phase of committing to a partner as unexciting, implied by his use of the word "settling." Although men actually seemed to prefer and appreciate being in and having sex in monogamous relationships (see Chapter 5), many, like Greg, described this stage of commitment with a tinge of regret—as if it was about giving up more than gaining. The loss of excitement that follows commitment is called habituation. The "spark" that spurred desire early in the relationship dims and as a result partners have less sex over the course of the relationship.

Yet qualitative studies of couples in long-term relationships show that it's a bit more complicated than that. Sociologists Amy Lodge and Debra Umberson studied sexual behavior among married couples and found that couples did in fact report less frequent sexual activity but, in some cases, couples noted that the quality of sex improved over time.[9] Sex was better because couples felt as if they knew and appreciated their partner and his or her sexual proclivities. However, Lodge and Umberson found that when husbands' interest or pursuit of sex diminished, midlife wives questioned *their* desirability. At the same time, their husbands worried about their ability to perform. The relevance of this study to the experiences of the men we spoke with is this: even though sex was described as more satisfying and key to satisfaction in long-term relationships, fixation on or internalization of gendered scripts about how sex is supposed to be and how men are supposed to perpetually keep it up mattered in how men assessed sex in their relationships and how they assessed themselves as men.[10] Simply, expectations about how husbands are supposed to be the desirers and pursuers of sex influenced both behavior and relationship satisfaction. Furthermore, because sex affirms manhood, the transition to having less sex means having fewer opportunities to affirm it that way.

Although not all the men we interviewed who'd been in long-term relationships talked about habituation as something that happened to them, many did. Those men acknowledged that the desire they once felt for their partners (or believed their partners felt for them) was no longer there—although there were many reasons they gave to explain this. As Josh (57, married, mechanic, white), who'd been married to his wife for twenty-five years, described it:

> Age itself slows down human life. Period. But—but I think another thing, too . . . when you're married for such a long time to the same person . . . her desire slows down and I think what that does is that puts your desire in a mode to slow down also. . . . You get to the point that [your wife is] just tired of putting something on that is really pretty or whatever. You know what I'm saying? We made it through another day [with no sex] and that's the way it goes, too bad. You know? And that attitude would slow you down at the same time.

When Josh felt that his wife was no longer putting in an effort in her appearance or in making him feel desired, he started to desire her less. Although he initially spoke of age and long-term marriage as catalysts for a decline in sex—attributing responsibility to his wife can also be a strategy for maintaining his masculine image. Josh implied that if she tried harder, his interest in sex might not have waned. Josh's wife was implicitly positioned as an agent of denial in that Josh saw her behavior and their long-term marriage as contributing to the change in their sexual activity.

Deon (60, separated, delivery driver, Black), said something similar. He said that sex within a relationship "is always [with] the same person, it gets boring. . . . You can always have sex with that person each and every day. Anytime you want to." Both of these men blamed monotony for the decline in their sexual relationships. They felt that it was too hard to keep it up when they no longer desired their partners as they had in the earlier days of their relationships. In this way, they infer that the problem resides, at least in part, in their wives, rather than in their own aging or changing attitudes. In so doing, they can still come across as interested in sex, as men are perpetually supposed to be, and support the stereotype that men need variety in sexual partners. Women, it seems, are expected to hold up their end of a gendered bargain, in which they continue to make themselves appealing and to "spice things up" for their men partners.

For other men habituation happened soon after getting married. Jose (61, dating/ previously married, retired, Latino), for instance, shared stories about the sexual exploits that occurred throughout his marriage. Fidelity was consistently a challenge for Jose because he found sex with the same partner "boring." Although he married the first person he had sex with and stayed married to her for almost thirty years, for most of that time he had other sexual partners.

Looking back, Jose said he learned about sex from "word of mouth, mostly, you know. The kids all talked, that's all they wanted to talk about when you're 14. . . . And some of the older guys explained to the younger guys. I never had it at home. See, I'm from the old times, at home nobody talked about it." Although he was born in the United States, he spent his adolescence and early teens (until the age of 23) in Western Europe, where his parents were from. He had sex for the first time at the age of 16, with his girlfriend of two years, whom he later married. Jose remembers it as a very positive experience because he was in love and saw sex as a "passage into manhood, great sensation." And although their relationship was good and satisfying for the first ten years, after a while, Jose felt that he and his now ex-wife might not have been on the same page as far as the importance of sex in their marriage. He explained, "I also think that I needed more, you know, like some people need more than others. . . . In my case in particular I think I had more desire than she had—more—a higher level of libido than my wife, or former wife, had." For this reason, he initiated sex most—if not all—of the time in their relationship.

Jose was particularly happy in his thirties, which he said was the best phase of his life as far as sex was concerned because "you're strong, you have the knowledge." He was pleased not due to the intimacy he shared with his wife but because of his self-assessed sexual prowess. When he says "you're strong," he implies that his ability to perform and keep it up was not an issue. It was during this time when he first pursued a sexual relationship outside of his marriage. For him, monogamy was not consistent with his sexual self-image. And although he felt somewhat guilty about cheating, he also accepted it as the way some people just are. He accounted for this by saying, "It depends on your life, you know, some people just accommodate the one person, other people, depending on their proclivities, like more than one partner. It's different strokes for different folks, sort of. For me, I always had trouble being loyal to just one person, frankly."

So Jose found himself taking advantage of extramarital sexual opportunities as they presented themselves. In midlife, keeping it up meant finding ways to make sex exciting, which included other partners, much to the devastation of his wife of 28 years. He struggled with following contradictory sexual scripts. As a married person, raised Catholic in a Latino family, monogamy was expected. But as a straight masculine man (and a Latino man with high sexual desire), he felt encouraged to take advantage of any sexual opportunity and justified his strong desires with scripts about varying libidos.

At 61, he looks back, however, and wishes he'd been faithful to his wife more of the time and curbed his desire a bit more, because he recognized the fallout for his family. Wistfully, he said, "Well, if I had to do it all over again, of course I would change. I guess I would be more loyal and try to—but then again, you know, what you think now you don't necessarily think when you're younger." In his current relationship, he finds fidelity easier because he doesn't have the same desires or libido he had when he was in his twenties and thirties.

Other men, like Geno (65, married for forty-two years, retired executive, white), turned to another partner because of feelings of frustration and rejection in what they described as sexless marriages. Being with a wife who would turn away from him in bed hit hard on Geno's self-esteem and made him feel lonely and unloved. Geno saw his wife as an agent of denial—he could not get what he wanted or felt he needed with regard to sexual satisfaction and saw his wife's lack of interest as the reason for this. As discussed in Chapter 5, men seemed to really depend on intimate partners for emotional support and validation. So, when it was lacking, some went out of their marriages to find a way to keep up their sex lives and redeem their sexual selves and manhood, rather than seeking sexual outlets that did not include infidelity.

When I asked Geno what sex was about for him in his forties and fifties, he said:

> There was a transition at that point in terms of the frequency of sexual activity. But in terms of my viewpoint it was always—it has always been about connecting. It was about the expression of affection. And so that feeling through my entire adulthood really hasn't changed. The frequency has certainly changed but the desire behind it, at least with my wife, has always been about the one idea of affection.
>
> Beth: How have you felt about the decline in frequency?
>
> Geno: Uh, pretty shitty. Yeah, that—I'm disappointed in that. That, that has decreased. And it has been a topic of conversation with my wife and I and it has led me to unfortunately have an affair at one time. So that was—and my wife knows about the affair—so that was a stressful—that has caused a stress in our relationship. . . . I talked before about opportunity and what—it was kind of almost the perfect storm of situation. Sex with my wife has always been—I said it before—about connecting. And as the sex diminished, that connection also diminished. And as I also said before, it's a void that needed to be filled. I retired in my mid-50s—had the opportunity to retire early and my wife encouraged me to do so. She is also a professional and so she continued to work. That unfortunately gave me the opportunity to have this span of time that needed to be filled. And, and so with the lack of affection that I was feeling, I sought out, uh, another opportunity. And as it presented itself, I took advantage of it.

Like Jose, Geno uses the idea of "opportunity" as a motivator for having an affair. Although they did so for different reasons, both suggested that once the possibility existed, they were inclined to act on it, which is consistent with sexual scripts that men never turn down a chance for sex.[11] The feeling of monotony for Jose and the disinterest Geno felt from his wife may be more similar than different. Sex, as many of the men we spoke with suggested, and as has been shown throughout this book, was about bonding and feeling loved or admired, which essentially translated into feeling affirmed as men. And when they felt they were not getting it at home, they sought it from other partners. They needed this affirmation from *women*—they needed to prove that they could catch a woman's eye and that women would have sex with them. Because older, partnered men have fewer opportunities to experience sexual conquest or show off that they are desired, the way their partners responded to them (or failed to respond to them) seemed to be the way they read their sexual allure. In this sense, women mattered as external sources of attribution of fault in men's sexual decline. Women partners could be held responsible for men's sense of themselves as "failed men." So men like Geno and Jose sought out other partners either to provide a feeling of conquest and status via garnering women's attention or to make up for what they felt was missing in their own relationships. When they saw their wives as agents of denial, they looked for other women to serve as objects or agents of affirmation.

In his marriage Geno was usually the one to initiate sex, which was a source of frustration. He wanted to feel wanted. He explained, "As I got older, and am now older, I experienced times of I could say anger that my wife wasn't the initiator. It was always me. And that I had to read the tea leaves. And so I wished as I grew older that my wife was more spontaneous and aggressive in that manner. And to her credit there have been times that she has indeed done that but less so in the last, let's say, ten years of our lives."

Geno never really felt sure whether his wife desired him, given her lack of sexual initiation. He felt he had to "read the tea leaves" to try to figure out when or if she wanted to have sex. When I asked Geno how important sex is in his marriage at this stage in his life, he explained:

> The lack of it caused me to have an affair so I think that says something. Is it important? Yeah, it is important. It's a way to show, for myself, a way to show how I feel. It's a way to express my love for her. It's— more than recreation now. . . . As you get older, I think minors become majors. So the things you took for granted that you can no longer do, now become things that, that maybe you look at more closely and wonder why we aren't doing that any longer? And so I look at that and say, "Do you feel the same way about me as I do about you?"

Geno's comments show the importance of intimacy, of connection, of closeness that partnered sexual activities bring to a relationship.[12] He wanted to continue to have a loving and active sex life with his wife, but it wasn't happening. As he said, as he got older, sex became more important to him, as did the feeling of being wanted and loved. He worried not just about the lack of sex but also about what it said about him as a person deserving of love. Feeling sexually desired was seemingly a way of affirming his manhood, particularly in his retirement.. He no longer had his professional work identity to define him. Geno noted how his daily routine changed entirely and how this made for a challenging adjustment. The lack of intimacy in his marriage was more salient than it had been when he was working.

In his research on men's failures of masculinity, sociologist Scott Melzer noted that "men must demonstrate mastery and control over their bodies and a sense of status and identity from their work to stake a claim to American manhood."[13] Melzer found that men who experience a masculine failure internalize it as part of their identity. In other words, they see themselves as "failed men." He found that men deal with masculine failures in several ways: repairing, compensating, and redefining. Men may seek to fix whatever the problem is by finding new ways to express masculinity. Alternatively, they may try to compensate for what's lacking by showing their manhood in other areas. Finally, men can redefine, they can write new scripts for manhood and for acceptance of modified or alternate masculinities.

At this stage, Geno's control over both body and work identity were in flux. Although he said he respected his wife a great deal, it seems having time on his hands made him lonelier and less sure of himself as a man. He was not the businessman commuting to the city with purpose every day, nor was he the younger man who enjoyed an active sex life with his wife. He was not feeling valued, seemingly, in the way that might affirm older men in "youth-oriented" societies.[14] So, what defined him as a man? What avenues did he have for demonstrating masculinity? Geno's affair thus functioned as compensation and repair. That is, Geno seemed to be making up for feelings of emasculation associated with not working, not being pursued by his wife, and with her lack of receptivity to his advances. He remedied the situation by having an affair as substantiation of his desirability.

Ultimately though, he ended the affair because he "came back to what was important to me. And I found that my wife was more important to me. My life was more important to me than what might be outside of it. And whatever potential or distraction it was—it didn't weigh favorably against what I already had." So Geno continues to work on his marriage and is committed to being faithful going forward. At the time of our interview, he strove to keep up the sexual aspect of their relationship even though, he shared, little had changed since the affair. Yet, he identified a silver lining in what he had gone through. He explained:

> In an odd way my wife has helped me directly and indirectly to develop my sexual awareness and sexual feelings. Because of our relationship . . . she has caused me to look at my sexuality, my need for sex, my desire for sex. She has caused me to think about this in a way other than having a spousal loving relationship. So, being married and going through the ebb and flow of a lifetime with a person has caused me to, to kinda

consider all elements of sex beyond that of a loving monogamous relationship.

With the affair Geno seemed to be proving to himself that he could be a valued sex partner. The other woman's interest in him made him feel good about himself and allowed him to satisfy unmet physical urges (which, surely, he might have satisfied in ways other than infidelity). He was also keeping up his masculine sense of self, though at the expense of his wife's feelings and the sanctity of their marriage. Ultimately, at least at the time of our interview, Geno chose love over sex. Perhaps he realized that fidelity and commitment were values he wanted to align himself with (or realign himself with) more than he wanted or needed affirmation from other women about his desirability. It could be that just knowing that he could be with another woman or had been with another woman was enough validation for him to accept the state of his marital intimacy.

Most of the long-married men we spoke with had not had affairs, though some of those men talked about how they understood the decision to do so, perhaps as a way of showing their work in keeping it up. They said this due to their own feelings of boredom or lack of intimacy or because they were not as attracted to their partners as they had been earlier in their relationships. Russell (65, married for thirty-five years, insurance agent, white), for instance, described feelings of attraction to other women and shared that he enjoys looking at younger women and sometimes going to strip clubs. He said:

> I have found that, you know, especially, too—I mean when you get into your older age, a man my age probably is more interested in a somewhat younger woman, and they usually have a different—I've never had any affair outside of my marriage. . . . But, like, I know this one woman and I could be easily very attracted to her. She's 20 years younger than me and she's actually now become single because she's divorcing her husband. But I mean she has so many issues going on. I mean I'm sure that she's not really exactly looking to dive into something, you know?

Men like Russell seemed to hold on to the idea that keeping it up is about showing active desire. In so doing, they retained at least a patina of youthful masculinity; they aged "successfully."[15] They followed scripts suggesting that being a man is about continuing to "look" and think about sex with multiple partners.

Finally, a handful of men remained committed and faithful to their spouses in essentially celibate marriages. These men expressed a deep sense of conflict. They seemed to truly care about their wives, children, and the families they had established. Yet they did not want to imagine that their sexual lives were over, nor did they want to give up hope that things might change. They spoke out as "failed men"; a defeated tone pervasive in their interviews.

Mick (56, married, retail manager, white), for example, a father of one, had been married to his wife for twenty-seven years. Mick loved his family very much; however, he and his wife were no longer intimate because, he confided, his wife dealt with both physical illness and responsibilities associated with career and motherhood that left her uninterested in sex. He explained:

> There's that one missing link. And growing up, on the totally other spectrum . . . from the time I was 12 or 13, [I was a] very physically and sexually active young man, all the way to the time we got married, and we were rather randy when we first got married. Once we had our daughter, years after that was like declining gains. We've confronted the situation numerous times and I gotta agree with her that yeah, there are times when my body hurts, and there are times when I know her body hurts. But it's not all the time. And we've discussed it actually, talked about it, without anything getting accusatory on either side. And, you know, we try to come to a center point and there's been times when we did try to connect and for one reason or another things just were not right. And it just kind of blows everything for the next couple of months. Either one decides maybe it's just not worth it. And

> it sucks because I want to be in this loving relationship. And I am in a loving married relationship but that physicality is missing and I dearly miss it.

Mick framed his current relationship with his wife using stories about his past sexual self. As I've noted elsewhere, men incorporate their younger sexual selves into their stories about their current lack of sex or sexual self-image as a means of constructing their sexual identity.[16] That he was, as a teenager and at the beginning of his marriage, "rather randy" is a way of saying that the way he is now does not encompass all he is as a sexual person or as a man, or all he has ever been. Linn Sandberg found something similar in her research on men's sexuality. She noted that men described their desire as once "strong, uncontrollable and direct." In so doing, their "narratives of a strong sexual desire in the past . . . establish[ed] them as masculine subjects."[17] In other words, men like Mick framed their desire as an important way of showing their manhood, in emasculating circumstances. Here, too, men can be seen as compensating for their current inability to meet manhood mandates with stories from their earlier days.

Mick wanted to keep up his relationship, but without sex or physical intimacy he didn't know how much longer he could. He characterized his partnership as out of sync and tried to talk through ways of improving it, but didn't feel as if he was getting anywhere. His wife was an agent of denial—denying him opportunity to prove himself as a man or to satisfy his sexual yearnings. Given his sadness over the state of their sexual relationship, I asked Mick whether he might end his marriage or seek another partner. He said:

> I did join into a bond of matrimony and I would prefer it to be that way. I really don't want to roam. But we have these conversations about this as our relationship progressed over the years. We've been married a long time. . . . I need to eventually tell her—and it's been awhile since we had one of these conversations—I can't do this much longer. I still have time. I'm not an old decrepit person yet. There's time for me to enjoy my life.

> You either want to be part of that with me . . . or we have an open relationship.

For Mick, marriage means commitment and sticking it out, whether with or without sex. But personally, his desire has not changed. Like other men, he craves not just physical pleasure or release but sensuality. He gets massages because he longs for the feeling of being touched. He said:

> I love physicality, I yearn for it. And as a long-time married man with a wife who's gone through lots of emotional and physical changes over the last couple years, especially with intense medical crap that's going on, times for being amorous are few and far between. . . . I don't often get a chance to express my sexuality as much as I would want to. But, that doesn't mean I don't yearn for it. . . . Not that I feel I'm due it because I'm married to a person. And I can understand reasons why that disjunct has happened. But it still doesn't do any good for my libido. . . . I don't need it every night. I'm easy to satisfy. At this point in my life, my birthday and Father's Day would be nice. And I'm more than happy to please you. . . . Time hasn't changed those inner yearnings. . . . . I still love women. I still yearn for companionship in that regard. But will I act on that? With somebody else other than my wife? Probably not. Unless there's a mutual understanding. We have this conversation, she says, "I like being married, I like the comfort of knowing you're here. I love you as a person. I'm just not a sexual being any more. I don't have the yearning or the craving. Things don't work that great any more down there." . . . So the environment around me, outside of my skin, is what's changed. Not how I feel inside me.

Mick's story is one of commitment and love, but also grief. When we spoke, he seemed at once resigned to this life and puzzled over how he could live out the rest of his days like this. This was not just about his sense of himself as a man, but as a person who longed to be touched and feel that sense of physical intimacy that he realized mattered so much to him. This was a common concern among the men we spoke with, particularly those who did not have partners later in life. Older men sometimes affirm the importance of closeness and intimacy, more so than of sexual pleasure, as means of recognizing and accepting decreased sexual activity, while still acknowledging that desire is there.[18] Mick would have found just being physically close to his wife gratifying, even if they rarely had intercourse. Because masculinity is so tenuous and because we discourage emotional expression for men in U.S. society, there are few places where men like Mick can feel physically and emotionally affirmed. When it was absent in his relationship, he discovered how important being touched was to him in making him feel supported and cared for.

When men like Mick are not able to keep it up, they are also unable to feel affirmed as men. In the same way that sex is an act of affirmation of worth—not having sex was perceived as a denial of worth. Yet, as Mick attributes this change to his environment, he also places responsibility for his sexual satisfaction in the hands of his wife. When he says he hasn't changed, he, like other older men interviewed for this study, keeps a hold on the masculine image of the "randy" young man he once was.

Walker (39, married fifteen years, works in information technology, biracial), a father of four, was going through a similar situation. In this case, however, it was his depression coupled with his wife's lack of interest in sex that created it. He labored to keep up his desire for sex as he entered into his thirties, in the wake of challenges he and his family faced. He shared:

> Our relationship just became very difficult and it's hard to, you know, when you're in a difficult situation relationship wise, sex definitely takes its toll. Sex takes a hit, put it like that, it's affected in a negative way. And, I—there were just so many factors in my 30s—working terribly long hours, having zero energy, being in a bad place with my wife. Stress from the kids, you know. Financial stresses. So, in my mid-late 30s sex was just almost like a memory. . . . When you're arguing about the stupid stuff in marriage, it's hard to take sex seriously and say, despite your

> marriage falling apart, you're concerned about sex. That conversation is not going to go well. So at some point you just stop trying.

Initially sex was a place for Walker and his wife to connect and come together and let go of some of the tensions, but,

> it stopped working, I'd say, maybe a year or two ago. That's when we just fell out of sync. . . . Sex became lackluster and also my wife was having trouble sleeping. She had hormonal issues with her thyroid. A bunch of things were happening at the same time. The stress of the kids. They went into a new school. My daughter got involved in some cyber-bullying crap at school so all kinds of stuff. We said if we're going to be in the bed, we're going to sleep. We don't have time. She couldn't keep her eyes open. She was sleeping on the couch.

For Walker keeping it up was untenable because there were so many other priorities to which he and his wife needed to direct their energy. Sex was just not an option when they weren't even sleeping in the same room. Walker said he learned, during that time, that he could be a "sex camel." By this he meant he realized he could go for a long time without it—which he would never have believed in his younger years could be the case later. He explained, "Early on in the relationship I think I would be clawing the walls in certain periods my wife would say, 'You have a cycle and certain times of the month you can't sleep unless you have sex.' And I really felt that way. I'd just be watching the clock all night. I'd be really excited and energized and ready. But I think as I've gotten older, maybe I've put sex in perspective, I don't know." Walker seemed to hope this was just a phase in their relationship—something not uncommon for couples to go through when there are young children and other priorities that supersede intimacy.[19] But accepting that he didn't feel the desire he felt he should was hard on him as a man.

In a study of sex in long-term relationships, sociologists Sinikka Elliott and Debra Umberson framed desire as something that is "performed." Consistent with the sexual scripting approach to sexuality, the desire of men and women is influenced by social norms about how they *should* feel, in conjunction with what they actually feel.[20] Elliott and Umberson also found that couples thought of sex as a measure of marital success. Part of the reason that Walker felt bad about his current sex life was likely because of what he thought it should be and how he should be feeling, as a man. Like some of the individuals in the Elliott and Umberson study, Walker (and Mick) worked to perform desire in a way that mitigated conflict over divergent sexual libidos.

There are some key differences between Walker and Mick as compared to Jose and Geno, which might explain why Walker and Mick did not have affairs. Walker and Mick were both younger and still had children living at home. They also had reasons other than habituation for the lack of sex in their marriages. Mick's wife's physical limitations due to surgery and Walker's wife's hormonal issues and family's stress due to troubles with their children were external factors—they were not about their own desire as men. And both referenced their younger, desirous selves to show that the problem did not rely solely with them.

For Geno and Jose, both in their sixties (though Jose had been having affairs for a longer period of time), their narratives were about how strong their own desire was compared with that of their partners. As men, they wanted more sex. Also Geno, at least, was in a stage of identity transition where he seemed to be navigating his place as a man who is not working *and* not having sex. He needed to do some repair work to make up for his appearance as a "failed man." Walker and Mick, in contrast, still had work identities to ground their masculine identities.

Keeping It Up through Life Transitions

Relationship Transitions: Breakups and Divorce

About half of the divorced men in this study said divorce didn't really influence their sexuality. Most of those in the other half said it only had a small impact. However, for a few, divorce had a significant bearing on their sexual selves. As it did for some women in my previous research, divorce resulted in both self-discovery and excitement, and, at times, feelings of inadequacy and fears that they might never have sex again. After divorce, some of the men talked of difficulty in finding other relationships or keeping it up and trying to date in an environment that was very different from the way it was before they got married.

For instance, when I asked Bruce (59, divorced, unemployed engineer, white) how things had been with him sexually since his divorce, he confided:

> It's been difficult, Beth. Since we broke up, I have not felt real comfortable about having sex with women. Because I still feel attached to my wife. And the other problem—I don't know if this is a subconscious issue, is that I have 3 daughters. . . . I think if you're a father of 3 boys it's not a problem. But if you're a father of three daughters and you're much more sensitive to women's needs and desires and you don't want to hurt them. . . . I just don't know if I'm ever going to get back into a relationship. And I know other professional men that have felt the same way as well. Do they need that in their life at this point? . . . I have desire to be intimate and loved, and love in return, but I'm having a tough time getting into a sexual relationship with a female. . . . I've been hurt very badly and I don't want to get hurt again. Am I not your best subject for this? . . . I'm apprehensive about getting into a relationship, spending time with a person, putting my ego out on a limb and then [finding] we're incompatible. I don't need that. Why even venture there?

As with "getting it," keeping it up involved the chance of being rebuffed by potential partners. Like Bruce, a couple of men we spoke with were thus resigned to not dating because they felt that they did not want to go through what they'd been through with their divorces. Fear of rejection was not just an issue for the young or inexperienced, not just a concern when "getting it." Many of the men we interviewed dreaded heartbreak and rejection throughout their lives. Giving up on keeping it up was thus a way to avoid being spurned.

Curtis (55, engaged/previously married, retired military, Black) felt the same way after his divorce. He married for the first time at 19 and was in that relationship for "eight tumultuous years." He explained that after his divorce, he took a two-year hiatus from dating and sex because he felt so deceived by his former wife, who had been unfaithful in their marriage. He shared, "When I eventually got divorced I couldn't really trust women as much as I used to. I felt a sense of really—betrayal, ok? And I felt that, you know . . . I didn't want to have any kind of sexual relationship or any type of relationship with a woman for a long time."

Curtis made it clear that he did not want to risk being brokenhearted or betrayed. His comment that he did not trust women also implies that he saw them as having the capacity to signify something important about him as a man. It was easier to stay away than take a chance of being denied or hurt by a woman. Curtis's decision not to have sex was also motivated by consciously focusing on looking for meaning in a relationship, rather than focusing on sex. He said he felt good about making that choice, as he explained,

> I felt . . . proud that I could do that, you know what I mean? Because I felt that . . . I needed a break. I needed to start focusing on just . . . me and the gratification aspect of love. You know what I mean? Because it's not all about just the sexual aspect. You know? You have to find the right person, at the right time in your life, in order for it to be the way you wanted it to be. . . . And I was at that point that that's what I was looking for.

Divorce allowed some of the men we spoke with a chance to experiment and have new sexual relationships and encounters, which were a welcome change. Men like Kirk (54, divorced/remarried, self-employed, white) said as much in response to questions about the effects of divorce on sexuality. Kirk said that divorce "sort of unleashed [my sexuality]. I was like okay, it's a finely tuned machine now, let's put it to work." He was eager for new experiences and felt that they helped him heal: "I crossed a bridge and I sort of took away the pain of—getting divorced was not my idea so there was a lot of pain there—it took away some of the pain. It was like well, at least something good has come out of it." Kirk could repair his failed sense of manhood—that he had not been able to keep up in his relationship—by successfully seeking out new sexual partners and making use of his "finely tuned machine."

In discussing divorce (and relationships in general) most of the men talked about failed relationships as emotionally agonizing and hard to get over. The men who were most affected by divorce were those who felt blindsided or heartbroken when it happened. These men seemed determined not to get hurt again. Contrary to stereotypes about men's disinterest in romantic attachment or desire for sex outside of relationships, for men, being in a failed relationship, being cheated on or rejected were great sources of pain. For some, however, new beginnings and new sexual partners were opportunities to restore some sense of masculinity and self-esteem. On the other hand, not venturing into relationships or dating was also a way to mitigate emasculation. In all these situations, women mattered in shaping men's sexual selves. If men did not feel so affirmed (or denied) by women partners, divorce might not have been such a blow. Women's rejection seemed particularly painful as it labeled men as less desirable and thus lower status in the hierarchy of men.

Fatherhood

When I interviewed women for *Deserving Desire*, motherhood had a major impact on women's sexual selves, both in negative (fatigue, loss of desire, decrease in frequency and time for sex) and positive (sexual awakenings, recognizing the power of women's bodies, and self-acceptance) ways.[21] For men, this was not the case. None of the men in this study said that their sexuality changed or evolved in any significant way as a result of becoming fathers. Some noted a temporary (mental) discomfort having sex when partners were pregnant, but that was the extent of their concerns.

More often, sexuality changes associated with fatherhood were due to partners' levels of interest in and time for sex. Other research corroborates this. Chelom Leavitt and colleagues studied parenting stress and sexual satisfaction among over 160 couples after the first year of their child's birth and discovered that when new mothers felt stress, this predicted decreased sexual satisfaction for both new moms and new dads.[22] This very situation happened for Mick. Between working long hours and raising their only child, his wife was exhausted and disinterested in sex. As Mick explained, "we knew we only wanted one child, so having sex was not a reason for procreation. It was more for my enjoyment, so it seemed. And that wasn't fun either. Because I think she kind of wasn't into it. Didn't have that mutual enjoyment, like it used to be before the baby was born. So, the baby I think was the tipping point of the change."

Even men who felt their level of attraction for their partner had not changed over the course of a long relationship recognized that life transitions associated with parenthood and adult responsibilities meant mid-life was a time they could not keep it up as they had when they were younger. For instance, Bradley (49, married, health-care administrator, white) said:

> It's been 20 years and I really love my wife. I still get fully, emphatically turned on when I see my wife naked. . . . When she's in her panties . . . I still get totally, totally turned on. And a lot of guys don't. I know a lot of guys who aren't turned on by their . . . wife anymore and I'm fully. I mean every guy wants more sex at my age, I would love to have it more often, you know? That's the thing—kids and the stress of both people working—it doesn't happen as often.

Bradley's comments show his internalization of sexual scripts about men's sexual desire, throughout their lives. When he said, "every guy my age wants more sex," he implies that men in their late forties are supposed to have strong desire but are also not likely to be keeping it up. This is a time during which men may question their manhood because they do not have the reassurances they might have had when they were younger and having more frequent sex or even more frequent sexual interaction with more women. Bradley seemed to accept that this was a stage in his life, but was also sure to emphasize that, unlike most guys, he still is easily aroused and has a wife who has kept up her level of desirability, too, despite having had kids.

A couple of men, such as Eli (64, divorced, consultant, white), recalled that the pressure of being a provider created a stressful situation and it was that, rather than the transition to fatherhood per se, that changed their sex lives. Eli stated:

> So it wasn't having children that was the impact. It was the fact that when she was pregnant—the realities of the economic demand that a family and moving from an apartment to a house and the facts of non-sexual life began to become overwhelming. And it was a burden I hadn't anticipated. Nobody explained it to me. I wasn't psychologically prepared for it. And that creates a barrier when it comes to sexuality. I just stopped asking for it and she stopped also asking or expressing interest in it. I mean if we did it, we did it once a month.

Eli's feeling of responsibility to financially provide for his family, coupled with his wife's decreased interest, meant they were unable to keep it up. He felt pressure to be a breadwinner and was not earning the kind of money his wife expected. In that way, he felt emasculated first by his financial status and then again by his wife's rejection. It seems he saw his wife as an agent of denial of his manhood, because she communicated that he was not good enough in either area. Their relationship suffered as a result. He explained:

> I think her expectation versus my expectation—even though we expressed what we wanted marriage to be like . . . we never talked about sex, and we certainly never discussed the timing of children. She apparently had a—I read in her diaries later—but she apparently had a game

> plan that I had no clue about, and so this was a terrible situation. . . . One of the things that I wanted to share with you is I knew when both children were conceived. I knew exactly the day and the time because we had such little sexual activity, so I knew exactly when they were conceived. And then when we went to the final throes of marital counseling, you know, she had initiated it when the marriage was falling apart, and the therapist said to us, she asked me directly, "How is your sex life?" And I just looked at her and I said, "It's terrible." I said, "It's nonexistent." And [my wife] looked like she had been smacked in the face. . . . And I think that was the last session we ever had. I think what I've learned is you've got to be consistently attracted to your partner or there is no, you know, the emotional portion of a relationship is gone and the sexual portion is likely to go at that time.

In retrospect, Eli thought his wife had married him because he was a nice Jewish man who could give her the life and children she wanted. But he didn't believe she was really attracted to him or loved him. So, in some ways, having children was the beginning of the end as far as Eli was concerned. Because once his ex-wife got what she wanted in terms of children, she no longer wanted sex. And then when she didn't get what she wanted financially, she no longer wanted him.

For Minjun (39, married, instructor, East Asian), it has been *not* becoming a father, despite trying, that has made it hard to keep up his interest in sex. Minjun and his wife married while in graduate school and both have academic careers. The stress of dissertations and finding work took a toll on their sex life, as well as on Minjun's level of desire. He shared, "About for two years when we [were] finishing our doctorate[s], and finishing our dissertation, we were virtually sexless. I was not interested and my wife was sort of disappointed, I guess. But we were really stressed and we were very depressed. So I was not interested anymore."

When I asked what in particular led to his depression, Minjun said he felt hopeless about the future given the grim prospects for jobs in his field, particularly as an immigrant competing against American candidates. After he secured a job, they started trying to conceive, as both really wanted a child. However, years later, they were still struggling with infertility, which added to the stress around sex in their relationship. At the time we met, Minjun was having a difficult time keeping up his interest in sex, which he said had become a "manufacturing process." He explained:

> [We were sexually active] like 10 days ago—that was my timing for babies, it required sex. And I did not enjoy it. . . . I think that [trying to get pregnant] has a big influence. . . . I guess it's been like 5 or 6 years and I'm tired. We don't have a big problem but my wife went to like fertility doctor. From the exam nothing is wrong. . . . I feel like we are stuck even though we are trying. It was just manufacturing process. Not for joy. Not much. So I guess to answer your question when I had to do it for that particular purpose, I don't enjoy it. . . . To me it's like homework. I have to do it now, because we have to have at least one. Otherwise we'll be lonely in later life. Something like homework. We have to finish it.

Describing sex as "homework" for serious students like Minjun and his wife reveals the lack of pleasure he now associates with it. He keeps it up not because he enjoys it, but because he feels that they need to have a child to feel like a family. Minjun has had a complicated sexual history, including childhood sexual abuse and an obsession with pornography, followed by a period of abstinence (see Chapter 2). His feelings about sex are more than conflicted. So, as he only had a short time period during which he really enjoyed sex without feeling guilt or shame, keeping it up is a strain on him and his relationship. He also felt emasculated by his inability to "get" his wife pregnant. He felt he was being punished for the homosexual encounters he endured during childhood sexual abuse and that this was the reason for the infertility. Minjun felt he should have been able to get his wife pregnant and that not doing so was an example of his failing as man. Sex was not a pleasurable act or an act of affirmation of manhood when it did not yield the desired result.

Single Heterosexual Male Seeking Single Heterosexual Female: Finding Partners in Later Life and in the Digital Era

Although narratives around gaining access to girls and sex mostly related to younger men's first or early experiences, a good number of men suggested this was an ongoing negotiation throughout men's lives. For older men—that is, men with sexual experience—getting it became keeping it up. What was different was that, in contrast to their younger peers or younger selves (when they were in their teens or twenties), the men we spoke with felt that money mattered more in keeping it up than it did in getting it. A few younger men alluded to spending money to *get* sex, but more in passing. Being involved in high school dating cultures, bar cultures, or peer networks where dating and hooking up were expected—and where men perceived good looks to be the most important capital—social class did not seem to matter much. But unpartnered men who were seen as old enough to be expected to have financial resources continued to struggle with the youthful dilemma of how to prove themselves as worthy men. Although they may have established their heterosexuality with previous relationships, not having partnered sex meant they did not participate in one of the processes most associated with manhood.

Expressions of masculinities change as men age and as their bodies and ability to communicate manhood shift.[23] Money can be a way to compensate for youth. Most men we interviewed felt that money was necessary for dating, with increased importance as men got older. As Russell (65, married, insurance agent, white) said, with laughter, "It's kind of funny and weird but I mean a lot of times you see these really attractive women in their late 20s or early 30s with some fat, bald, ugly looking guy in his mid-60s and you know there's the one common denominator, the guy's got a lot of money and they're looking to get it. And they don't care that he doesn't look like much, you know? They figure maybe . . . he'll try something, he'll have a heart attack and then she'll be [rich]."

For working class or poor men, money was an issue in their ability to keep it up. Dating was characterized as expensive. So although men like Gary (68, widower, photographer/information technology worker, white), were still interested in sex, finding a partner was not viable. When asked if sexuality was an important part of who he is, Gary replied:

> Not as much as it used to be. It's still something I would—I haven't been with anyone since my wife passed. I'm going to be very honest, since it's confidential. Much as I'm trying to meet ladies I guess I'm not pushing that hard because my budget doesn't allow dating. One date and then the rest of the month I can barely take care of [my bills]. . . . The first date, if you try to make it a simple one, someone will say—we'll go to dinner the first time. Wait a minute—whoa! Hold on! Even if I was making good money, the first things got to be a big dinner to start off?! The first time I took [my wife] to dinner my financial situation was a lot better. . . . I think it all has to be based on better finances. I can't get out there.

Money factored into decision making regarding dating for many of the men when it came to keeping it up, as it did when it came to getting it. The difference here is these men—mostly older/ midlife men—were concerned with both getting it *and* keeping it up. They had trouble finding partners after breakups and for some, like Gary, not having money made it nearly impossible to have sexual intimacy or sustain it. Gary seemed to feel that he couldn't see a woman choosing him over other men, because he could not afford to date in the way he thought women expected.

Older men also felt that if they didn't get it now, they were running out of chances to keep it up. For many of the men we interviewed in their forties and older, the idea of dating and entering into a relationship was daunting. For those who ended a long-term relationship, dating in the digital era was quite different from when they'd last been in the erotic marketplace. Older men, in their late fifties and sixties, felt the challenge of finding partners and navigating new platforms. Some men found older women either sexually unappealing or incompatible. Eli (64, divorced, consultant, white), the man who had a short marriage with a partner whom he felt didn't desire him, struggled regarding where his sexual future would end up. Although he's put a lot of effort into learning how to be the best sexual partner and performer he can, he lamented:

> One thing I have concluded is that women my age have an inverse response to [sex]—that maybe they're willing to engage, but that's gonna be a rarity and there has to be something else involved in that engagement. And so, you know, I kind of resent the reality that women in their 40s are more where I'm at and women in their 60s are not. And women in their 40s are not interested in men in their 60s. So with all of the knowledge I have and all of the skill and desire that I have, it's useless when there's no one there to participate.

Other men, who felt undesirable for one reason or another, struggled even more so as they entered their sixties and realized the pool of potential partners had dwindled to almost none. Wesley (68, single/never married, unemployed, white), for instance, explained that he is disappointed about how his sex life has turned out and that while he's tried online dating—it has not yielded any positive results. Although he kept trying to keep it up, his limitations as a disabled person made him an undesirable partner. He explained:

> I wish someone would give me the instruction manual as to here's what to do to get you sex. But I don't—I don't know what to do. Or even at age 68, is there anything you can do? I'm bald. Does any woman want a bald-headed man? Plus I'm blind. Plus, I'm unemployed, you know? There may not be anything I can do at this point. . . . I always feel like I should be doing something about things, you know? I'm an active, forward-motivated person. I always think don't just sit home and brood about it. Anybody can do that, you know? But take action—take a step. Get out of the house. Have a plan. And right now I don't have a plan.

> I tried one of those internet—eHarmony was the brand I tried. I had a cheap 3 month membership. Never met anybody. . . . On the very last day of my membership I said I'm going to answer every ad on this website. Match or no match. I sent out like 140 emails in one day. Never got a reply because most of the women had expired memberships so they didn't read my messages either. So that was my lesson in how internet dating really works.

Gary, Eli, and Wesley, all in their sixties, struggled to keep it up. They all lacked things they saw as critical in signifying manhood—money, looks, youth. They were all also retired, unemployed, or marginally employed, so they did not have a career to fall back on to secure their place as men. Adding in the awkwardness and challenges associated with online dating—using technologies designed for younger markets—made it difficult for these men to use sex as a medium for affirming manhood.

The vast majority of interviewees wanted to keep up their sex lives. Financial responsibility, habituation in relationships, sexless marriages, and finding and keeping partners complicated the way men felt about their sense of self as both partners in relationships and as men. Rejection, whether active or passive, weighed heavily on the sexual self-images of the men in this study. Getting and keeping it up are markers of manhood that leave some men, like Wesley, Eli, and Minjun, with a masculinity deficit when they are unable to fulfill cultural scripts. Such men internalized this "flawed man" identity and grappled with how to repair, redefine, or compensate.[24]

Although not always intentionally or explicitly, men often placed the blame for indiscretions and failures on their women partners. They framed women as agents of denial—actively preventing men from engaging in sex and thus from being able to signify a masculine self. Men who cheated described the circumstances around doing so as the result of not having enough excitement in their marriage or not getting enough sexual attention. Most of the men were sure to point out that they still had strong desire—which can be a way of compensating with masculine feelings for what they were not getting in experience.[25] They wanted to keep it up, they shared, but it was their partners' issues that made it a challenge. So powerful are scripts about men's desire and sexual activity as a marker of manhood that even men in their fifties and sixties are guided by them, and men of all ages and generations saw this as a motivator for keeping it up.

CHAPTER 7

Keeping *It* Up

MAINTAINING AGING AND CHANGING BODIES

I realize things are slowing down. And while I look at my wife and I love her, I don't want to have her every day (laughs). And it's not derogatory in the slightest. It's like I said, when I go to bed, a lot of times I just want to sleep. And it has nothing whatsoever to do with her. It's just that things are, are going—nature's way. Back in the '60s there was this—there was a poem. It was called "Desiderata" and it kind of talked about like a philosophy on life, you know? And one of the sentences I remember is like, "gradually surrendering the things of youth." Something along that line. And that always kind of pops into my head every now and again. Well, this is one of the things I gradually surrender, this thing of youth. I have no problem with it. I know kind of where it's headed.

—*Dennis (67, married, retired, white)*

Dennis, married for thirty-nine years, seemed to have made peace with the idea that his desire was leveling off. Like other men going through a similar phase, he accepted a redefinition of intimacy at this stage in his life.[1] He had a good marriage and was happy with the closeness and affection he shared with his wife. Yet this doesn't mean it was easy to let go of the youthful sexual self of his past or that he didn't care about his sexual performance. As he said, self-consciously, "I started to notice myself, like in my late 50s . . . I would not be as erect, you know, as I could be. And then it wasn't till maybe only a couple years ago I tried some [medications] and for me they didn't work. Actually, I had some goofy reactions to them but, you know, you always want to be that virile man that you were."

As Dennis talked about experimenting with performance drugs to try to keep up the stamina and erectness of his younger years, he admitted his uneasiness discussing this with me ("I feel a little a nervous talking like this to a woman—like I never, I've never spoke to a woman like this.") But his statement "you always want to be that virile man that you were," tells of the importance to him of keeping it up, even when he knew that his body was slowing down. That Dennis was willing to go through the embarrassment of talking about his erectile dysfunction (ED) with a woman he did not know shows how significant this was to him. Like most other men we spoke with, aging and declining sexual function was a major concern for Dennis.

And although Dennis saw a sexual double standard where women were judged more for how their appearance changed as they aged, he also believed that "men, even older men, I think are concerned about it. I know, even as a married man I kind of like to look nice and I kind of like, you know, people to say, 'Hey Dennis, he looks pretty good. He's 67.' . . . I think it's something we always kind of think about." Looks mattered to him and were something to keep up, so he, at least publicly, put forward an image of an attractive, masculine man. It may be that looking attractive—looking good *for 67 years old*, is a way of compensating for or making peace with the fluctuations in his sexual functioning.

When I asked if there was anything he'd like to change at this stage in his life with respect to his sexuality, he replied:

> Just the normal male insecurities of, uh, gee I wish I was better. Gee, I wish I could last longer (laughs). . . . I still kind of can laugh about it. Yeah well, you got what you got, you gotta live with it. But nothing else besides that. It's been great, you know. It's slowing down considerably so when we do have sex, it's on an average of maybe once a month now. Maybe a little longer sometimes, a little less sometimes. It still feels great. Feels wonderful. And then, usually after it's not like "Oh, gee, let's do that again." When you're in your 20s, it's like, "Hey, that was great, what are you doing in an hour?" No, that part's gone.

This other way of keeping it up, is keeping *it* up; having the ability to get and maintain an erection and to have intercourse with regularity. With men's sexuality judged by erectile function and rooted in scripts likening masculine sexual performance to working machinery and the penis to a tool, it's not at all surprising that all of the men in this study had something to say about keeping it up throughout their lives.[2] Most of the men we interviewed—young, old, having had problems with stamina, premature ejaculation or not—worried about keeping it up.

Being able to perform was not only a measure of manhood but also a means of aging "well."[3] Consistent with a "successful aging" narrative, where appearing aged is something to be actively resisted, the men we spoke with did not seem to want to be labeled as old.[4] They equated being old with diminished sexual capabilities and, thus, diminished manhood. With sexuality such a key aspect of masculinity, men had to grapple with who they were if they could no longer have sex in a way consistent with dominant sexual scripts. In this chapter, I conclude the study of *Getting It, Having It, Keeping It Up*, by looking at how aging and different types of experiences with ED impacted men's sexual selves.

Health Issues and Situational ED

Of those interviewed, 12 of the 15 men in their sixties, 6 of the 20 men in their fifties, 4 men in their forties, and 2 men in their thirties (for a total of 26 percent of the 94 men) said that they experienced ED at some point in time. A few men, like Dennis, accepted or tolerated this as part of the aging process. For others, ED was devastating. All the men who talked about ED noted either explicitly or implicitly that it was emasculating or humbling and thus had a significant impact on their sexual self-image. Men seemed to see ED as an indication of frail or failed manhood.

In some cases, ED was neither chronic nor related to aging. A few interviewees who took mental health-related medications spoke of how the drugs interfered with their sex lives. For example, Trevor (39, dating, warehouse worker, Black) was shot in the leg and seriously injured. This left him with a permanent limp that made him doubt his sexual desirability. During this time, he was prescribed medicine to combat his anxiety and paranoia. For a while, he felt as if no woman would ever want to be with him. He explained:

> My insecurity was at an all-time [high] because I didn't think I would be able to attract what I needed to attract to accomplish my agenda, which was to have sex. I mean, sure, I can masturbate, but how long am I going to be doing that? . . . My physical appearance only bothered me, nobody else. That's why I had the insecurity. I'm not paralyzed anymore; I just walk with a limp. I was taking . . . [an anti-]psychotic drug and I guess one of the side effects was to decrease your sexual desire. But being who I am, it's hard to decrease because it's always on my mind. And even when I took that medication and the opportunity presented itself . . . I would not be able to ejaculate.

Trevor was frustrated with this turn of events but recognized the need for the medication. In his case, being able to continue having sexual partners and confirm his desirability after his injury, was his way of keeping it up. Even if he couldn't climax, the feeling of being wanted was important to him. It was hard for Trevor to accept that women might still be sexually interested in him when he walked with a limp, because this did not fit with his image of a desirable man. In this way, his injury emasculated him and then the medications exacerbated the situation by affecting sexual performance.

Troy (39, single/never married, printer, white), who also dealt with anxiety, had a different response to medication. For him, anything that was going to interfere with sexual performance was not going to work. Troy's doctor prescribed Xanax. But when taking it he, "could not get it up. So I cut that out immediately." Rather than try another pharmaceutical treatment, he just dealt with the anxiety. Troy felt relieved when things went back to normal after he stopped the Xanax. Knowing it was the medicine (rather than his body failing) made him feel better about his sexual performance and about himself as a man. He said, "I knew I didn't have a problem. So I just stopped taking the medicine and I didn't have a problem after it, so it didn't affect me at all. At the time I was still really horny, I just could not get it up." His repeated "I didn't have a problem" was a way to shape the narrative around his sexuality and assert that this was caused by external factors, not his own desire. Showing that he still had desire and that the problem disappeared after stopping the Xanax is a way for Troy to frame himself as in control and masculine. Men with ED can use such discourses of desire as way of retaining sexual subjectivity.[5]

Gavin (48, single/never married, therapist, biracial) participated in a clinical study with an experimental mood-stabilizing medication with the consequence that he "was unable to ejaculate through my trial. . . . Every other time in my life I was able to. So, it's probably the [medicine]." Like Trevor, he dealt with the complications because it was worth it to finish the trial and find a medicine that worked for him. But, like Troy, being able to ascribe his ED to the medicine made him feel better about it because it seemed he felt a greater sense of control over his body and lesser feeling of loss of his masculine identity. All these men were able to distance themselves from the stigma of ED because they could attribute it to something outside of their own bodies and then also within their control (whether they took drugs or not).

Aging Bodies: Perceptions and Fears

Sociologist Laura Carpenter found that at the beginning of their sexual "careers," some people (more men than women) viewed virginity as a stigma they wanted to shed.[6] Here, at the other end of their sex lives, men framed ED as a stigma they hoped to avoid. Most men shared that they did not talk about ED at all with others. Rather, some resisted accepting that they had it. Like men described in another study, who worried about the size of their penis and sought out online support to "fix" this flaw of manhood, men with ED worked to remedy it by searching for "cures."[7]

Men's sexual identities and bodies are tied up in their erectile proficiencies.[8] Western culture is inundated with messages about improving and upholding erectile performance and keeping up a youthful sexual energy.[9] As Susan Bordo has noted, men are described as *being* impotent, rather than *having* impotence.[10] There is a cultural expectation for men to be in control of their bodies and bodily functions throughout their lives.[11] Thus, aging was a chief concern because the men we interviewed believed aging would likely bring ED and ED would bring emasculation. Indeed, one study found that men with ED had lower ratings on *multiple* quality-of-life measures—not just those related to sexuality.[12]

Drugs like Viagra may be changing the way we think about aging and sexuality and who is considered "old." People may now feel that they should have sexual intercourse for longer periods of time in their lives because of medical innovations promoted to the public as "cures" for ED.[13] In her study of Viagra, sociologist Meika Loe discovered that middle-aged men took the "little blue pill" as though they were following sexual scripts that connected successful sexual intercourse and masculinity.[14] Other research has documented the use of Viagra among men of younger and younger age groups, consistent with the change in Viagra's marketing from featuring silver-haired seniors to younger, more active, middle-aged looking men.[15] The push to perform like a teenager or young man has extended to a wider age range of men, with men between the ages of 18 and 45 the most rapidly increasing group of ED medication users.[16] In other words, because medication exists and is believed to be easily accessible, and because the discussion and control of erectile function is now in the everyday public domain, men should aim to continue to have intercourse with stamina, regardless of age or level of desire. Men should be in control of their erectile function—if they are not, it signifies failed manhood.

And though the men we spoke with rarely talked with others about their own ED, Viagra was sometimes discussed. Josh (57, married, mechanic, white) said that at his work there is often sex talk and, from time to time, problems or issues will come up. He said, "There you are eating lunch with a whole bunch of guys . . . like one guy would sit there, you know, you talk and . . . he says, 'I have a buddy of mine that tried Viagra.' And everyone is sitting there talking and one said, 'Oh, how did it work?' . . . And [you think] 'Would I want to try something like that?' I don't know. I think every man would kinda want to in a way, at least where I work."

In this conversation, I found it striking that Josh didn't share a story about someone talking about their own ED or Viagra use but instead talked about it in a roundabout way, through the experience of friends. Like the indirect socialization that happens when men are getting how sex works that I wrote about in Chapter 2, men can infer that other men are experiencing some level of ED when the conversation is related to Viagra. They don't have to talk about it directly or about their own issues to learn something about the prevalence of ED. In so doing, they can maintain a public masculine presentation without the emasculation that comes from admitting private manhood failures.

And though men said they would not talk about ED publicly, it was clear that they were very aware of it and the available treatments. Even men we interviewed in their twenties and thirties spoke about being cognizant of Viagra and Cialis, saying they would eagerly use it if the time came when they could not perform. Randy (35, engaged, trader, white), for example, said he would be quick to take Viagra or anything that would allow him to continue to have sex. When John said, "Let's project in the future. How would you feel if you had to take . . ." Before he could finish his question, Randy blurted, "I would take them daily—(John: Viagra or Cialis?) I would take them daily. Without issue . . . I would get a penis pump implanted and make it work." Although few of the younger men in the sample had any personal experience with ED, they were part of a generation that had grown up knowing there were tools to help them keep it up and that doing so was normal. This, in turn, shapes sexual scripts around sexual performance for men of all ages and reinforces the association of penile function and masculinity.

Most of the men in the study demonstrated their internalization of such messages, telling of fears about losing their ability to perform as they aged. When asked if he had any concerns about how sex might change for him as he got older, Jerod (22, dating, student, Black) replied, "I don't want to get ED when I grow up." His worry seemed unrelated to decline in sensation or pleasure or intimacy. Rather, his remark, "I feel like if you can't get it up, then you won't want to do it as much. . . . Because you don't want to be embarrassed," implicitly references intercourse as an act of affirmation of virility and manhood. Men who cannot keep up erections (and thus cannot perform) are stigmatized and low-ranking in the hierarchy of men.

For other men, like Issac (30, married, case manager, Black), the idea of suffering from ED was not just worrisome but devastating. When asked how he'd feel if he could no longer get an erection or have intercourse, Issac said, "I'll just need to kill myself. I will lose my purpose. I have a wife that needs to be pleased. Like, I don't know, there['s] just no purpose. It would be bad. . . . I have always said if I was in a wheelchair where my dick isn't working you just need to finish me off."

Although likely an exaggeration, the idea that Issac has "no purpose" and would "kill himself" if could not get erections shows how deeply entrenched sexual function is in Issac's sense of himself as a man. Throughout his life, sexual performance has been a chief means of demonstrating manhood and proving himself to others. Issac, first introduced in Chapter 1, thought of sex as coming "naturally" to him, due to his Jamaican roots. Before getting married he had many sexual partners. He relied on women's "reviews" and reactions to improve upon his sexual techniques and seemed to garner a large part of who he was as a man and as a person from knowing that he was a skilled sexual partner. Not being able to get that confirmation from women partners, not being able to use sex as an act of affirmation of who he was, was inconceivable to Issac.

Barry (44, engaged, postal worker, Black) had a comparable reaction. In response to the same question, he exclaimed, "Oh man! Ech! Oh man! I don't know what I would do man. How would I feel about that? God! Get a gun? (laughs) If I can't perform anymore, I don't even know how to answer. It's never happened. But if it happened, I would pray that she would stay with me, but I don't know." Like Issac, Barry's identity is embedded in his sense of himself as masculine, which is clearly rooted in his sexual capabilities.

However, when asked how he'd react if his partner couldn't have sex, he replied, "It would be fine. I wouldn't go nowhere. I'm beyond [being] worried about that." In Barry's comments, it's clear how much he ties sexual performance to manhood. He sees ED as a fatal flaw in himself, but not being able to be sexually intimate as understandable for his fiancé. For women partners, a lack of interest in sex or sexual failings may be more expected given gendered sexual scripts around desire and performance. It also seems that for Barry, it is more forgivable. He can see his love for his fiancé as more important than her ability to be sexual; yet, he doesn't extend the same understanding to himself. The message here is that men are supposed to be able to get erections and have intercourse, and if they cannot women will leave. If they don't have women and sex to uphold their manhood, is it even worth living?

Hector (55, single/divorced three times, truck driver, biracial [Latino and white]) also expressed horror at the idea of a sexless relationship, but was less sympathetic to a partner who had issues. He exclaimed, "I don't think I could be with her, without being able to please her or doing something. That would be fucking horrible." He said he'd rather be single than in a relationship without sex. Unlike Barry, he would not stay with a partner if she could not satisfy him sexually or, critically, if *he* could not satisfy *her*. Hector clearly saw his women partners' orgasms and pleasures as measures of his sexual skill. He needed to be able to use sex (and his partner) as affirmation of his manhood. If he cannot please his partner, he cannot affirm himself as a man.

For all these men, ED was perceived as a demoralizing diagnosis. Furthermore, as with men who spoke of concerns about performance and penis size in general, these men seemed to imagine a community of women with high sexual needs that could only be satisfied by regular or copious amounts of intercourse and who would not put up with a man who had ED. Women, as agents of affirmation, matter in keeping it up because men see their satisfaction as critical to men's sense of themselves as men. Karen Pyke suggests that men who lack the ability to display or perform hegemonic or culturally valued forms of masculinity may compensate by exaggerating other aspects of masculinity.[17] Straight men who lack wealth and economic stability or racial privilege might feel more threatened by ED because their sexuality may be more salient as a manhood act.[18]

This may also be why some men, like Issac and Barry, were quick to say they did not want to live if they couldn't have intercourse or an erection-capable penis. Most of the men quoted above were Black, Latino, or biracial (with Latino identities). The identities of Black and Latino men are hypersexualized and these men face racialized stereotypes about their sexual performance.[19] Therefore, they may have attributed more weight to what they perceived as a compromised demonstration of manhood that comes along with ED. Hector, who is half Puerto Rican, said this explicitly: "Latin men are more—in relationships sex has a lot to do with it. A Latin guy who can't have sex, that's fucking horrible." For these men, being seen as virile was a critical part of their racialized sexual identities and their displays of masculinity. Not having that was apparently associated with not feeling like a man and not living up to expectations.

Keeping Up with Women's Expectations

Along with ED, participants often spoke regarding their worries about not having the stamina to keep up with sex as they had when they were younger. These concerns were about performing in the way they believed women expected men to perform. As with "getting" and "having" it, men worried there were other more skilled and virile men waiting to take their place. Women shaped men's expectations about sexual performance, even in the abstract.

Jermaine (40, dating/never married, unemployed, Black), who'd just started dating a new woman in the weeks prior to the interview, worried about being able to keep her interested, given recent fluctuations in his sexual performance. He said:

> I'm going through a change right now, where I wonder if I'm still the same, sexually. . . . I got a new girl right now that I met. And I really, I think I like her—I know I like what she has. She has it going on for herself. . . . She's 2 years older than me. I wonder will that make a difference? . . . I don't want her to leave because sex ain't good. So I'm thinking right now I am a little, like, I wonder did I change because I'm not—I'm not no wild bunny rabbit no more, just hopping all over the place like I used to. You know I would hate to lose her because my sex ain't all that.

Jermaine's comments underscore the notion that women's first concern in sexual relationships is men's ability not only to perform, but to perform like machines. He imbues his partner with the agency to reject him and, in turn, deny him as a man.

Other men, most of whom were in their forties and older, also mentioned feeling uneasiness around performance and pleasing women, echoing sexual scripts that suggest a hierarchy of men based on sexual skill.[20] A number of men mentioned this as a particular concern with younger partners. Gavin (48, single/never married, therapist, biracial), for one, feared, "To be honest with you if I had an opportunity to be in a sexual friendship with a young [woman] I don't think I could keep up with them. . . . Eventually they would say, 'Hey, what's going on?' You know? I would just be like I can't do it anymore, I physically can't keep up. And in the bed, too, because if she was a 30-year-old girl, you know, and I'm 48, am I gonna be able to physically keep pace with her?" Both Gavin and Jermaine imagined potential partners with ravenous sex drives and high expectations for men's sexual performance. Neither talked about other qualities they might bring to a relationship. Gavin implies that the days for "friends with benefits" types of encounters are in the past because he doesn't think he has much to contribute.

Even men in committed relationships worried about keeping partners sexually satisfied. We asked whether men felt a sexless relationship would last. Hugh (33, dating/divorced, graduate student, white) who'd been in a serious relationship for a year and a half at the time of our interview, said he'd feel upset and insecure if he had any issues with performance. I asked if he'd be insecure about himself or the relationship and he responded, "Both. I would obviously wonder if my girlfriend would stay with me, if I was being selfish in having her stay with me. Even if she *would* stay with me, I'm not sure. I think she would. But I would still, myself, even if she didn't feel any problems, I would—inside—still feel like I wasn't good enough for her."

When we discussed the scenario of an accident or prostate cancer, Hugh, like most other men we spoke with, had a hard time imagining a relationship working out without sexual intercourse. Like the men with ED, Hugh could not imagine feeling self-confidence without being able to please his girlfriend. And it's striking that he said even if she was fine with it, he didn't think he would be. Once again, so internalized is the idea that sex affirms manhood that it is hard for Hugh to feel he would be enough without being able to keep it up. Although there are certainly other assets he brings to their relationship, his comment that it would be selfish to deprive his girlfriend of a functioning penis shows how central a concern this was.

One final thing I noticed about men's apprehensions in regard to maintaining a partner's interest: social class and other markers of desirability seemed to factor into men's concerns, as did longevity and stability of relationships. Upper-middle class men, white men, and men in long-term marriages or committed relationships, like Dennis, quoted at the start of the chapter, did not express concerns about their partners leaving if they could not have intercourse, even when they were actively experiencing issues associated with ED. Working class men, some middle class men, and racial minority men were more likely to share their apprehensions about relationship stability, as were men in newer relationships or men who were not in relationships. Younger men, too, were more likely to have these worries about potential future situations, which demonstrates the proliferation of sexual scripts about erectile function and manhood.

Not Surrendering Gracefully: Clinical ED

Although most men worried about ED and some had it situationally, other men were living with ED caused by aging or prostate issues. Most of the men who'd been diagnosed with clinical ED spoke with embarrassment or shame about their disorders. They felt stigmatized by these diagnoses. Unlike the men with mental health issues or those whose ED was a side effect of another condition, these men could not explain away their inability to get an erection or ascribe its cause to something within their control. They were thus coming to terms with living as men for whom intercourse was problematic or a thing of the past, and with a body that they could not control.

Alex (41, dating/divorced, painter, white) was the youngest man to reveal that he had (more than situational) ED. At 41, he told John he felt like less of a man because he'd lost his hair and his sex drive wasn't as strong as it used to be. He shared that his problems began in his late twenties, but weren't consistent and he implied that he was able to hide them. But now, "It's getting more noticeable. . . . When I can't function right, it makes me feel like less of a man. That's because I feel that's something I feel I should be able to do. When I can't do it, it just makes me feel like less of a man. . . . Like I can't do what I'm supposed to do."

Alex's statement is a textbook-like example of how linked men's sexuality is to erectile function. Simply, with ED, his manhood, not just his sexuality, was compromised. Alex worried about how this was affecting his relationship with his girlfriend. In notes from the interview, John noted that Alex "repeatedly told me that his erectile dysfunction makes him feel like less of a man, mainly because he feels he cannot please his girlfriend and feels she might leave." Like the men quoted above, the fear that women will not accept men who experience ED weighed on Alex. Impotence became a "master status" in defining manhood.[21]

ED in Relationships. Most of the men we spoke with who had clinical ED were in their sixties. Partnered men seemed to feel a great deal of pressure (coming from themselves and their internalization of what men's bodies are supposed to do) to "fix" ED, even when doing so required significant effort and intervention. Harry (61, married forty-two years, maintenance worker, white), for example, required surgery due to prostate cancer and this experience seemed to challenge his sense of himself as a man. He confided, "I struggled, went through a time where . . . I didn't know. I just—I was searching for answers. And . . . I actually strayed a little bit to try to prove that to myself, and learned that it was me."

Like the men I wrote about in Chapter 6 who cheated on their partners because they wanted to prove they were still desirable, Harry's first response to ED was to attribute it to something external. He felt he needed to try to have sex with another partner so he could be sure that the problem was actually *his* problem. Maybe his wife was no longer desirable enough (and was thus acting as an object of denial), he thought, and that was why he was experiencing ED. Because if the problem was him, then, well, what did that say about him as a man? Consistent with research examining times during which manhood is tested or compromised, Harry sought to repair this failure.[22] He tried to have sex with another partner, but ultimately nothing changed. He still could not sustain an erection.

Harry was so anxious about keeping it up that he not only cheated on his wife but also developed an addiction to pornography (because he believed, initially, that if he was aroused enough, he could get and maintain an erection that would last long enough for him to ejaculate). In the aftermath, he ended up joining a sex addicts support group because he wanted to show his wife he was trying to deal with this preoccupation and remain faithful. Through that group, he came to terms with the fact that this was not a problem he could control, "that it wasn't a mental thing. It was definitely a physical thing. . . . I would have to say that I probably felt less a man at that point because I couldn't perform."

After surgery, Harry finally accepted his diminished sexual function as the result of nerve damage from prostate cancer. When he accepted that his ED was not going to be fixed organically, he sought out other alternatives to have erections. At the time of the interview he confided that though he is still able to have intercourse, it's become more complicated. He explained:

> We tried pills. We tried this, we tried that. And injections, which go right in the penis, and that works. And I use a pump and, you know, I can do things to perform but it's just a hassle to get set up to get things going. The spontaneity has gone away. . . . Even though it's been so many years, I still would like to overcome this some way at some point. I mean I've met with doctors about an implant, you know. I've looked at every avenue there is. The implant just wasn't gonna do it . . . it wasn't gonna increase anything size wise or, you know. So I've been using the methods I have now. It wasn't gonna change my ability—it just would have, the only thing [an implant] would change, you know, partially change would be the ability to be spontaneous. I wouldn't have needed apparatuses with me.

Harry pointed out that his desire has not decreased, indicating his masculine sex drive.[23] His wife's interest, however, has declined. Harry feels, in turn, that he is even more preoccupied with sex because he wants to "fix" this problem and figure out a way to "overcome" ED. What it seems he really wants to do is to *control* his sexuality, to feel masterful over his body and to have the physical response he had before the prostate problems. Like many men, he equated masculinity and control.[24] Like Alex, he also said he felt "less a man" with a penis that could not become erect at will. He wanted the spontaneity of youthful sexuality and held out hope that there will be some way he can get back to that, despite the realities of his aging body and prostate cancer.

Geno (65, married, retired, white), whose recent affair I detailed in Chapter 6, also had been diagnosed with ED. Although he was able to have sex with his affair partner, it seems, like Harry, he was looking to keep it up by trying to forestall the decline in sexual activity that happens as men age. An affair was a way to test the waters to see one—if he was still desirable, and two—if his body's functionality was truly in decline. Although he said his decision to cheat was spurred by his wife's lack of interest in sex and his increased interest in it postretirement, this was also happening at a time when his sexual ability was not what it once had been.

Geno remained optimistic about sex after his ED diagnosis because he'd been able to use medicine to keep it up, consistent with a "successful aging" narrative. He was luckier than Harry in that respect—he had a simple solution to his problem. He opined:

> I have been diagnosed with ED but it has not changed my expression of my sexuality. At least I'm not aware of that changing my expression. . . . Having ED although it's a problem—there is a correction for that problem that does work. So that problem is not a problem. And the mental side hasn't changed. It hasn't pushed the mental side—maybe it has pushed the mental side more than the physical side. I'll share with you a line that I used jokingly with many people. And the line is, "It takes me all night, now, to do what I used to do all night" (laughs). . . .

[ED]'s changed the frequency of ejaculation, not my mental attitude toward sex, if that makes sense.

Like other men, Geno made sure to emphasize that his desire is consistent. Even if he can't respond in the way men are supposed to, he could *think* and *feel* in the way men are supposed to. Like other men, Geno spoke of ED using language that demonstrated his masculinity, underscoring the idea of masculinity as discursive practice.[25] Stories of desire can show they are masculine, even if their actions do not.[26]

Single Men and ED. For unmarried and unpartnered older men, struggles with ED presented a different set of trials. Although they did not have partners to perform for or judge them, they had to grapple with knowing that they could not get an erection should the opportunity present itself. They also had to come to terms with what this said about them as men in a culture that ties manhood to sexual performance. Not having women partners to affirm them was one blow to their sense of selves. Not being able to get or sustain an erection was another.

Wesley (68, single/never married, unemployed, white), for instance, explained the troubles he'd been having since being diagnosed with a prostate condition. He bemoaned:

[I have] benign prostate hyperplasia. Enlarged prostate. It's a very common thing. I think about a third of all American men have it. . . . It occupies more of my medical attention than anything else. I've had 3 biopsies. I'm on 2 different medications. . . . So they are always watching it. If it's not cancer their attitude is just live with it. And they know it affects my sex life. But I keep saying I don't have a partner. And if you don't have a partner that's the end of the talk. . . . So sex is more of an embarrassment for me than a pleasure. If I'm going to bed with a woman and she's 20 and she expects a man to get an erection every night, she's not going to be very happy with me.

Even though the doctors did not want to talk to him about sex when he told them he was unmarried (which underscores the stereotypical assumption that older people, particularly those without partners, are asexual), he was concerned with his ability to get an erection—despite the fact that he has not been sexually active much in his life and not at all in many years. During his interview he frequently spoke of not being able to imagine finding a partner who'd be with him and how, throughout his life, "getting it" was consistently an issue due to his self-reported low ranking in the hierarchy of desirability. Yet even Wesley worried about keeping it up (and held onto the idealized young woman as the prized potential partner). Even in celibacy he wanted to know he could, just in case.

Eli (64, divorced, consultant, white) whose marital and relationship struggles I detailed in Chapter 6, also struggled with ED. For him, this diagnosis was "horrible, it is devastating. . . . It's such a masculinity hit it's unbelievable, you know?" Eli told me how, because he's not in a relationship, he doesn't have the opportunity to test his ability to have intercourse. So instead, he frequently uses pornography as stimulation. Doing so, he said, "is really an attempt to constantly check to see if I can still deliver." Like Geno and Harry with their affairs, Eli felt he needed to be sure that he really had ED. All these men seem to be resisting aging and the idea that this part of their life could be changing in such a dramatic way. They want to be ready to affirm their manhood at the moment that opportunity arises.

Also, like other men, Eli explained he is reluctant to talk about what's happening because of what it implies about him and his signification of masculinity. He remarked, "When a man gets older the volume of semen, you know, cuts in half to a third. And that is also a big shock and a big hit on a man's ego. That's why a lot of them say, 'I'm not gonna do this anymore because I don't want to go through that.' . . . It's debilitating to the ego, it's very much so. And we can't—it's nothing you can talk about. Guys don't ever talk about it, at least the guys I am affiliated with."

When I asked why he didn't talk about it, he explained, "It's a failure component, we don't talk about failures. Even if nine out of 10 have it, it's a failure component." Clearly men like Eli, and most of the other men we spoke with who had ED, felt stigmatized by it. Not talking about it allowed them to "pass" as virile men, in a manner parallel to the way virgin men used silence as a strategy for passing as sexually experienced.[27]

When men are hesitant to talk about ED or even more broadly about issues related to keeping it up, they reinforce sexual scripts that connect erectile function and manhood. Not talking about it—even if, as Eli suggested, 90 percent of older men are dealing with it—shows how much of men's sexuality is focused on a very narrow aspect of sexuality: their ability to have intercourse and how much the ability to have intercourse with an erect penis is a manhood act. As I've noted throughout this book, when sex is an act of affirming manhood, and men can no longer have it in the way that mirrors dominant sexual scripts, it is no surprise they feel not just sexually inadequate, but inadequate as men. They know they can no longer count on women as objects or agents of affirmation because they know they can no longer have sexual intercourse with them. When men's response to ED was to hide it, contest it, or confirm it with infidelity or copious consumption of pornography, it's clear that phallic performance is vital to these men. Most of the men with ED did not "gradually surrender" their ability to get or maintain an erection.

Not Letting Yourself Go: The Importance of Physical Fitness and Appearance

In addition to concerns about erectile function and physical stamina, men also worried about keeping up their physical appearance and fitness so that they looked desirable. In this way, they upheld a masculine image, publicly. Men suggested that taking care of themselves in terms of weight and musculature was manly behavior. In contrast to research showing that straight men were concerned with decline in function rather than looks, several of the older men (fifties and older) reinforced the script that men who remain sexually active are those who take care of themselves.[28]

In other words, they had a hard time imagining that men who "let themselves go" would be able to keep it up or find partners. In particular, many of the white, middle and upper-middle class men participants in their fifties and sixties spoke a great deal about staying in shape as a means of retaining desirability and keeping up their skills as sexual partners.

Bruce (59, divorced, unemployed, white), for example, described how essential exercise is in his overall sense of himself as a man and potential sexual partner. By way of contrast, he spoke about his belief that a friend's failure to do the same has contributed to his friend's lack of luck with women. He pronounced:

> I know men—there's a civil engineer friend of mine—he doesn't exercise. I can't get him on a bicycle. . . . I think age, a marriage that ended in divorce and he . . . was out of work for a while. . . . I said, "Jim, I want to see you settle in with someone socially so perhaps the foursome can do something." [He said] "Well, I don't have a job and no woman will want me because I don't have a job." Well, he got a job. So I said "What's your excuse now, Jim?" "Well, I'm not attractive." He's balding and he's overweight. I said, "Well, balding you can't do much about. But what about cutting back on your calories?" He said, "I'm trying to lose one pound a month." I said, "Well, that's a goal." But I don't see him doing anything. . . . I think the reason my sexuality has maintained itself over all these years is because I feel that I'm attractive.

Despite his own hesitancy about dating and risking getting hurt (see Chapter 6), Bruce wanted to keep up his appearance and physical fitness so that he remains interested in sex and women remain interested in him. He distinguishes himself from his friend Jim, by indicating that he cares about how he looks and will do what he needs to do to keep that up. He has put in the work to still feel attractive. In so doing, he shows his higher ranking compared with other men peers.

As men like Bruce enter their fifties and sixties and careers shift or end due to unemployment or retirement, men seek out ways to continue to perform masculinity and attempt to align with hegemonic ideals. Men (mostly middle- and upper-middle class) with fast-paced or identity-defining occupations may turn to other means of proving who they are when work identities fade from the forefront. Staying sexually viable and desirable is one of these things, and one that is becoming increasingly more important as narratives around staying youthful and resisting visible signs of aging become more normative.[29]

Geno (65, married, retired executive, white), the married man I wrote about earlier in the chapter who dealt with ED and had an affair, experienced this kind of identity shift when he retired. When he worked, he commuted for three hours each day and didn't have time to exercise. Upon retirement, he hired a personal trainer when he realized "my body wasn't where it needed to be." The trainer and exercise "helped me not only physically but it also helped me mentally. So I saw my body change. I saw my health change positively. And that did and does play a part in developing my confidence and my sexual thoughts about me." It was, in fact, this new self-confidence that propelled Geno to go through with his infidelity.

Again, it is important to note that most of the men who talked about not "letting themselves go" or expressed this focus on physical fitness as a measure of masculinity were white, middle and upper-middle class men. Men like Geno, who had access to trainers and gym memberships, as well as time to exercise and keep up their appearance were in a different socioeconomic class than the men who did not talk about this as an important aspect of keeping it up. Their resources allowed them the opportunity to keep up their public masculine appearance, even if their private masculinity was compromised by ED or diminishing sexual stamina.

Indeed, there may be different social class expectations about maintaining one's appearance and complying with notions of "successful aging."[30] As Kristen Barber noted in her study of men's patronage of haircutting establishments, upper-middle class men were more likely to go to "salons" rather than barber shops because they felt they had a professional image or look to uphold.[31] They justified crossing into these "feminine" spaces by explaining the importance of their appearance as an aspect of their identity. This may extend to differences in appearance norms and standards for some straight men's sexual body image and how they perceive older men's place in the hierarchy of desirability, as some scholars have noted.[32]

In contrast, other men felt they had "let themselves go." Those who said they knew they were not in good shape anymore described insecurities about having sex with new partners or about changes in their sexual relationships. One case in which this happened was with Tyrone (61, separated, entrepreneur, Black), who said he stopped working out after he got married. Now that he is back in the world of dating he wonders if he will find someone, given his appearance. He said, "I'm 5'5. I'm a short guy. I wear a size 11½ shoe. I'm knock-kneed. I have man boobs. I have a gut, you know? And I didn't always look that way. I had a six pack when I was like 19, 20 years old, like most people. I think over time the more active you stay, it does give you that confidence. But you know the way I look at it is I already had my woman so why would I have to stay looking that way? I already got the girl, you know? (laughs)." Tyrone didn't worry as much about keeping it up when he was married. But once separated, he saw himself as relatively low on the hierarchy of desirability given his height, his soft body, and overall look.

Dean (33, married, building manager, biracial) went through a hard time emotionally and financially and that made it difficult to have the energy or desire to have sex. He gained about thirty pounds during that period and the extra weight and being out of shape made him feel less desirable, too. He explained:

> [My wife and I] have gone through a lot of stuff, physically. When we met I was working out, I was lifting weights. I just kind of stopped doing that because of the difficult times we were going through. I lost my job, et cetera, et cetera. And so it was really hard for me and ever since then I've had difficulties maintaining an erection. It's incredibly, incredibly embarrassing. . . . It's a strain on my relationship, because

> it's not my wife. It's the fact that I've been lethargic, and not moving, not getting my blood moving. We both smoke too much weed sometimes. There's a lot of factors there and as a result of that it's been very difficult.

Dean clearly saw himself as someone who hadn't kept up his appearance in the way he felt he should and this has resulted in issues with keeping up erections. He has not compartmentalized his sex life from his lack of energy and depression. What is a bit different with this example is that Dean's problems were not physical initially—he felt emasculated by his experiences and inability to provide financially, which caused him to stop exercising, and that seeped into his ability to keep it up. For Dean and Tyrone, like others we spoke with, appearance mattered a great deal in their assessment of their value in the hierarchy of men. When they felt they weren't keeping up their bodies consistent with sexual scripts, they felt insecure about their desirability, even within committed relationships.

Men's embodied sexualities are firmly rooted in having high-functioning penises. By and large, the men we spoke with believed that without control over their erections they would be compromised as men. Men of all ages spoke as if they were haunted by the idea of ED and the man they might become if they had it. Even younger men spoke of their readiness to take Viagra or have surgical implants or do anything they could to maintain erectile function. They thought that women would not tolerate men with ED and that having intercourse was central to any intimate relationship. If men could not keep it up, they could not keep women satisfied or committed. Although some men in this situation found that this was not actually true, most still had a hard time letting go of the notion that men with ED were failed men.

Some men (most of whom were not in relationships) also worried about aging bodies and emphasized the importance staying physically fit has on men's sex lives. Men who had made this point connected looking good with being desirable to women. In this chapter (and in the interviews overall) no men told stories about women who broke up with them because they couldn't get it up or didn't last long enough. But men imagined that women would reject them and that rejection would indicate their low status in the hierarchy of desirability. So, in keeping it up, women acted as both agents and objects of affirmation. In women's response to men's ED or lack of stamina or to their soft bodies, women could also function as agents of denial. When women stayed with their men partners as their bodies and sex lives changed, they affirmed that men still mattered and that they were still men, even if they could no longer have intercourse. Women—both as partners and in men's imagination—influenced men's sexual selves because, even at later stages in their sex lives, women's affiliation with them served to affirm their manhood.

Conclusion

WRAPPING IT UP

I'm at a point now where my attorney says you've got to do your estate planning and HIPPA releases and health proxies. So I have to leave instructions of how I want to leave this world. My last memory, if I have a choice, I want to bury my face in a woman's breasts and just forget there's a world out there. Forget about responsibilities and duties and chores and so on and just let that be my last experience of life.

—Wesley, 68

I began this book with Wesley's story and so it seems fitting to end with it as well. His first quote, in Chapter 1, suggested that what he wanted most was to have a woman willing to be intimate with him as a means of confirming that he mattered as both a man and a person. In the above quote, the same message holds true. He wanted to die feeling a woman's affection—shutting out everything else but the sensual experience of touch. It seems that who the woman is does not matter so much—she's an object in this fantasy, but knowing that any woman would choose to be with him sexually is what he craves most. Throughout Wesley's life, because he rarely had sexual relationships with women, he longed for affirmation of his worth. Other accomplishments did not fill the void associated with not succeeding in getting it, having it, or keeping it up. Wesley's story encapsulates how much sex affirmed manhood and how much women made a difference in the sexual selves and self-worth of the men we interviewed.

Getting, having, and keeping up with sex are predicated on getting, having, and keeping up relations with women. And this, in turn, is a large part of keeping up manhood for straight men in twenty-first-century U.S. society. Straight men are discouraged from having emotionally close relationships with one another and expressing affection or intimacy toward anyone other than a woman intimate partner.[1] Thus, relationships with women are critical for allowing men emotional expression and closeness. As Peggy Orenstein noted in her study of teenage boys and sex, boys most frequently confided in girlfriends and mothers, which taught them that "women are responsible for emotional labor, for processing men's emotional lives in ways that would be emasculating for guys to do themselves."[2] This leaves women in the position of being not only caretakers but also care-keepers—that is, the ones in relationships who do the care work to support, encourage, and reassure their men partners that they are men enough in a world when manhood is fragile.[3] In turn, this reinforces gender hierarchies, as it is women's job to support and uphold hegemonic masculinity. When men believe that other men are likely to judge them for expressing a preference for having sex in a loving context, or for having affection for one another, and when they turn to women to fulfill these roles, the notion that men and women are different, feel different things, and that men should be publicly emotionally closed off is reinforced.

My research confirmed that for the men we spoke with, engaging in sexual activity was an act of affirmation. Sex was not just—or even mostly—about pleasure or gratification. Sex was a manhood act that affirmed men's worth as straight men.[4] It was a way boys, young men, midlife men, and aging men proved themselves to other men and also to themselves. To do so, men needed women as agents and objects of affirmation. For many of the men we spoke with, women (as girls) started as objects of desire and tools for gaining status with other men. They were bodies to use as conquests and to talk about as a means of showing off knowledge. They were images from pornography that served as anatomical models. They were imagined partners as boys masturbated and learned how their bodies worked, or as they desperately sought information to help them gain currency in conversation with peers or to prepare them for anxiety-ridden early encounters.

Only girls and women could validate men's worth by choosing them as sexual companions. When they rejected men, they served, implicitly or explicitly, as either objects or agents of denial of manhood. Men seemed to feel they were constantly competing with other men—real and imagined—for women's attention because it was so critical in determining who they were among men. Regarding women in this way reinforces gender inequalities, as women are constructed as tools for achieving status. Men's frequent emphasis on women's appearance or "hotness" in stories about sexual conquests and relationships highlights the ways in which women can function as trophies or objects of affirmation.

Getting, Having, and Keeping as Acts of Affirmation of Manhood

The importance of looking at men's sexuality as collective action (rather than something natural or individualistic) is underscored in the three main themes for this book. "Getting It," in the form of learning about sex, was important not just so that boys and men understood sex but so they would not be embarrassed or emasculated in sexual situations or in conversation with their peers. In addition, "getting" girls or women for their early sexual experiences was critical to interviewees' sense of themselves as masculine. They spoke of feeling as if they had "joined a club" or "scored their first three-pointer," of feeling *like men*, after losing their virginity. Whether they did or did not have sexual experience (and with which girls or women) influenced the ways men saw themselves in comparison to others in the hierarchy of men.

Women (and men peers, in conversation about sex) were seen as mechanisms for avowing men's desirability and establishing their social status. In this way, interaction with women partners was not the only important interaction in establishing sexual selves. Men imagined other men as competition and their narratives revealed worries that other men were more virile, valued, and viable. This is likely because to succeed at manhood is to "elicit deference from others in concrete situations."[5] Knowing that women were with them rather than with other men was a way of feeling that they had won.

As men got out of high school or college, they were likely to be spending less time in the homosocial peer cultures that flourished in adolescent and teen years. They were no longer sitting around a video screen together looking for images of naked women. Simply, there is less time and there are fewer forums for engaging in the type of posturing sex talk that scholars like C. J. Pascoe and others have written about.[6] Furthermore, a point comes when men are supposed to be knowledgeable about sex, so the time for and nature of discussion changes as well.

At the same time, as men entered into relationships with women, they started to shift their thinking about women, now as people to please and gratify. They were no longer just entities of fantasy or imagination, but real people with sexual responses. At this stage, in addition to and sometimes instead of men peers, women become agents of affirmation—arbiters of manhood perceived as having the power to judge a man's sexual prowess. Women act as affirmers of masculinity, manhood, and, in turn, self-worth. In "Having It," men's assessment of their own performance was not just about how they lived up to cultural standards associated with stamina and confidence, but also about whether they felt they were able to satisfy partners. In those early experiences, manhood is put to the test—men are acting, usually for the first time, without the support or audience of their peers. If women did not "come back for more" or affirm men through praise of their sexual skills, men took this as a sign that they were doing it wrong. This is similar to what Scott Melzer found in his study of men who sought out online support when they had insecurities about their penis size or function. Men, he wrote, "internalize their performance activities and failures as reflections on their manhood . . . any single failure raises possibilities in men's minds they are total failures."[7] The way that the men we interviewed did not forget individual experiences of rejection or criticism, that they shared these when asked about negative experiences, shows that these men internalized their failures in the same way.

Even men in committed, long-term relationships relied on women to affirm them, though their presentation of manhood was often different than when they were younger or with peers. They seemed to feel pressure to be like both fictional men "studs" from popular culture and their younger selves. Men needed women—as objects and agents—to assuage their concerns about whether they were "proficient" or "failed" men. Having it was also a way that they felt gratified and valued as men and people, particularly in loving and committed relationships. In these relationships, interviewees told of showing some level of vulnerability when they believed that they could trust their partners not to shame or embarrass them if their sexual skills were not always the best. In these relationships, men knew there was always another opportunity to have sex, so they worried less about the impression made in each individual encounter. As other research has noted, even teenage boys have described "good sex" in an "emotional context," characterized by "feeling close and secure."[8] Boys and young men crave intimacy and affection and realize that sex is a socially acceptable way to seek it out.[9]

Finally, the men in this sample worried a great deal about "Keeping It Up." They worried that partners would leave them if they were not strong, consistent performers. They also worried about balancing sexual desire with love and affection for partners with whom their sexual libidos were incompatible. Men dealt with habituation in long-term relationships. Some men lived in sexless marriages and felt as if their sex lives might be over well before they wanted them to be. Single men fretted over finding partners in middle age and later life, particularly when they felt they had little to offer in terms of sexual performance or financial support. Most of all, men worried about whether "failing" bodies meant that they were failed men. Men who'd struggled in their relationships, who lacked economic or social capital to compensate for declining sexual function, had difficulty believing they would be desirable sexual partners. When it came to relationships with women, men had trouble imagining that a woman would choose to be or stay with them rather than seeking a man with a high-functioning penis. In all these cases, the way women partners viewed them mattered a great deal.

Men went to great lengths to prove that they could keep it up or to resist clinical diagnoses of erectile problems. A few had affairs as a way of "testing the equipment." Men held out hope they could attribute ED to partners who let themselves go or who failed to initiate or respond to sexual advances. Yet most men confided that they did not talk with anyone about their ED or about any issues associated with keeping it up. Here, too, they were concerned about how other men would view them if they were exposed as failed men. As in the case of having it, men's comments about keeping it up revealed that having control over their bodies was a key element of manhood.

Sexual accomplishment and affiliation with women (especially beautiful women) was a means of establishing status among men. Gender hierarchies were thus not just reinforced between women and men, but also among men. Men assessed and sometimes denigrated men who were less successful in these pursuits as lesser men. The number of men who described themselves as "late bloomers" or who noted that they hid their lack of experience or sexual failures from others shows the awareness of how subordination could result if they did not get, have, or keep up with sex.

Signifying Masculine Sexual Selves

Sociologists Douglas Schrock and Michael Schwalbe noted that "learning to signify a masculine self entails learning how to adjust to audiences and situations and learning how one's other identities bear on the acceptability of a performance."[10] Men's race, class, ability, and age all affected the way they did masculinity. For instance, men were cognizant of racial hierarchies of desirability—Asian men in particular spoke out the most on feeling that they were automatically seen as less sexually appealing and thus less manly than other men. Black men recognized that some women (most often white women) pursued them because of a curiosity or fetishizing of Black men as well-endowed and hypersexual. Almost all of the participants spoke of the importance of having money in getting the attention of girls, though more so when men were past college age.

When it comes to sex, men in this study also learned to "adjust to audiences and situations" in their presentation of manhood. In their stories, it was evident that the performance of manhood they needed to give to their peers was different from the presentation they gave to sexual partners. Men's remarks indicated that they knew peers generally expected them to engage in (or at least not protest the use of) objectifying talk about female bodies and getting sex. Even when they framed themselves as "not like other guys," most men in this study noted they kept quiet around peers about their preference to have sex in loving contexts or about their lack of knowledge about how sex works because they knew doing so would cost them in their attempted signification of a masculine self, which is consistent with other research.[11] Here, manhood was a team act of men working together to demonstrate public masculinity. It was an interactive "front stage" performance of posturing for men peers.[12]

Men also seemed to realize that when they took on the identity of boyfriend, partner, or husband, they were expected to prove their manhood differently from when they were single. When in committed relationships with women, men could be masculine simply by being in those relationships. In that way, women were objects that affirmed manhood. But in those relationships they also had a space for the performance of private masculinities—those performances that happen only in front of their sexual partners. To be sure, men worried about their sexual performance and how it would be received and reviewed by partners, but their primary concern was erectile function and stamina. And men worried less during midlife (thirties and forties) when they were in serious relationships. With women partners, objectifying talk about female bodies or past sexual experiences was not a strategy for showing off who they were as men.

Men could show emotion and vulnerability in these situations, sometimes in tandem with demonstrating manhood through sexual performance. Susan Bordo noted that men are permitted to be "soft" after they have already proven that they are "hard." She wrote that the show of emotion in conjunction with a demonstration of manhood is "like the soft penis after satisfying sex. They don't demean the man but make him lovable and human—because he's proved his strong manly core."[13]

In her book *Performing Sex*, Breanne Fahs, a professor of gender and women's studies, wrote that "women's performances of sex—and their internalization of the sexual scripts that dictate those performances—represent one of the major ways to trace the continued iteration of sexism, male dominance, hegemonic notions of gender, and lopsided power relations."[14] In other words, women follow patriarchal scripts that privilege men's sexual pleasures and desires. In sexual interactions women's *performances*—whether in faking orgasm, making noises to indicate pleasure, or engaging in sex acts that they do not desire but they believe will please men partners—undergird these dominant sexual scripts.

Men are part of these performances, too. The men we interviewed typically described sexual encounters that followed the same type of sexual scripts that, as Fahs suggested, guide women's performance. Men were expected to have sexual skill, stamina, and the ability to maintain sexual interest. They were generally expected to be initiators—even though most men did not become regular initiators of sex until after they gained sexual experience.[15] Above all, they were expected to manage and control erectile function. Some men spoke of reconciling intrapsychic scripts focused on multiple partners and adventurous sexual practices with interpersonal and cultural scripts that favored monogamy and respect for partners. Others managed their desire for commitment and their discomfort with sexual objectification with scripts that suggested feeling these ways made them lesser men. They, too, needed to perform *masculine* desire, aptitude, and pleasure. They labored *to be seen as* proficient sexual partners who were hopefully better than, but at least as good as, previous or imagined future partners of the women with whom they were intimate. Their concern with and discussion of partners' reactions and "reviews" shows how much they viewed sex as a presentation of manhood.

As women talk of "receiving" orgasms as "gifts" from their partner, men talked about giving or providing them as part of their job as men. Fahs noted that women's constructions of orgasm turn into a "product rather than experience."[16] In turn, this makes men the producers of orgasms, and the men we interviewed certainly agreed with this characterization. They believed they were expected to put on a good show and many, particularly in early experiences, felt they needed to emulate what they saw in pornography in order to do so.

Performance was also important in getting it—both understanding and gaining access to sex—although here men were most often performing for their men peers. Men described pressure to perform in ways consistent with cultural scripts that positioned them as dominant over women, to be sure, but also in competition with other men. They postured for their peers and for women partners, rarely disclosing ignorance, innocence, or inexperience. As boys and teenagers, interviewees recalled "passing" as sexually knowledgeable or experienced when they were not because they wanted to avoid the embarrassment or emasculation they believed would follow if they admitted a lack of knowledge. They stayed silent during discussions about masturbation or female bodies because they believed they were supposed to know what they did not know. Several men talked about lying that they had lost their virginity or that they had had sex during a hookup because they knew they'd be seen as weaker or feminine if they did not. Getting and sharing and showing interest in a copy of *Playboy* or a pornographic video affirmed their straightness, their manhood, and their place of belonging among other boys and men. Talking about girls and women as objects of sexual desire or voyeuristic pleasure allowed men to discursively perform heterosexual masculinity.

Of course, there were generational, racial, ethnic, age, class, and religious variations in some of the performances. Younger men, those who grew up learning about sex from online pornography, felt a different kind of performance pressure than older men, whose early exposure to sex was that of still images. Men who grew up in conservative religions or cultures with anti-premarital sex scripts had to resolve conflicting values and cultural ideals. Men who lacked class privilege often spoke of sex in the language of compensatory masculinity, of having to make up for what they lacked, and recognized their lack of privilege as something that disadvantaged them in the erotic marketplace.

Although men's performances of masculinity and the importance of sex as an affirmation of manhood generally upheld dominant sexual scripts that reinforce gender stratification and androcentrism, in some ways men challenged existing scripts. Many of the men we spoke with talked at length about how sex was an act of love and how they greatly enjoyed seeing their partners experience sexual pleasure and gratification. They were open (at least to us, as interviewers) about the importance of affection and intimacy. In my analysis of interview transcripts, the theme of "closeness" was frequently mentioned as a major motivator for and benefit of sex. Although men often framed their way of thinking as "like women" or "not like other guys," many mentioned how much better sex was when they had strong feelings or love for partners.

In this way, men constructed sexual scripts framing sex as an act of love and intimacy. Using a closeness narrative, they highlighted the importance of partnered sex as a means of expressing love and feeling affirmed as people, not just as specific sexual partners or as men. It was easier for men in committed relationships to espouse these narratives because they had already signified masculinity through being in the relationships.

Affirming Manhood versus Deserving Desire

This book project started as a companion or follow-up to my research on women's sexualities through the life course, *Deserving Desire: Women's Stories of Sexual Evolution*. As I did interviews and research for that book, people often asked questions such as, "What about men?" and "How do marriage and parenthood impact men's sexualities?" I thought about these questions, too. In part, I thought that hearing what men had to say would help enhance understandings of women's experiences. However, given the depth and breadth of information shared in interviews, I realized how much men have their own story to tell.

Men's stories were different in critical ways that shifted the focus of this book from a story about significant life transitions to one focused on how sex and women are central in the affirmation of manhood. Although marriage and parenthood—two major experiences in women's sexual development—were not inconsequential, they were less formative experiences for men in thinking about their sexual selves. And although femininity played some role in women's sexualities, it was much less significant in their overall expression of sexuality than masculinity was for men. This makes sense because conforming to femininity norms involves controlling rather than expressing sexuality, whereas the opposite is true for masculinity. We monitor and negatively label girls and women as "sluts" for the same behavior that garners boys and men adulation.[17]

Because of these ideas about women's sexuality, most women I interviewed were slow to develop sexual self-assurance and entitlement to desire. For men, this was not the case. Although the vast majority of men we interviewed lacked confidence in early sexual encounters and most did not initiate their first sexual experiences, they never struggled with the *right* to sexual desire.[18] Many expressed feeling confident relatively soon after their first experiences. Experience made them feel more like men, which boosted their sexual self-assurance. Positive experiences and messages about sexuality in early life provided advantage for men in later sexual situations, and negative experiences yielded disadvantage.[19] How men *got* sex influenced how they *had* it, and the importance they attributed to *keeping it up*. In this way, sexual experience was certainly cumulative in their stories.

Furthermore, women were central in men's stories about their sexual selves in ways that men were not in women's stories in *Deserving Desire*. I found that though women struggled to feel entitled to their sexual desire and sexual pleasure, this was mostly an internal problem. Although men were sometimes instrumental in women's gradual acceptance of their own desire, some women came to self-acceptance through motherhood, personal accomplishments, and career successes. In other words, most of the women I spoke with came to the feeling that they *deserved* desire independent of men. This is where men's stories were very different. Women wanted men to confirm their desirability; men needed women to confirm their manhood.

Moreover, among the women I interviewed for *Deserving Desire*, only a few talked about or were concerned about their sexual skills. They wanted to please their partners but rarely expressed anxiety or apprehension about how to have sex or how they would be judged for their sexual talents. The women I interviewed never spoke about how they thought other women would judge their sexual abilities in intimate relationships or being esteemed for their aptitude. There was no imagined community of other women to compete with to be better than (only better looking, at times, but not better at sex). Furthermore, they did not see themselves as judges in the way men perceived they were being judged by women. Most women did not talk much about men's skill. Some (mostly older women, born before 1960) had complaints about partners who ignored their sexual needs and desires or who lacked sexual skills when it came to pleasing women, but, overall, very few spoke of incompetent partners. That is not to say they didn't experience this, but, it was not impactful in the development of their sexual selves in the way it was for men. Simply, they saw themselves as reactors more than initiators and had less to say about the actual experience of sex than did men.

In spite of these differences, the men interviewed for this book and the women interviewed for *Deserving Desire* both saw sex as an act that determined something important about who they were as people. I was frequently surprised and fascinated by the similarities in men's and women's stories. At the root of their sexual experiences both men and women interviewees yearned for confirmation of their worthiness as sexual partners and as people. Like Wesley, they all wanted to know that they mattered.

The men interviewed for this study internalized dominant sexual scripts and saw sex and the attention of women as yielding feelings of accomplishment or failure. In U.S. society women's appearance is a chief aspect of their value and so men choosing them as sexual partners confirmed their desirability. For men, demonstrating manhood requires action. So, for them, it was through sexual behavior or display of sexual knowledge in talk with peers that they attempted to prove themselves. When they successfully showed off their sexual conquests, knowledge, or skill—when they showed that they could get what other men could not—then their manhood and status were affirmed. In other words, women worried about how they compared to other women in terms of looks, whereas men worried about how they compared to other men in terms of behavior and skill. The men we spoke with also talked significantly more frequently about threats to manhood during their sexual lives than women talked about threats to femininity related to sexual experience during their lives.

In summary, men's stories revealed that having sex is a critical way of affirming manhood. Men, particularly men not in relationships or men with less sexual experience, seemed to see each sexual experience as a test and competition. Men worked to prove themselves to each other and to their partners. Sexual achievement was a major factor in jockeying for position in the hierarchy of men and avoiding marginalization. Women were necessary and instrumental in men's ability to use sex as a manhood act. Through affiliations with "hot" women, straight men showed compliance with compulsory masculinity. Female bodies were objectified as tools that aided in manhood acts. Women also served as agents of affirmation. When women chose or rejected men, when they gave good reviews of or responses to men's sexual performance, when they comforted men as they experienced erectile dysfunction, they provided men with evidence that they were man enough.

APPENDIX A

Descriptive Table of Research Participants

Age	*% (N)*
20–29	21 (20)
30–39	19 (19)
40–49	21 (20)
50–59	21 (20)
60–68	16 (15)
Race/ethnicity	
White	52.1 (49)
Black (African American, Caribbean)	26.5 (25)
Asian	8.5 (8)
Latino	7.4 (7)
Biracial	5.3 (5)
Socioeconomic status	
Working class	31.9 (30)
Middle class	52.1 (49)
Upper-middle class	14.8 (14)
Upper class	1 (1)

Education	
High school education or less	20.2 (19)
Some college	24.4 (23)
Associate's degree	3.1 (3)
Bachelor's degree	24.4 (23)
Graduate degree	23.4 (22)
Marital status at time of interview	
Married	37.2 (35)
Never married	32.9 (31)
Divorced	18.1 (17)
Separated	4.2 (4)
Widowed	1 (1)
Engaged	6.3 (6)
Parental status	
Fathers	59.5 (56)
Not fathers	40.5 (38)
Residential location	
Urban	43.6 (41)
Suburban	52.1 (49)
Rural	4.2 (4)
*Current religious identification**	
Christian (other than Catholic)	37.2 (35)
Catholic	14.8 (14)
None/Atheist	29.8 (28)
Jewish	6.3 (6)
Agnostic	7.4 (7)
Buddhist	1 (1)
Muslim	2.1 (2)
Hindu	1 (1)

* Self-reported current religious identification. Most of the men with no current religious identification were raised with formal religious influences.

APPENDIX B

Demographic Characteristics of Research Participants

Aaron is a 37-year-old white man with a high school education who works in transportation. He defines himself as middle class and has been dating his girlfriend for nine years. He was raised Jewish but is now agnostic. He lives in a northeastern U.S. suburb.

Adam is a 46-year-old white administrator with a BA. At the time of the interview he was separated from his wife, with whom he has three children. He was raised Catholic but does not consider himself religious. He defines himself as middle class. He lives in a northeastern U.S. suburb.

Akshay is a 41-year-old South Asian researcher with a PhD who identifies as middle class. He has been married for thirteen years and has two children. He was raised and identifies as Hindu and practices weekly. He lives in a northeastern U.S. suburban area.

Alex is a 41-year-old white man with a high school education who works as a painter. He considers himself working class. He is divorced, but at the time of the interview had been dating his girlfriend for two years. He has four children. He was raised Baptist and identifies as Christian. He lives in an urban area on the U.S. West Coast.

Arjun is a 20-year-old South Asian college student who works part-time at his college. He is single, middle class, and was raised and identifies as

Catholic. He was born and raised in India and presently lives in a northeastern U.S. suburban area.

Barry is a 44-year-old Black man with a high school education. He works for the post office and identifies as working class. At the time of the interview he was engaged to his girlfriend of two years. He was raised and identifies as Catholic. He has two children. He lives in a suburban area in the U.S. mid-Atlantic region.

Bradley is a 49-year-old white man with a college education, who works as a health-care administrator. He identifies as middle class and has two children with his wife of twenty years. He was raised and identifies as Protestant. He lives in a northeastern U.S. suburb.

Brett is a 42-year-old white divorced father of one child. He has a bachelor's degree and considers himself middle class. He was raised and identifies as Catholic. He works in sales and lives in a northeastern U.S. suburb.

Brian is a 26-year-old white college-educated man who works in sales. He is dating his girlfriend of seven years. He was raised and identifies as Christian. He lives in a northeastern U.S. suburb.

Bruce is a 59-year-old white unemployed engineer who identifies as upper-middle class. He was married for eighteen years, has three children, and is currently divorced. He has a master's degree. He was raised Christian but considers himself ecumenical. He lives in a northeastern U.S. suburb.

Bruno is a 41-year-old Latino man with a high school education, who works as a manual laborer. He has been married for twenty-six years and has two children. Although he was raised Catholic, he identifies as an atheist. He considers himself middle class and lives in a southeastern U.S. suburban area.

Cameron is a 32-year-old white graduate student with a bachelor's degree. He has been dating his girlfriend for seven years and does not identify with a religion, nor was he raised with one. He considers himself working class and lives in a large northeastern U.S. city.

Casey is a 29-year-old white man who works in media and who identifies as middle class. He has a college education. He is engaged to his girlfriend of two and a half years. He considers himself Christian and was raised Protestant. He lives in a northwestern U.S. suburban area.

Chad is a 33-year-old white educator who identifies as working class. He's been married for four years and has three children. He has a master's degree, identifies as Catholic, and was raised Protestant. He lives in a northeastern U.S. suburban area.

Clyde is a 52-year-old Black office manager who considers himself upper-middle class. He has a bachelor's degree and is divorced. He's been dating his girlfriend for eight years and has one child. He was raised Baptist but now identifies as Catholic, though he says he rarely attends religious services. He lives in a northeastern U.S. suburban area.

Craig is a 31-year-old East Asian project manager. He has been dating his girlfriend for seven years. He has a master's degree and considers himself upper-middle class. He was raised Buddhist but does not identify with a religion. He lives in a large U.S. West Coast city.

Curtis is a 55-year-old Black man with an associate's degree. He is retired from the military and considers himself middle class. He is engaged to his girlfriend of six years. He was previously married. He was raised and identifies as Baptist. He lives in a southeastern U.S. urban area.

Daniel is a 46-year-old Black electrician with some college education. He defines himself as working class and is currently single, though he was married for eight years. He was raised and identifies as Baptist and attends religious services weekly. He lives in a large U.S. city on the West Coast.

Darren is a 37-year-old Black (Caribbean American) government employee with a bachelor's degree who considers himself middle class. He is single and was raised and identifies as Christian. He lives in a large northeastern U.S. city.

Dean is a 33-year-old biracial (white and Native American) building manager with a high school education. He considers himself working class and has been married for a year. He was raised and identifies as Christian, though he does not attend religious services. He lives in a western U.S. rural area.

Dennis is a 67-year-old white retired information technology worker with an associate's degree. He considers himself upper-middle class. He's been married for thirty-nine years and has two children. He served in the military. He was raised Catholic and identifies as Episcopalian. He goes to church weekly. He lives in a northeastern U.S. suburban area.

Deon is a 60-year-old Black delivery driver who identifies as working class. He has a high school education and took some college classes. He was married for thirty years, but is now separated. He has two children. He was raised Baptist and attends religious services on a weekly basis. He lives in a southwestern U.S. urban area.

Devar is a 42-year-old Black (Caribbean American) researcher with a master's degree. He identifies as working class. He has been married for five years and has one child. He was raised Catholic but identifies as Baptist and says he attends religious services a couple of times a month. He lives in a southeastern U.S. city.

Devin is a 56-year-old Black middle class surveyor, who has never been married. He has been dating his girlfriend for two years. He has four children. He was raised and identifies as Baptist, but rarely attends religious services. He lives in a large northeastern U.S. city.

Donny is a 20-year-old East Asian college student. He considers himself working class. He does not consider himself religious, nor did he have a religious upbringing. He is single and lives in a northeastern U.S. city.

Doug is a 28-year-old white man who works for a cable company. He has been married for six years and has one child. He considers himself middle class and has a high school education. He was raised Christian, though he does not consider himself religious. He lives in a northeastern U.S. suburb.

Dylan is a 21-year-old white college student who works several jobs part-time. He is working class. He is single and though he does not consider himself religious, he was raised Christian. He lives in a northeastern U.S. suburb.

Eli is a 64-year-old white consultant, who considers himself middle class. He is single, though he was previously married for five years. He has two children. He was raised and identifies as Jewish, and lives in a large north-eastern U.S. city.

Fred is a 30-year-old Black production worker, who considers himself middle class. He has a GED. He has been married for one year and has three children. He was raised and identifies as Baptist. He lives in a south-eastern U.S. urban area.

Gary is a 68-year-old white photographer and information technology worker, who considers himself working class. He has a GED. He is wid-owed and was married to his wife for thirty-nine years. He was raised Catholic and considers himself agnostic, but he does not go to church. He lives in a large northeastern city.

Gavin is a 48-year-old biracial (East Asian and white) therapist who has a bachelor's degree. He thinks of himself as middle class and is single/never married. He has never identified with a religion. He lives in a large U.S. city on the West Coast.

Geno is a 65-year-old white retired executive. He has been married for forty-two years. He has one child. He has a bachelor's degree and took some graduate classes. He considers himself upper-middle class. He was raised and identifies as Catholic. He lives in a northeastern U.S. suburb.

George is Black and 67 years old. He did not complete high school and thinks of himself as working class. He is retired. George is divorced and single, and has four children. He was raised Jewish but now identifies as Baptist. He says he goes to religious services on a daily basis. He lives in a southeastern U.S. city.

Glenn is a 58-year-old biracial (Pacific Islander and white) retired carpenter. He completed some college classes and sees himself as working class. He is dating (his girlfriend of two years) and divorced (he was married for ten years). He has three children. He was raised and identifies as Christian and attends religious services on a monthly basis. He lives in a large U.S. city on the West Coast.

Gordon is a 58-year-old white, retired, middle class man. He has a high school education and is currently divorced, though he was married for ten years. He has one child. He considers himself agnostic, though he was raised Baptist. He lives in a southeastern U.S. suburban area.

Greg is a 20-year-old South Asian college student who considers himself middle class. He has been dating his girlfriend for one year. He considers himself agnostic and was raised Christian. He lives in a northeastern U.S. suburban area.

Harry is a 61-year-old white maintenance worker with a high school and trade school education. He considers himself middle class. He has been married for forty-two years and has two children. He was raised Catholic and Baptist though he now identifies as Methodist. He lives in a northeastern U.S. suburban area.

Hector is a 55-year-old biracial (Latino and white) truck driver with some college education. He identifies as working class. He is currently single, though he was married three times, most recently for ten years. He has one child. He was raised and thinks of himself as Catholic, though he rarely attends religious services. He lives in a large midwestern U.S. city.

Henry is a 59-year-old white middle class consultant who has been married for twenty-one years. He does not have any children. He was raised Catholic, identifies as Catholic, and goes to religious services on a regular basis. He lives in a northeastern U.S. suburban area.

Hugh is a 33-year-old white graduate student who considers himself working class. He was in the military and has a bachelor's degree. He is divorced and has one child. He has been dating his girlfriend for about a year and a half. He was raised Christian but does not identify with a religion. He lives in a northeastern U.S. suburban area.

Hunter is a 51-year-old white artist who considers himself working class. He has a high school education. He is divorced and a stepparent to a child from his marriage. He was raised Christian but does not identify with a religion. He lives in an urban area in the U.S. mid-Atlantic region.

Ian is a 51-year-old white information technology worker who has been married for twenty-four years. He has a master's degree and considers himself upper-middle class. He was raised and identifies as Christian, and regularly attends religious services. He lives in a western U.S. suburban area.

Issac is a 30-year-old Black (Caribbean American) case manager with a bachelor's degree (as well as some graduate courses). He is middle class, and has been married for four years (though together with his wife for ten years). He was raised Christian and identifies as Protestant, though he rarely attends religious services. He lives in a northeastern U.S. city.

Jack is a 32-year-old Black middle class man who works in media. He has a bachelor's degree and has been dating his long-distance girlfriend for one and a half years. He was raised Christian but identifies as Jewish, though he does not attend religious services. He lives in a southwestern U.S. suburban area.

Jamal is a 21-year-old Black college student who identifies as upper-middle class. He was raised and identifies as Catholic and attends religious services on a weekly basis. He is single and lives in a northeastern U.S. suburban area.

Jamie is a 56-year-old white engineer with a bachelor's degree. He considers himself upper-middle class and has been married for twenty-five years. He is a father of two and was raised Baptist, though he is currently Methodist and goes to church a couple of times a month. He lives in a northeastern U.S. suburban area.

Jay is a 60-year-old white retired upper-middle class man who has been married for thirty-two years and has one child. He has a master's degree and was raised and identifies as Christian, though he does not go to church. He lives in a northeastern U.S. rural area.

Jermaine is a 40-year-old Black, unemployed, working class man. He has a trade school education and has never been married. He has one child and is in a new relationship. He was raised and identifies as Muslim and practices weekly. He lives in a northeastern U.S. urban area.

Jerod is a 22-year-old Black college student who works in production. He identifies as working class. He's been dating his girlfriend for five months. He was raised Christian but does not consider himself religious. He lives in a northeastern U.S. suburb.

Jerry is a 41-year-old white scientist who has been married to his second wife for four years. He considers himself working class. He was raised Catholic but does not identify with any religion as an adult. He lives in a northeastern U.S. suburb.

Jose is a 61-year-old Latino man with a high school education and some college classes. He is retired, considers himself working class, and has two children. He is divorced and dating casually. He identifies as an atheist, but was raised Catholic. He lives in a large northeastern U.S. city.

Josh is a 57-year-old white mechanic with a high school education who identifies as working class. He has been married for twenty-five years and has two children. He was raised Catholic and though he does not consider himself religious, he occasionally attends church. He lives in a suburb of a large northeastern U.S. city.

Juan is a 55-year-old Latino man who works as a manager. He has an MBA and identifies as upper-middle class. He has been married for twenty-five years and has three children. He was raised and identifies as Catholic, but rarely attends religious services. He lives in a southeastern U.S. suburban area.

Justin is a 28-year-old white medical assistant. He has an associate's degree and considers himself middle class. He has been dating his girlfriend for five years. Although he was raised Catholic, he identifies as an atheist. He lives in a large midwestern U.S. city.

Kenneth is a 26-year-old Black warehouse worker with a high school education. He is engaged to his girlfriend of five years, with whom he has one child. He was raised and identifies as Christian, though he does not attend religious services. He considers himself middle class and he lives in a northeastern U.S. urban area.

Kent is a 47-year-old white sales manager who has been married for four years. He has a bachelor's degree, and considers himself middle class. He was raised Christian but does not identify with a religion. He lives in a northeastern U.S. suburban area.

Kirk is a 54-year-old white self-employed upper-middle class man who has been married for twenty years and has three children. He has two master's degrees. He was raised Catholic, though he does not currently identify with a religion or attend religious services. He lives in a northeastern U.S. suburban area.

Kurt is a 48-year-old white educator with a PhD who identifies as middle class. He is divorced. He was raised Christian but does not identify with a religion. He lives in a northeastern U.S. suburban area.

Lance is a 45-year-old white man who works in real estate. He has a master's degree and considers himself middle class. He has one child and is separated from his wife. He has been dating his girlfriend for about a year. He was raised Christian and considers himself spiritual, though not religious. He lives in a southeastern U.S. suburban area.

Louis is a 60-year-old Black researcher who has a master's degree and is middle class. He has been married for eighteen years (in his second marriage) and has five children. He was raised Christian but identifies as Muslim and practices his religion on a daily basis. He lives in a northeastern U.S. suburban area.

Luke is a 42-year-old white financial professional with a master's degree who identifies as upper class. He has been married for eight months (in his second marriage) and has one child. He identifies as Buddhist and practices daily, though he was raised Christian. He lives in a southwestern U.S. urban area.

Marcus is a 20-year-old Black college student. He is single and considers himself working class. He was raised and identifies as Christian, though he rarely attends religious services. He lives in a large northeastern U.S. city.

Mario is a 23-year-old Latino college student who considers himself middle class. He is single. He was raised and identifies as Catholic, though he never attends religious services. He lives in a northeastern U.S. urban area.

Max is a 21-year-old Latino college student. He is single and considers himself middle class. He was raised and identifies as Christian but rarely attends religious services. He lives in a northeastern U.S. urban area.

Mick is a 56-year-old white retail manager with a high school diploma, as well as some college classes, and considers himself middle class. He has been married for twenty-seven years and has one child. He was raised and identifies as Jewish and observes the Jewish holidays. He lives in a northeastern U.S. suburban area.

Minjun is a 39-year old East Asian educator who was born and raised in East Asia. He has a PhD and considers himself working class. He has been married for eight years. He was raised and identifies as Christian and attends church weekly. He lives in a northeastern U.S. suburban area.

Neil is a 47-year-old white retired lawyer with a graduate/professional degree. He considers himself upper-middle class and has been married (to his second wife) for four years. He has four children. He doesn't consider himself to be religious, but was raised Evangelical. He lives in a northeastern U.S. rural area.

Nick is a 52-year-old Black man who is unemployed. He considers himself to be working class and did not complete high school. He has never been married but has been dating his girlfriend for six years and has two children. He was raised Baptist but does not consider himself religious. He lives in a large city in the U.S. mid-Atlantic region.

Patrick is a 25-year-old white educator and graduate student. He considers himself middle class and has been dating his girlfriend for six years. He was raised and identifies as Jewish and observes Jewish holidays. He lives in a northeastern U.S. urban area.

Peter is a 48-year-old white man who works in higher education, has a master's degree, and considers himself middle class. He has been married for twenty-two years and has two children. He was raised and identifies as Christian and goes to church weekly. He lives in a northeastern U.S. suburban area.

Randy is a 35-year-old white trader with a bachelor's degree who considers himself middle class. He is engaged and his been dating his fiancé for seven years. He does not identify with a religion though he was raised in a conservative Christian faith. He lives in a northeastern U.S. urban area.

Reggie is a 50-year-old Black contractor with a high school education who considers himself working class. He is dating and previously divorced, and the father of two children. He does not consider himself religious though he was raised Baptist. He lives in an urban area in the U.S. mid-Atlantic region.

Rex is a 45-year-old Black college student who considers himself middle class. He has been married for five years and has two children. He was raised and identifies as Baptist, though he rarely attends religious services. He lives in a southeastern U.S. suburban area.

Ron is a 62-year-old Black health professional with a bachelor's degree who identifies as middle class. He is single (never married). He identifies as a Jehovah's Witness, practices twice a week, and was raised Christian. He lives in a suburban area in the U.S. mid-Atlantic region.

Ruben in a 35-year-old Black customer service representative. He has a high school education and identifies as middle class. He is single and has one child. He was raised and considers himself Christian and attends church weekly. He lives in a southeastern U.S. urban area.

Russell is a 65-year-old white insurance agent who considers himself middle class. He has been married for thirty-five years and has three children. He was raised and identifies as Catholic, though he rarely attends religious services. He lives in a northeastern U.S. suburban area.

Ryan is a 53-year-old white cleaner with a bachelor's degree. He considers himself middle class. He is single (never married). He was raised Catholic but does not identify as religious. He lives in a northeastern U.S. city.

Samuel is a 30-year-old white counselor with a master's degree who thinks of himself as working class. He has been married for ten years and has four children. He was raised Christian and is a Jehovah's Witness, who practices regularly. He lives in a midwestern U.S. suburban area.

Scott is a 37-year-old white educator with a master's degree who considers himself middle class. He has been married for nine years and has one child. He was raised and identifies as Protestant. He lives in a northeastern U.S. rural area.

Shane is a 21-year-old South Asian man who came to the United States as a teenager. He considers himself middle class. He is a single college student and works part-time as a medical assistant. He was raised and identifies as Christian. He lives in a northeastern U.S. suburb.

Stuart is a 59-year-old white educator with a master's degree who identifies as upper-middle class. He has been married for sixteen years and has two stepchildren. He was raised Catholic but is not religious. He lives in the northeastern United States.

Timothy is a 25-year-old white florist, who is single and defines himself as working class. He has a high school education and has taken some college classes. He was raised Catholic, thinks of himself as agnostic, and does not attend religious services. He lives in a northeastern U.S. suburb.

Todd is a 35-year-old white middle class compliance officer who has been married for six years and has two children. He has a bachelor's degree. He was raised and identifies as Christian and occasionally attends religious services. He lives in a northeastern U.S. city.

Trevor is a 39-year-old Black working class warehouse worker. He has a GED. He has never been married but has been dating his girlfriend for one year and he has two children. He was raised Christian and currently identifies with Catholicism and Islam, though he rarely attends religious services. He lives in a mid-Atlantic U.S. city.

Troy is a white 39-year-old printer who considers himself middle class. He has a high school education and is single (never married). He has one child. He was raised and identifies as Christian but never goes to church. He lives in a midwestern U.S. urban area.

Tyrone is a 61-year-old Black entrepreneur who identifies as middle class. He has a high school diploma and has taken some college classes. He is separated from his wife of twenty-five years with whom he has four children. He was raised and identifies as Pentecostal and goes to religious services twice weekly. He lives in a northeastern U.S. city.

Victor is a 20-year-old Latino college student who considers himself middle class. He was raised and identifies as Catholic, though rarely attends religious services. He is single and lives in a northeastern U.S. city.

Vishan is a 24-year-old South Asian college student who defines himself as middle class. He was raised and identifies as Catholic. He attends religious services about twice a year. He is single and lives in a northeastern U.S. urban area.

Vlad is a 20-year-old white (Russian) college student who considers himself upper-middle class. He was raised and identifies as Jewish but does not attend religious services. He is single and lives in a northeastern U.S. suburb.

Walker is a 39-year-old biracial (Black and Native American) middle class information technology worker. He has been married for fifteen years and has four children. He was raised and identifies as Episcopalian. He goes to religious services a couple times each month. He lives in a southwestern U.S. city.

Walter is a 60-year-old white middle class manager. He has a high school diploma as well as some college classes. He is divorced and was married for five years. He was raised Protestant but does not consider himself religious. He lives in a U.S. urban area on the West Coast.

Warren is a 40-year-old Latino (Central American) consultant who considers himself middle class. He is engaged and has been with his fiancé for about a year. He has a doctoral degree. Although he was raised Catholic, he does not consider himself religious or attend services. He lives in a southwestern U.S. urban area.

Wesley is a 68-year-old white unemployed real estate professional who considers himself middle class. He has a master's degree. He is single (never married). He was raised Jewish but does not identify with a religion. He lives in a northeastern U.S. city.

Zack is a 34-year-old white educator with a doctoral degree. He considers himself working class and has been married for eight years. He was raised Lutheran but now identifies as agnostic. He lives in a western U.S. suburb.

APPENDIX C

Methods

Between 2014 and 2016, I, along with several research assistants, conducted in-depth interviews with ninety-five straight men aged 20 to 68 living in the United States. My goal was to interview a minimum of fifteen and a maximum of twenty participants in each of the following age groups: twenties, thirties, forties, fifties, and sixties. I selected these age ranges given that mid-life is the time that men are most likely to be sexually active and that midlife men's sexuality is less studied than adolescent/teen/college-aged boys' and men's sexualities or senior men's sexualities. I also sought out a racially diverse sample; establishing a quota that at least thirty percent of the sample be men of color (48 percent of the final sample were men of color). I also made sure that most participants were or had been married or were fathers, consistent with demographic trends for men in these age groups as confirmed by the U.S. census.

Recruitment was challenging. Unlike my study on women's sexuality, where women were eager to refer other women, and I readily used snowball sampling as a means of finding participants, in this study none of the men referred other participants. Thus, I needed to be creative with recruiting. I first began recruitment through email/social media solicitations to existing social networks and through posting in a university research participant pool. This made it relatively easy to find men in their twenties.

However, as I sought diversity in terms of race and relationship status as well as age, I needed broader recruitment.

So, I next posted on Craigslist, which is a United States online bulletin board or classified advertisement website which features job listings, rentals, personal ads, and, as relevant for this study, a section on "Volunteer Opportunities," which includes solicitations for participants in research studies. Recruiting through Craigslist had advantages and disadvantages. First, it allowed me to find participants throughout the country, as I posted advertisements on boards for major cities in different regions of the United States (e.g., Philadelphia, New York, Boston, Miami, Dallas, Phoenix, Washington D.C., Chicago). Doing so, I was able to find racially diverse participants that I would not likely have found recruiting only locally. The downside of Craigslist is there was about a 50 percent interview yield rate based on those who replied to advertisements. Many people never responded to email contacts or did not show up to take the call for the interview at the scheduled time. One interview was completed and discarded due to the participant's apparent lack of concern with the subject matter and inappropriate and abusive comments (this brought the final sample to 94 participants). Yet, the vast majority of the men who were interviewed from Craigslist (and through all other means) seemed to take the interview seriously and had a lot to say about their sexual selves. Finding men in their sixties was most challenging, as they were less likely to be looking on Craigslist. So, I also posted flyers in public places like senior centers and supermarkets and found a few participants that way.

Although some interviews were conducted face-to-face (n=27), about two-thirds of interviews were conducted via phone/audio call (n=67). Phone interviews yielded rich data, and we surmise that many men felt comfortable with the "anonymous" feel of the phone interview. Some interviewees commented that they would not have shared as much intimate information had the interview been face to face. Overall, I was surprised that interviews with men were longer, on average, than interviews with women for *Deserving Desire*. Interviews averaged about two hours and were audio recorded and transcribed. Identifying information such as names and specific locations were removed during transcription and/or coding. Participants were paid $25 for their time, with an additional $5 for each half-hour, when the interview extended beyond two hours (approximately one-third of interviews were more than two hours).

Initially, I thought men would be more comfortable talking with other men, so I recruited men students who I trained to work as interviewers. Most interviews were conducted by John Jackson, a nontraditional student in his early thirties who did forty interviews, and Jonathan Magill, a nontraditional student in his late thirties, who conducted twelve interviews. Along the way, however, some men expressed a preference to be interviewed by me—sometimes because I was a woman, and sometimes because I was a professor. So, after about the first twenty interviews, we offered participants a choice of interviewer (me or one of the men RAs). I conducted one-third of the interviews, most of which were with older men in their fifties and sixties who were more likely than younger men to request me as the interviewer. While I would need to take a much closer look to make any statements about an interviewer-gender effect, in analysis I did not detect much difference in responses based on the gender of the interviewer. In a few cases, I think the language used with men interviews was a bit coarser, but that did not have material impact on the content of the interview. Also, as I interviewed most of the older men in their fifties and sixties, I do wonder if they may have been more candid with me about erectile dysfunction than they may have been with men interviewers.

At the start of interviews, demographic information including age, race, religion, religiosity, social class, education, and occupation was collected by self-report (See Appendix A for full demographics). Interviewees provided consent by emailing, signing in person, or mailing in consent forms, following procedures of Penn State University's Institutional Review Board. Interviews were conducted using a semi-structured, open-ended interview guide containing questions on attitudes about sexualities and sexual development, sexual selves, and sexual relationships. Most questions focused on the development of sexual selves. Following a grounded theory perspective, questions were open-ended and revised throughout data collection, as new themes became salient in interviews. Follow-up questions were added for clarification or for more information during interviews.

I analyzed data in NVivo, using a grounded theory approach. With the help of my research assistants, I began by doing open coding and microanalysis. This process involved reading through interview transcripts multiple times, labeling data with codes, and writing memos about emergent themes. After I identified dominant themes, I went back and reviewed those themes, often sub-coding within them to identity patterns and variations based on demographic differences like age and relationship status, as well as race and ethnicity. Through this process, the concepts of getting it, having it, and keeping up with sex and with women emerged as the primary concerns among participants, and I began to sort data and themes again into these broad categories. I frequently read and re-read interview transcripts to challenge or confirm evolving patterns and theories about the role of women in men's sexualities.

Acknowledgments

First, I would like to offer my deep and sincere gratitude to the ninety-four men who shared their stories as material for this book. It was not easy to find men willing to talk about such a personal topic, so I greatly appreciate those who took the time and spoke with candor to my research team and me. These men had such diverse and interesting experiences, which certainly provided depth and richness to the book.

This project would not have been accomplished as readily without my excellent research assistants. First, John Jackson conducted forty interviews—more than anyone else on the team. John was capable, reliable, and enthusiastic. He approached each interview with curiosity and openness and was always eager to chat about participant comments and emerging themes. I enjoyed and appreciated the opportunity to work with him over the course of two years of data collection. Jonathan Magill started working on this research as part of the team for Abington College's Undergraduate Research Activities (ACURA) program. Jon continued to work on the project after ACURA was over and conducted twelve interviews. Jon was affable, disciplined, and also genuinely curious about the research process and this research project. Both John and Jon, as non-traditional college students, connected with the project and with research participants and it was apparent that they made participants feel comfortable talking about an uncomfortable topic.

I was fortunate to have a number of excellent undergraduate research assistants through the ACURA program over several years. I greatly appreciate the work of all of these students. Alongside Jon Magill, Clarence Bryant and Victoria Pirenoglu were involved in the initial stages of data collection and helped with interviewee recruitment, data collection, transcription, and analysis. Clarence conducted seven interviews, and I appreciated his sincere desire to do his best work in interviews. Victoria also conducted several interviews and recruited a couple of participants. Steven Henao and Hayley Payne also were helpful in coding data and doing data analysis in a later stage of the project. Alejandra Barmash and Madeline Richard both worked on transcription and analysis as ACURA students. Through that year of ACURA, I was also fortunate to work with Penn State Abington librarian Christina Riehman-Murphy, who was a tremendous help with mentoring the students and with analysis of data. Christina coded many interviews, was enthusiastic, and brought creativity and structure to data analysis. It was a pleasure to coauthor a paper with her using preliminary findings from this research.

Additionally, several other students assisted with recruitment, interviewing, and transcription. I thank Daniel Fogarty, Thomas Lafferty, and Joshua Paris-Santana for their work in these capacities. I would also like to recognize Susan Tomko for her fast, accurate, excellent transcription work, as well as Pamela Anticole and Chali Maughan, who also did transcriptions. I also sincerely thank my sister, Christina Montemurro, who transcribed several interviews and offered support throughout the project.

Next, I recognize my wonderful colleagues at Penn State Abington, especially those in the Psychological and Social Sciences program. Every year I realize more and more how fortunate I am to be in an interdisciplinary program with supportive, congenial faculty. Jake Benfield, Michael Bernstein, Meghan Gillen, and Judy Newman, in particular, have always been go-to colleagues and sources of encouragement. My sociology colleagues and writing group, Liz Hughes, David Hutson, and Laura Orrico, were very helpful in working through chapter drafts. I am grateful for all of their suggestions and discussions, especially to Liz Hughes, who has always been only a text away from sharing her insight and fresh perspective.

Many colleagues have helped me talk through and develop this project over the past six years. I thank David Knox, Nicole Stokes, Alicia Walker, and Dennis Waskul for their suggestions and support at various stages in the project. In particular, I so appreciate the many conversations with Rebecca Plante about all things men's sexualities and masculinities and the encouragement she provided.

I owe tremendous gratitude to Laura Carpenter. As reviewer, Laura's careful reading, push to make the book stronger, and exceptionally helpful suggestions really transformed the book. I feel fortunate to have the insight of a gender scholar of her caliber.

I also acknowledge the support of my Society for the Study of Symbolic Interaction besties, Andrea Laurent-Simpson and John Pruit. I've never had sociology friends like these two and having them to run ideas by, to vent to about the challenges of book writing, and to go over ideas for titles has been a comfort and joy while working on this book.

I am also grateful for my friend readers, sounding boards, and interviewee recruiters: Julie Wielehowski, Kim Maialetti, Rebecca Fishkin, Colleen Rahill, and Jennifer Hawley. Thank you to all my friends who showed interest, asked questions, and offered encouragement, support, and needed distractions.

My work was very generously supported by several grants from Penn State University, all of which helped accelerate the pace of data collection and analysis. I received a grant from the Rubin Fund, which supported interview costs, and two faculty development grants from Penn State Abington, which supported wages for John and Jon, data analysis software, and professional transcription of interviews.

Additionally, I would like to thank the staff at Rutgers University Press. Although initially I wasn't sure where this book would land, I know this is where it belongs. I am grateful to have the support of this excellent team for a third time. I thank Peter Mickulas for enthusiastically welcoming me back and championing this project. Thanks, too, to Mary Ribesky and the production team at Westchester Publishing Services for making the process of getting the book to publication a smooth one.

Finally, thanks to my family for always supporting, encouraging, and understanding. Thanks to my parents Susan and Tony Montemurro for always believing and being proud.

Madison and Kate, your smiling faces at the end of a writing day meant the world. Madison, thanks for being my in-house expert. Kate—thanks for telling me to keep going so you could have my office after I finished writing.

Notes

CHAPTER 1 — INTRODUCTION

1. Scott Melzer, *Manhood Impossible: Men's Struggles to Control and Transform Their Bodies and Work* (New Brunswick, NJ: Rutgers University Press, 2018), 228.

2. Jane Ward, *The Tragedy of Heterosexuality* (New York: New York University Press, 2020).

3. Alexsandar Stulhofer, Luana Cunha Ferreira, and Ivan Landripet, "Emotional Intimacy, Sexual Desire, and Sexual Satisfaction among Partnered Heterosexual Men," *Sexual and Relationship Therapy* 29 (2014): 229–244.

4. Michael Flood, "Men, Sex, and Homosociality: How Bonds between Men Shape their Sexual Relations with Women," *Men and Masculinities* 10, no. 3 (2008): 339–359; Melzer, *Manhood Impossible*; and Peggy Orenstein, *Boys and Sex: Young Men on Hookups, Love, Porn, Consent and Navigating the New Masculinity* (New York: Harper, 2020).

5. I use the terminology straight rather than heterosexual here because straightness is a better indication of sexual identity, while heterosexual is a better indication of sexual practice. Although all men identified as straight, several had same-sex sexual encounters at some point during their lives. Thus, their sexual behavior or practice was not exclusively heterosexual.

6. Douglas Schrock and Michael Schwalbe, "Men, Masculinity, and Manhood Acts," *Annual Review of Sociology* 35 (2009): 281.

7. Melzer, *Manhood Impossible.*

8. James W. Messerschmidt, *Masculinities in the Making: From the Local to the Global*, (Lanham, MD: Rowman & and Littlefield, 2016); and Schrock and Schwalbe, "Men, Masculinity, and Manhood Acts," 278–279.

9. R. W. Connell, *Masculinities* (Berkeley: University of California Press, 1995); Flood, "Men, Sex, and Homosociality"; Melzer, *Manhood Impossible*; and Schrock and Schwalbe, "Men, Masculinity, and Manhood Acts."

10. Gary Alan Fine, *With the Boys: Little League Baseball and Pre-adolescent Culture* (Chicago: University of Chicago Press, 1987); Orenstein, *Boys and Sex*; and C. J. Pascoe, *Dude You're a Fag: Masculinity and Sexuality in High School* (Berkeley: University of California Press, 2007).

11. Tristan Bridges and C. J. Pascoe, "Masculinities and Post-Homophobias?" in *Exploring Masculinities: Identity, Inequality, Continuity, and Change*, ed. C. J. Pascoe and Tristan Bridges, (New York: Oxford University Press, 2016), 412.

12. Chiara Bertone and Raffaella Ferrero Camoletto, "Beyond the Sex Machine? Sexual Practices and Masculinity in Adult Men's Heterosexual Accounts," *Journal of Gender Studies* 18, no. 4 (2009): 369–386; David Grazian, "The Girl Hunt: Urban Nightlife and the Performance of Masculinity as Collective Activity," *Symbolic Interaction* 30, no. 2 (2007): 221–243; Diane Richardson, "Youth Masculinities: Compelling Male Heterosexualities," *British Journal of Sociology* 61 (2010): 737–756; Brian Sweeney, "Masculine Status, Sexual Performance, and the Sexual Stigmatization of Women," *Symbolic Interaction* 37 (2014): 369–390; Ward, *Tragedy of Heterosexuality*; and Amy Wilkins, "Stigma and Status: Interracial Intimacy and Intersectional Identities among Black College Men," *Gender & Society* 26 (2012): 165–189.

13. For example, Orenstein, *Boys and Sex;* Pascoe, *Dude*; and Ward, *Tragedy of Heterosexuality.*

14. Orenstein, *Boys and Sex.*

15. Schrock and Schwalbe, "Men, Masculinity, and Manhood Acts," 282.

16. William Simon and John H. Gagnon, "Sexual Scripts: Origins, Influences, and Change. *Qualitative Sociology* 26 (2003): 491–497; William Simon and John H. Gagnon, "Sexual Scripts: Permanence and Change," *Archives of Sexual Behavior* 15 (1986): 97–120; and William Simon and John H. Gagnon, "Sexual Scripts," *Society*, November/December (1984): 53–60.

17. Bertone and Camoletto, "Beyond the Sex Machine?"; and Ronald F. Levant, "Nonrelational Sexuality in Men," in *Men and Sex: New Psychological Perspectives*, ed. Ronald F. Levant and Gary R. Brooks, 9–27 (New York: Wiley, 1997).

18. Orenstein, *Boys and Sex*; and Schrock and Schwalbe, "Men, Masculinity, and Manhood Acts."

19. Christopher Vito, Amanda Admire, and Elizabeth Hughes, "Masculinity, Aggrieved Entitlement and Violence: Considering the Isla Vista Mass Shooting," *NORMA* 13 (2018): 86–102.

20. Michael Kimmel, *Angry White Men: American Masculinity at the End of an Era* (New York: Nation Books, 2013).

21. Simon and Gagnon, "Sexual Scripts."

22. Anthony Chen, "Lives at the Center of the Periphery: Chinese American Masculinities and Bargaining with Hegemony," *Gender & Society* 13 (1999): 584–607; Connell, *Masculinities*; and Lisa Wade and Myra Marx Ferree, *Gender: Ideas, Interactions and Institutions*, 2nd ed. (New York: W. W. Norton, 2019).

23. Chen, "Lives at the Center"; Flood, "Men, Sex, and Homosociality"; C. Marie Harker, "Fat Male Sexuality: The Monster in the Maze" *Sexualities* 19, no. 8 (2016): 980–996; Nguyen Tan Hoang, *A View from the Bottom: Asian American Masculinity and Sexual Representation* (Durham, NC: Duke University Press, 2014); Beth Montemurro, "'If You Could Just See Me': The Construction of Heterosexual Men's Sexual Selves and the Hierarchy of Desirability," *Sexualities* 24, no. 3 (2021): 303–321; Orenstein, *Boys and Sex*; Rashawn Ray and Jason A. Rosow, "Getting Off on Getting Intimate: How Normative Arrangements Structure Black and White Fraternity Men's Approaches toward Women," *Men and Masculinities* 12, no. 5 (2010): 523–546; Jesus G. Smith, Maria Cristina Morales, and Chonh-Suk Han, "The Influence of Sexual Racism on Erotic Capital: A Systemic Racism Perspective," in *Handbook of Sociology of Racial and Ethnic Relations*, ed. Pinar Batur and Joe R. Feagin, 389–399 (New York: Springer, 2018); and Kris Taylor and Sue Jackson, "'I Want That Power Back': Discourses of Masculinity within an Online Pornography Abstinence Forum," *Sexualities* 21, no. 4 (2018): 621–639.

24. Connell, *Masculinities*; Pascoe, *Dude*; Richardson, "Youth Masculinities"; Sweeney, "Masculine Status"; and Ward, *Tragedy of Heterosexuality.*

25. Taylor and Jackson, "I Want That Power Back."

26. Janet Holland, Caroline Ramazanoglu, Sue Sharpe, and Rachel Thomson, *The Male in the Head: Young People, Heterosexuality, and Power* (London: Tuffnell, 2004), 136.

27. As cited in Bridges and Pascoe, "Masculinities and Post-Homophobias?," 417.

28. Sweeney, "Masculine Status," 373.

29. Gary R. Brooks, "The Centerfold Syndrome," in Levant and Brooks, *Men and Sex*, 28–57.

30. Brooks, "Centerfold Syndrome."

31. Glen Elder, Gary Brooks and Susan L. Morrow. "Sexual Self-Schemas of Heterosexual Men," *Psychology of Men & Masculinities* 13, no. 2 (2012):166–179; and Paul Wright, "Show Me the Data! Empirical Support for the 'Centerfold Syndrome,'" *Psychology of Men and Masculinities* 13, no. 2 (2012): 180–198.

32. Elder, Brooks, and Morrow, "Sexual Self-Schemas," 170.

33. Breanne Fahs, *Performing Sex: The Making and Unmaking of Women's Erotic Lives* (Albany: State University of New York Press, 2011); Robert Jensen, *Getting Off: Pornography and the End of Masculinity* (Cambridge, MA: South End Press, 2007); Jackson Katz, *The Macho Paradox: Why Some Men Hurt Women and How All Men Can Help* (Naperville, IL: Sourcebooks, 2006); Rachel O'Neill, *Seduction: Men, Masculinity and Mediated Intimacy* (Cambridge: Polity, 2018); Orenstein, *Boys and Sex*; Pascoe, *Dude*; Sweeney, "Masculine Status"; Wade and Ferree, *Gender*; and Ward, *Tragedy of Heterosexuality.*

34. For example, Grazian, "Girl Hunt"; Orenstein, *Boys and Sex*; Pascoe, *Dude*; Richardson, "Youth Masculinities"; and Sweeney, "Masculine Status."

35. Ward, *Tragedy of Heterosexuality.*

36. Pascoe, *Dude*; Julie Reid, Sinikka Elliott, and Gretchen R. Webber, "Casual Hookups to Formal Dates: Redefining the Boundaries of the Sexual Double Standard," *Gender & Society* 25, no. 5 (2011): 545–568.

37. Niobe Way, "Boys as Human," *Contexts* 12, no. 1 (2013): 16–17; and Niobe Way, Jessica Cressen, Samuel Bodian, Justin Preston, Joseph Nelwo, and Diane Hughes, "'It Might Be Nice to Be a Girl . . . Then You Wouldn't Have to Be Emotionless': Boys' Resistance to Norms of Masculinity during Adolescence," *Psychology of Men & Masculinities* 15, no. 3 (2014): 241–252.

38. Pascoe, *Dude*; Louisa Allen, "Girls Want Sex, Boys Want Love: Resisting Dominant Discourses of (Hetero)Sexuality," *Sexualities* 6 (2003): 215–236; and Louisa Allen, "'Sensitive and Real Macho All at the Same Time': Young Heterosexual Men and Romance," *Men and Masculinities* 10 (2007): 137–152.

39. Toby Keith, *Masculinities in Contemporary Culture: An Intersectional Approach to the Complexities and Challenges of Male Identity* (New York: Routledge, 2017).

40. For example, Allen, "Girls Want Sex"; Laura Carpenter, *Virginity Lost: An Intimate Portrait of First Sexual Experiences* (New York: New York University Press, 2005); Brooks, "Centerfold Syndrome"; Karin A. Martin, *Puberty, Sexuality and the Self: Girls and Boys at Adolescence* (New York: Routledge, 1996); Orenstein, *Boys and Sex*; Pascoe, *Dude*; Ray and Rosow, "Getting Off"; Amy Schalet, *Not Under My Roof: Parents, Teens, and the Culture of Sex* (Chicago: University of Chicago Press, 2011); and Andrew P. Smiler, "'I Wanted to Get to Know Her Better': Adolescent Boys' Dating Motives, Masculinity Ideology, and Sexual Behavior,'" *Journal of Adolescence* 31 (2008):17–32.

41. For example, Allen, "Girls Want Sex"; Allen, "Sensitive and Real Macho"; Martin, *Puberty, Sexuality and the Self*; Orenstein, *Boys and Sex*; and Richardson, "Youth Masculinities."

42. Shari Dworkin and Lucia F. O'Sullivan, "'It's Less Work for Us and It Shows Us She Has Good Taste': Masculinity, Sexual Initiation, and Contemporary Sexual Scripts," in *The Sexual Self: Construction of Sexual Scripts*, ed. Michael Kimmel, 105–121 (Nashville, TN: Vanderbilt University Press, 2007); and David Wyatt Seal, Lucia F. O'Sullivan, and Anke A. Ehrhardt, "Miscommunication and Misinterpretations: Men's Scripts about Sexual Communication and Unwanted Sex in Interactions with Women," in Kimmel, *Sexual Self*, 141–161.

43. Carpenter, *Virginity Lost*.

44. Elizabeth A. Armstrong, Paula England, and Allison C. K. Fogarty, "Accounting for Women's Orgasm and Sexual Enjoyment in College Hookups and Relationships," *American Sociological Review* 77 (2012): 435–462; Bertone and Camoletto, "Beyond the Sex Machine?"; Linn Sandberg, "Just Feeling a Naked Body Close to You: Men, Sexuality and Intimacy in Later Life," *Sexualities* 16 (2013): 261–282; Stulhofer, Ferreira, and Landripet, "Emotional Intimacy"; and Andrew S. Walters and Ivan Valenzuela, "More Than Muscles, Money, or Machismo: Latino Men and the Stewardship of Masculinity," *Sexuality & Culture* 24, no. 3 (2020): 967–1003.

45. Shawn Patrick and John Beckenbach, "Male Perceptions of Intimacy: A Qualitative Study," *Journal of Men's Studies* 17 (2009): 47–56; Sandberg, "Just Feeling"; and Stulhofer, Ferreira, and Landripet, "Emotional Intimacy."

46. Sandberg, "Just Feeling."

47. Beth Montemurro and Christina Riehman Murphy, "Ready and Waiting: Heterosexual Men's Discourses on Decision Making in Initiation of Sexual Intimacy," *Men and Masculinities* 22, no. 5 (2019): 872–892.

48. Lisa Diamond, *Sexual Fluidity: Understanding Women's Love and Desire* (Cambridge, MA: Harvard University Press, 2008); Pepper Schwartz, "The Social Construction of Heterosexuality," in Kimmel, *Sexual Self*, 80–92.

49. Antoine Lassaigne, *Love and Sex in Japan DVD* (Boulogne-Billancourt: Java Films, 2016); O'Neill, *Seduction*; and Ward, *Tragedy of Heterosexuality*.

50. Brenda Goodman and Caitlin Krapf, *Sex (Ed), the Movie: How Did You Learn about Sex?* (New York: First Run Features, 2015).

51. Goodman, *Sex (Ed)*; Schalet, *Not Under My Roof*; and John S. Santelli, Leslie M. Kantor, Stephanie A. Grilo, Ilene S. Speizer, Laura D. Lindberg, Jennifer Heitel, Amy T. Schalet, Maureen E. Lyon, Amanda J. Mason-Jones, Ph.D., Terry McGovern, Craig J. Heck, Jennifer Rogers, and Mary Ott, "Abstinence-Only-until-Marriage: An Updated Review of U.S. Policies and Programs and Their Impact," *Journal of Adolescent Health* 61, no. 3 (2017): 273–280.

52. Martin, *Puberty, Sexuality and the Self*; Beth Montemurro, *Deserving Desire: Women's Stories of Sexual Evolution* (New Brunswick, NJ: Rutgers University Press, 2014); and Schalet, *Not Under My Roof.*

53. Susan Bordo, *The Male Body: A New Look at Men in Public and Private* (New York: Farrar, Straus and Giroux, 1999); and Melzer, *Manhood Impossible.*

54. Meika Loe, *The Rise of Viagra: How the Little Blue Pill Changed Sex in America* (New York: New York University Press, 2004); Stephen Katz and Toni Calasanti, "Critical Perspectives on Successful Aging: Does It 'Appeal More Than It Illuminates?'" *Gerontologist* 55, no. 1 (2015): 26–33; Barbara Marshall, "Older Men and Sexual Health: Post-Viagra Views of Changes in Function," *Generations* 32, no. 1 (2008): 21–27; and Kathleen Slevin, "'If I Had Lots of Money . . . I'd Have a Body Makeover': Managing the Aging Body," *Social Forces* 88, no. 3 (2010): 1003–1020.

55. Richard M. Carpiano, "Passive Medicalization: The Case of Viagra and Erectile Dysfunction," *Sociological Spectrum* 21, no. 3 (2001): 441–450; Stephen Katz and Barbara Marshall, "New Sex for Old: Lifestyle, Consumerism, and the Ethics of Aging Well," *Journal of Aging Studies* 17 (2003): 3–16; Marshall, "Older Men and Sexual Health"; and Slevin, "'If I Had Lots of Money.'"

56. Amy C. Lodge and Debra Umberson, "Age and Embodied Masculinities: Midlife Gay and Heterosexual Men Talk about Their Bodies," *Journal of Aging Studies* 27 (2013): 225–232; and Amy C. Lodge and Debra Umberson, "All Shook Up: Sexuality of Mid- to Later Life Married Couples," *Journal of Marriage and the Family* 74 (2012): 428–443.

57. See Appendixes A and B for demographic table and summaries.

58. More than half of the 33 men who had never married were in their 20s (19 men). According to a Pew study in 2014, 23 percent of men age 25 or older have never been married, https://www.pewsocialtrends.org/2014/09/24/record-share-of-americans-have-never-married. My sample includes 13 men under the age of 25, so, it is close to par with the general population.

59. Given anticipated (and actual) difficulties recruiting men to participate in an interview study talking about their sexuality, I used Craigslist as a means of recruiting more men, in larger markets. This allowed for the large and diverse sample. See Appendix C for more detail on methods.

CHAPTER 2 — *GETTING* IT: UNDERSTANDING SEX AND BECOMING SEXUALLY AWARE

1. James K. Beggan and Scott T. Allison, "What Sort of Man Reads *Playboy*? The Self-Reported Influence of *Playboy* on the Construction of Masculinity," *Journal of Men's Studies* 11, no. 2 (2003): 189–206.

2. Tristan Bridges and C. J. Pascoe, "Masculinities and Post-Homophobias?" in *Exploring Masculinities: Identity, Inequality, Continuity, and Change*, ed. C. J. Pascoe and Tristan Bridges (New York: Oxford University Press, 2016); Karin A. Martin, *Puberty, Sexuality and the Self: Girls and Boys at Adolescence* (New York: Routledge, 1996); Richard Mora, "'Do It for All Your Pubic Hairs!' Latino Boys, Masculinity, and Puberty," *Gender & Society* 26 (2012): 433–460; Christin L. Munsch and Kjerstin Gruys, "What Threatens, Defines: Tracing the Symbolic Boundaries of Contemporary Masculinity," *Sex Roles* 79, no. 7–8 (2018): 375–392; and C. J. Pascoe, *Dude You're a Fag: Masculinity and Sexuality in High School* (Berkeley: University of California Press, 2007).

3. Emily W. Kane, "'No Way My Boys Are Going to Be Like That!': Parents' Responses to Children's Gender Nonconformity," *Gender & Society* 20, no. 2 (2006): 149–176; and Karin A. Martin, "Normalizing Heterosexuality: Mothers' Assumptions, Talk, and Strategies with Young Children," *American Sociological Review* 74, no. 2 (2009): 190–207.

4. Mora, "'Do It.'"

5. This number would likely have been higher, if the sample had not included men in their fifties and sixties, who lacked easy access to pornography when they were younger.

6. Ian Cook, "Western Heterosexual Masculinity, Anxiety, and Web Porn," *Journal of Men's Studies* 14, no. 1 (2006): 47–63; and Gail Dines, *Pornland: How Porn has Hijacked our Sexuality*, (Boston: Beacon Press, 2010).

7. See also Beggan and Allison, "What Sort of Man?" and Cook "Western Heterosexual Masculinity."

8. Cook, "Western Heterosexual Masculinity"; Dines, *Pornland*; and Maggie Jones, "What Teenagers Are Learning from Online Porn," *New York Times*, February 7, 2018.

9. Beggan and Allison, "What Sort of Man?"; and Jones "What Teenagers Are Learning."

10. Mora, "'Do It'"; Munsch and Gruys, "What Threatens, Defines"; Pascoe, *Dude*; and Amy Wilkins, "Masculinity Dilemmas: Sexuality and Intimacy Talk Among Christians and Goths," *Signs* 34 (2009): 343–368.

11. Anne-Frances Watson and Alan McKee, "Masturbation and the Media," *Sexuality & Culture* 17, no. 3 (2013): 449–475.

12. Robert Jensen, *Getting Off: Pornography and the End of Masculinity* (Cambridge, MA: South End Press, 2007).

13. Chiara Bertone and Raffaella Ferrero Camoletto, "Beyond the Sex Machine? Sexual Practices and Masculinity in Adult Men's Heterosexual Accounts," *Journal of Gender Studies* 18, no. 4 (2009): 369–386; Michael Kimmel, *Guyland: The*

Perilous World Where Boys Become Men (New York: Harper, 2008); Pascoe, *Dude*; Brian Sweeney, "Masculine Status, Sexual Performance, and the Sexual Stigmatization of Women," *Symbolic Interaction* 37 (2014): 369–390; and Amy Wilkins, "Stigma and Status: Interracial Intimacy and Intersectional Identities among Black College Men," *Gender & Society* 26 (2012): 165–189.

14. Beggan and Allison, "What Sort of Man?"

15. Pascoe, *Dude*; and Amy Wilkins, "Masculinity Dilemmas: Sexuality and Intimacy Talk among Christians and Goths," *Signs* 34 (2009): 343–368.

16. Martin, *Puberty, Sexuality and the Self*; Mora, "'Do It'"; Munsch and Gruys, "What Threatens, Defines"; and Watson and McKee, "Masturbation and the Media."

17. Amy Schalet, *Not Under My Roof: Parents, Teens, and the Culture of Sex* (Chicago: University of Chicago Press, 2011).

18. Beth Montemurro, *Deserving Desire: Women's Stories of Sexual Evolution* (New Brunswick, NJ: Rutgers University Press, 2014).

19. Schalet, *Not Under My Roof.*

20. Beggan and Allison also found this in their study of men's use of *Playboy*, "What Sort of Man?"

21. For data, see https://victimsofcrime.org/media/reporting-on-child-sexual-abuse/child-sexual-abuse-statistics. International samples report comparable results; see, for example, Elya E. Moore, Helena Romaniuk, Craig A. Olsson, Yasmin Jayasinghe, John B. Carlin, and George C. Patton, "The Prevalence of Childhood Sexual Abuse and Adolescent Unwanted Sexual Contact among Boys and Girls Living in Victoria, Australia," *Child Abuse & Neglect* 34, no. 5 (2010): 379–385; and Mannat Mohanjeet Singh, Shradha S. Parsekar, and N. Nair Sreekumaran, "An Epidemiological Overview of Child Sexual Abuse," *Journal of Family Medical Primary Care* 3, no. 4 (October–December 2014): 430–435.

22. Montemurro, *Deserving Desire.*

23. Kristin Carbone-Lopez, "The Life Course Consequences of Childhood Sexual Assault: Effects on Relationship Formation and Intimate Violence across Relationships," in *Sex for Life: From Virginity to Viagra, How Sexuality Changes Throughout Our Lives*, ed. Laura M. Carpenter and John DeLamater, 88–106 (New York: New York University Press, 2012).

24. Carbone-Lopez, "Consequences of Childhood Sexual Assault."

25. Watson and McKee, "Masturbation and the Media."

26. See also Watson and McKee, "Masturbation and the Media."

27. Pascoe, *Dude.*

28. Lisa Jean Moore, *Sperm Counts: Overcome by Man's Most Precious Fluid* (New York: New York University Press, 2008); Dines, *Pornland.*

29. Martin, *Puberty, Sexuality and the Self*; Peggy Orenstein, *Boys and Sex: Young Men on Hookups, Love, Porn, Consent and Navigating the New Masculinity* (New York: Harper, 2020); and Pascoe, *Dude.*

30. Martin, *Puberty, Sexuality and the Self*; Mora, "'Do It'"; and Pascoe, *Dude.*

31. Michael Flood, "Men, Sex, and Homosociality: How Bonds between Men Shape Their Sexual Relations with Women," *Men and Masculinities* 10, no. 3 (2008): 339–359.

32. Laura Carpenter, *Virginity Lost: An Intimate Portrait of First Sexual Experiences* (New York: New York University Press, 2005); and Mora, "Do It."

33. Orenstein, *Boys and Sex*; Lisa Wade, *American Hookup: The New Culture of Sex on Campus* (New York: W. W. Norton, 2017).

34. Janet Holland, Caroline Ramazanoglu, Sue Sharpe, and Rachel Thomson, *The Male in the Head: Young People, Heterosexuality, and Power* (London: Tuffnell, 2004); Martin, *Puberty, Sexuality and the Self*; Mora, "'Do It'"; and Pascoe, *Dude.*

35. Holland et al., *Male in the Head*; Martin *Puberty, Sexuality and the Self*; Mora, "'Do It'"; Munsch and Gruys, "What Threatens, Defines"; and Pascoe, *Dude.*

CHAPTER 3 — GETTING *IT*: GAINING ACCESS TO SEX

1. Neil Strauss, *The Game: Penetrating the Secret Society of Pickup Artists* (Regan Books: New York, 2005).

2. Rachel O'Neill, *Seduction: Men, Masculinity and Mediated Intimacy* (Cambridge: Polity, 2018) and Jane Ward, *The Tragedy of Heterosexuality* (New York: New York University Press, 2020).

3. O'Neill, *Seduction*; and Ward, *Tragedy of Heterosexuality.*

4. Christin L. Munsch and Kjerstin Gruys, "What Threatens, Defines: Tracing the Symbolic Boundaries of Contemporary Masculinity," *Sex Roles* 79, no. 7–8 (2018): 375–392; and Peggy Orenstein, *Boys and Sex: Young Men on Hookups, Love, Porn, Consent and Navigating the New Masculinity* (New York: Harper, 2020).

5. Chiara Bertone and Raffaella Ferrero Camoletto, "Beyond the Sex Machine? Sexual Practices and Masculinity in Adult Men's Heterosexual Accounts," *Journal of Gender Studies* 18, no. 4 (2009): 369–386; Glen Elder, Gary Brooks, and Susan L. Morrow, "Sexual Self-Schemas of Heterosexual Men," *Psychology of Men & Masculinities* 3, no. 2 (2012): 166–179; O'Neill, *Seduction*; C. J. Pascoe, *Dude You're a Fag: Masculinity and Sexuality in High School* (Berkeley: University of California Press, 2007); and Lisa Wade, *American Hookup: The New Culture of Sex on Campus* (New York: W. W. Norton, 2017).

6. Orenstein, *Boys and Sex*; Rashawn Ray and Jason A. Rosow, "Getting Off on Getting Intimate: How Normative Arrangements Structure Black and White Fraternity Men's Approaches toward Women," *Men and Masculinities* 12, no. 5 (2010): 523–546; and Wade, *American Hookup*, 34.

7. Bertone and Camoletto, "Beyond the Sex Machine"; O'Neill, *Seduction*; and Orenstein, *Boys and Sex*.

8. Michael Kimmel, *Guyland: The Perilous World Where Boys Become Men* (New York: Harper, 2008); Pascoe, *Dude*; and Wade, *American Hookup*.

9. Tristan Bridges and C. J. Pascoe, "Masculinities and Post-Homophobias?" in *Exploring Masculinities: Identity, Inequality, Continuity, and Change*, ed. C. J. Pascoe and Tristan Bridges, 412–423 (New York: Oxford University Press, 2016); Gary Brooks, "The Centerfold Syndrome," in *Men and Sex: New Psychological Perspectives*, ed. R.F. Levant and Gary R. Brooks, 28–57 (New York: Wiley, 1997); Munsch and Gruys, "What Threatens, Defines"; O'Neill, *Seduction*; Pascoe, *Dude*; and Wade, *American Hookup*.

10. Elder, Brooks, and Morrow, "Sexual Self-Schemas"; David Grazian, "The Girl Hunt: Urban Nightlife and the Performance of Masculinity as Collective Activity," *Symbolic Interaction* 30, no. 2 (2007): 221–243; Pascoe, *Dude*; and Beth Quinn, "Sexual Harassment and Masculinity: The Power and Meaning of 'Girl Watching,'" *Gender & Society* 16, no. 3 (2002): 386–402.

11. Bridges and Pascoe, "Masculinities and Post-Homophobias"; and Munsch and Gruys, "What Threatens, Defines."

12. Brooks, "Centerfold Syndrome."

13. Thomas Hendricks, "Race and Desire in the Porno-Tropics: Ethnographic Perspectives from the Post-Colony," *Sexualities* 17, no. 1–2 (2014): 213–229; Amparo Lasen and Antonio Garcia, "'But I Haven't Got a Body to Show': Self-Pornification and Male Mixed Feelings in Digitally Mediated Seduction Practices," *Sexualities* 18, no. 5–6 (2015): 714–730; and Wade, *American Hookup*.

14. Bertone and Camoletto, "Beyond the Sex Machine"; Brooks, "Centerfold Syndrome"; Breanne Fahs, *Performing Sex: The Making and Unmaking of Women's Erotic Lives* (Albany: State University of New York Press, 2011); Robert Jensen, *Getting Off: Pornography and the End of Masculinity* (Cambridge, MA: South End Press, 2007); Orenstein, *Boys and Sex*; and Ward, *Tragedy of Heterosexuality*.

15. Beth Montemurro and Christina Riehman Murphy, "Ready and Waiting: Heterosexual Men's Discourses on Decision Making in Initiation of Sexual Intimacy," *Men and Masculinities* 22, no. 5 (2019): 872–892.

16. Douglas Schrock and Michael Schwalbe, "Men, Masculinity, and Manhood Acts," *Annual Review of Sociology* 35 (2009): 277–295.

17. O'Neill, *Seduction*; and Ward, *Tragedy of Heterosexuality*.

18. Nicola Gavey, Kathryn McPhillips, and Marion Doherty, "'If It's Not On, It's Not On': Or Is It? Discursive Constraints on Women's Condom Use," *Gender & Society* 15, no. 6 (2001): 917–934.

19. Sara E. Thomas, "'What Should I Do?': Young Women's Reported Dilemmas with Nude Photographs." *Sexuality Research and Social Policy* 15 (2018): 1–16.

20. Bertone and Camoletto, "Beyond the Sex Machine"; Brooks, "Centerfold Syndrome"; Fahs, *Performing Sex*; Jensen, *Getting Off*; and Orenstein, *Boys and Sex*; Ward, *Tragedy of Heterosexuality*; and Paul Wright, "Show Me the Data! Empirical Support for the 'Centerfold Syndrome,'" *Psychology of Men and Masculinities* 13, no. 2 (2012): 180–198.

21. O'Neill, *Seduction*, 98.

22. O'Neill, *Seduction*, 98; See also Ward, *Tragedy of Heterosexuality.*

23. Brooks, "Centerfold Syndrome"; Kimmel, *Guyland*; Michael Kimmel, *Angry White Men: American Masculinity at the End of an Era* (New York: Nation Books, 2013); O'Neill, *Seduction*; and Ward, *Tragedy of Heterosexuality.*

24. Bridges and Pascoe, "Masculinities and Post-Homophobias; Pascoe, *Dude*; Peggy R. Sanday, *Fraternity Gang Rape: Sex, Brotherhood and Privilege on Campus*, 2nd ed. (New York: New York University Press, 2007).

25. Montemurro and Riehman Murphy, "Ready and Waiting."

26. Religion did not play a significant role in the way most of the interviewees felt about their sexuality. A few, such as Casey and Minjun (discussed in Chapter 2), noted that they felt guilt or shame associated with sexual thoughts or looking at pornography. Most who identified as religious said that while they knew that premarital or extramarital sex went against their religion, it didn't stop them from thinking about it or doing it. This is in sharp contrast to women I interviewed for *Deserving Desire*. The women I interviewed felt guilt and shame associated with sexual activity and experiences and it inhibited many of them. This is likely related to the fact that men are encouraged to be sexual and women are not. So men who overlooked religious proscriptions to have sex before or outside of marriage were still conforming to sexual scripts and gendered expectations. Women, in contrast, would be going against both sexual scripts for gender and religion rules; Beth Montemurro, *Deserving Desire: Women's Stories of Sexual Evolution* (New Brunswick, NJ: Rutgers University Press, 2014).

27. Laura Carpenter, *Virginity Lost: An Intimate Portrait of First Sexual Experiences* (New York: New York University Press, 2005).

28. Janet Holland, Caroline Ramazanoglu, Sue Sharpe, and Rachel Thomson, *The Male in the Head: Young People, Heterosexuality, and Power* (London: Tuffnell, 2004).

29. Carpenter, *Virginity Lost.*

30. Teela Sanders, "Male Sexual Scripts: Intimacy, Sexuality, and Pleasure in the Purchase of Commercial Sex," *Sociology* 42, no. 3 (2008): 400–417.

31. Montemurro and Riehman Murphy, "Ready and Waiting."

32. Lasen and Garcia, "'But I Haven't Got a Body'"; Jesus G. Smith, Maria Cristina Morales, and Chonh-Suk Han, "The Influence of Sexual Racism on Erotic Capital: A Systemic Racism Perspective," in *Handbook of Sociology of Racial and Ethnic Relations*, ed. Pinar Batur and Joe R. Feagin, 389–399 (New York: Springer, 2018); and Lisa Wade and Myra Marx Ferree, *Gender: Ideas, Interactions and Institutions*, 2nd ed. (New York: W. W. Norton, 2019).

33. Brooks, "Centerfold Syndrome."

34. Wade and Ferree, *Gender*; and Wade, *American Hookup*.

35. Smith, Morales, and Han, "Influence of Sexual Racism."

36. For studies that also discussed sex as an affirmation of social worth, see Linn Sandberg, "Just Feeling a Naked Body Close to You: Men, Sexuality and Intimacy in Later Life," *Sexualities* 16 (2013): 261–282; and David Wyatt Seal and Anke A. Ehrhardt, "Masculinity and Urban Men: Perceived Scripts for Courtship, Romantic, and Sexual Interactions with Women," *Culture, Health, and Sexuality* 5, no. 4 (2003): 295–319.

37. Brooks, "Centerfold Syndrome."

38. Patricia Hill Collins, *Black Sexual Politics: African Americans, Gender, and the New Racism* (New York: Routledge, 2005); Nguyen Tan Hoang, *A View from the Bottom: Asian American Masculinity and Sexual Representation* (Durham, NC: Duke University Press, 2014); and Brittany C. Slatton and Kamesha Spates, eds., *Hyper Sexual, Hyper Masculine? Gender, Race and Sexuality in the Identities of Contemporary Black Men* (New York: Routledge, 2014).

39. Hoang, *Asian American Masculinity*; see also C. Winter Han, *Geisha of a Different Kind: Race and Sexuality in Gaysian America* (New York: New York University Press, 2015), which looks at intersections of race and sexual orientation among gay Asian men.

40. Amanda E. Lewis, "'What Group?' Studying Whites and Whiteness in the Era of 'Color-Blindness,'" *Sociological Theory* 22, no. 4 (2004): 624–646.

41. Amy C. Lodge and Debra Umberson, "All Shook Up: Sexuality of Mid- to Later Life Married Couples," *Journal of Marriage and the Family* 74 (2012): 428–443; and Scott Melzer, *Manhood Impossible: Men's Struggles to Control and Transform Their Bodies and Work* (New Brunswick, NJ: Rutgers University Press, 2018).

42. Chip Brown, "Making a Man," *National Geographic* 231, no. 1 (2017): 74–76.

43. See Carpenter, *Virginity Lost*, for a comprehensive exploration of meaning of first sex.

44. Carpenter, *Virginity Lost*, also found that some virgin men felt the need to try to pass as sexually experienced so they would not be stigmatized for their virginity.

45. Bridges and Pascoe, "Masculinities and Post-Homophobias."

46. Ward, *Tragedy of Heterosexuality*, 108.

47. Schrock and Schwalbe, "Men, Masculinity, and Manhood Acts," 287.

48. Brooks, "Centerfold Syndrome."

49. For a similar finding, see also Ray and Rosow, "Getting Off on Getting Intimate."

50. For more discussion of the significance of retrospective accounts of sexual self-worth, see Beth Montemurro, "'If You Could Just See Me': The Construction of Heterosexual Men's Sexual Selves and the Hierarchy of Desirability," *Sexualities* 24, no. 3 (2021) 303–321,

51. Ray and Rosow, "Getting Off on Getting Intimate."

52. O'Neill, *Seduction*; and Ward, *Tragedy of Heterosexuality.*

CHAPTER 4 — HAVING IT: PROFICIENCY, PRESSURE, AND PERFORMANCE

1. Steve Garlick, "Taking Control of Sex? Hegemonic Masculinity, Technology, and Internet Pornography," *Men and Masculinities* 12, no. 5 (2010): 597–614; Robert Jensen, *Getting Off: Pornography and the End of Masculinity* (Cambridge, MA: South End Press, 2007); Maggie Jones, "What Teenagers Are Learning from Online Porn," *New York Times*, February 7, 2018.

2. See, for example, Sarah H. Murray, "Heterosexual Men's Sexual Desire: Supported by or Deviating from Traditional Masculinity Norms and Sexual Scripts?" *Sex Roles* 78 (2018): 130–141; J. K. Sakaluk, L. M. Todd, R. Milhausen, N. J. Lachowsky, and the Undergraduate Research Group in Sexuality, "Dominant Heterosexual Sexual Scripts in Emerging Adulthood: Conceptualization and Measurement," *Journal of Sex Research* 51 (2014): 516–531; and Erin Watson, Lea J. Seguin, Robin R. Milhausen, and Sarah H. Murray, "The Impact of a Couple's Vibrator on Men's Perception of Their Own and Their Partner's Sexual Pleasure and Satisfaction," *Men and Masculinities* 19, no. 4 (2016): 370–383.

3. Ian Cook, "Western Heterosexual Masculinity, Anxiety, and Web Porn," *Journal of Men's Studies* 14, no. 1 (2006): 47–63; Gail Dines, *Pornland: How Porn has Hijacked our Sexuality*, (Boston: Beacon Press, 2010); Garlick, "Taking Control"; Shayne Lee, *Erotic Revolutionaries: Black Women, Sexuality and Popular Culture* (Lanham, MD: Hamilton Books, 2010); Jensen, *Getting Off*; Sut Jhally, producer and director, *Dreamworlds III: Desire, Sex, and Power in Music Video* (DVD) (Northampton: Media Education Foundation, 2007); Jae Woong Shim, Mahnwoo Kwon, and Hong-In Cheng, "Analysis of Representation of Sexuality

on Women's and Men's Pornographic Websites," *Social Behavior and Personality* 43, no. 1 (2015): 53–62; Alicia M. Walker, *Chasing Masculinity: Men, Validation, and Infidelity* (New York: Palgrave Macmillan, 2020); and Watson et al., "Impact of a Couple's Vibrator."

4. Nicola Gavey, Kathryn McPhillips, and Marion Doherty, "'If It's Not On, It's Not On': Or Is It? Discursive Constraints on Women's Condom Use," *Gender & Society* 15, no. 6 (2001): 917–934.

5. Garlick, "Taking Control; Jensen, *Getting Off*; and Dan J. Miller, Kerry Anne McBain, and Peter T. F. Raggatt, "An Experimental Investigation into Pornography's Effect on Men's Perceptions of the Likelihood of Women Engaging in Porn-Like Sex," *Psychology of Popular Media Culture* 8, no. 4 (2019): 365–375.

6. Alexsandar Stulhofer, Luana Cunha Ferreira, and Ivan Landripet, "Emotional Intimacy, Sexual Desire, and Sexual Satisfaction among Partnered Heterosexual Men," *Sexual and Relationship Therapy* 29 (2014): 229–244.

7. Gary Brooks, "The Centerfold Syndrome," in *Men and Sex: New Psychological Perspectives*, ed. Ronald F. Levant and Gary R. Brooks (New York: Wiley, 1997), 32.

8. Scott Melzer, *Manhood Impossible: Men's Struggles to Control and Transform their Bodies and Work* (New Brunswick, NJ: Rutgers University Press, 2018); and Douglas Schrock and Michael Schwalbe, "Men, Masculinity, and Manhood Acts," *Annual Review of Sociology* 35 (2009): 277–295.

9. Brooks, "Centerfold Syndrome," 33.

10. Melzer, *Manhood Impossible*.

11. Walker, *Chasing Masculinity*.

12. Breanne Fahs, *Performing Sex: The Making and Unmaking of Women's Erotic Lives* (Albany: State University of New York Press, 2011).

13. Andrea Waling, "'We Are So Pumped Full of Shit by the Media': Masculinity, Magazines, and the Lack of Self-Identification," *Men and Masculinities* 20, no. 4 (2017): 427–452.

14. Sakaluk et al., "Dominant Heterosexual Sexual Scripts."

15. R. W. Connell, *Masculinities* (Berkeley: University of California Press, 1995); Sinikka Elliott and Debra Umberson, "The Performance of Desire," *Journal of Marriage and Family* 70, no. 2 (2008): 391–406; Michael Flood, "Men, Sex, and Homosociality: How Bonds between Men Shape Their Sexual Relations with Women," *Men and Masculinities* 10, no. 3 (2008): 339–359; Murray, "Heterosexual Men's Sexual Desire"; and Diane Richardson, "Youth Masculinities: Compelling Male Heterosexualities," *British Journal of Sociology* 61 (2010): 737–756.

16. Toby Keith, *Masculinities in Contemporary Culture: An Intersectional Approach to the Complexities and Challenges of Male Identity* (New York: Routledge, 2017).

17. Melzer, *Manhood Impossible*, 106.

18. Cook, "Western Heterosexual Masculinity"; see also Jensen, *Getting Off*.

19. Melzer, *Manhood Impossible*, 96.

20. Cook, "Western Heterosexual Masculinity," 56.

21. Dines, *Pornland*; Garlick, "Taking Control"; Jensen, *Getting Off*; Peggy Orenstein, *Boys and Sex: Young Men on Hookups, Love, Porn, Consent and Navigating the New Masculinity* (New York: Harper, 2020); and Jae Woong Shim, Mahnwoo Kwon, and Hong-In Cheng, "Analysis of Representation of Sexuality on Women's and Men's Pornographic Websites," *Social Behavior and Personality* 43, no. 1 (2015): 53–62.

22. Dines, *Pornland*; Jensen, *Getting Off*; and Orenstein, *Boys and Sex*.

23. Nicholas C. Borgogna, Ryon C. McDermott, Brandon R. Browning, Jameson D. Beach, and Stephen L. Aita, "How Does Traditional Masculinity Relate to Men and Women's Problematic Pornography Viewing?" *Sex Roles* 80 (2019): 693–706.

24. Dines, *Pornland*; Jones, "What Teenagers Are Learning"; and Miller, McBain, and Raggatt, "Experimental Investigation."

25. See Miller, McBain, and Raggatt, "Experimental Investigation."

26. Borgogna et al., "How Does Traditional Masculinity Relate?"

27. Dines, *Pornland*, Jensen, *Getting Off*; Jones, "What Teenagers Are Learning"; Orenstein, *Boys and Sex*; Regina Kulik Scully, Paul Blavin, Kirby Dick, Amy Ziering, Thaddeus Wadleigh, Aaron Kopp, and Miriam Cutler, *The Hunting Ground* (Sausalito, CA: Ro*Co Films Educational, 2015); Brian Sweeney, "Masculine Status, Sexual Performance, and the Sexual Stigmatization of Women," *Symbolic Interaction* 37 (2014): 369–390; and Waling, "'We Are So Pumped.'"

28. Flood, "Men, Sex, and Homosociality"; Janet Holland, Caroline Ramazanoglu, Sue Sharpe, and Rachel Thomson, *The Male in the Head: Young People, Heterosexuality, and Power* (London: Tuffnell, 2004), 136; Melzer, *Manhood Impossible*.

29. See also Beth Montemurro and Christina Riehman Murphy, "Ready and Waiting: Heterosexual Men's Discourses on Decision Making in Initiation of Sexual Intimacy," *Men and Masculinities* 22, no. 5 (2019): 872–892.

30. Gavey, McPhillips, and Doherty, "If It's Not On."

31. Fahs, *Performing Sex*.

32. See, for example, David L. Bell, Joshua Rosenberger, and Mary Ott, "Masculinity in Adolescent Males' Early Romantic and Sexual Heterosexual Relationships," *American Journal of Men's Health* 9, no. 3 (2015): 201–208; Tristan Bridges and C. J. Pascoe, "Masculinities and Post-Homophobias?" in *Exploring Masculinities: Identity, Inequality, Continuity, and Change*, ed. C. J. Pascoe and Tristan

Bridges, 412–423 (New York: Oxford University Press, 2016); Holland et al., *Male in the Head*; Flood, "Men, Sex, and Homosociality"; David Grazian, "The Girl Hunt: Urban Nightlife and the Performance of Masculinity as Collective Activity," *Symbolic Interaction* 30, no. 2 (2007): 221–243; Pascoe, *Dude*; Richardson, "Youth Masculinities"; and Schrock and Schwalbe, "Manhood Acts," 281.

33. Murray, "Heterosexual Men's Sexual Desire."

34. Susan Bordo, *The Male Body: A New Look at Men in Public and Private* (New York: Farrar, Straus and Giroux, 1999); and Meika Loe, *The Rise of Viagra: How the Little Blue Pill Changed Sex in America* (New York: New York University Press, 2004).

35. Melzer, *Manhood Impossible*.

36. Bordo, *Male Body*; Jared Del Rosso, "The Penis as Public Part: Embodiment and the Performance of Masculinity in Public Settings," *Sexualities* 14, no. 6 (2011): 704–724; Melzer, *Manhood Impossible*; and Paul Simpson and Julie Adams, "A Structured Review and Critical Analysis of Male Perceptions of the Penis: A Comparison between Heterosexual Men and Men Who Have Sex with Men (MSM)," *Men and Masculinities* 22, no. 4 (2019): 658–693.

37. Bordo, *Male Body*; Del Rosso, "Penis as Public Part"; Janet Lever, David A. Frederick, and Letitia Anne Peplau, "Does Size Matter? Men's and Women's Views on Penis Size across the Lifespan," *Psychology of Men & Masculinities* 7, no. 3 (2006): 129–143; Melzer, *Manhood Impossible*; and Simpson and Adams, "Structured Review and Critical Analysis."

38. Simpson and Adams, "Structured Review and Critical Analysis."

39. Bordo, *Male Body*; and Simpson and Adams, "Structured Review and Critical Analysis."

40. See Alicia Walker, *The Secret Life of the Cheating Wife: Power, Pragmatism, and Pleasure in Women's Infidelity* (Lanham, MD: Lexington Books, 2018). Walker found that size mattered to some women. In an interview study of women who used the website Ashley Madison to find affair partners, ten of the forty-six women sought out men with large penises because their own partners were lacking in that area.

41. Lever, Frederick, and Peplau, "Does Size Matter?"; Lever, Frederick, and Peplau found that 84 percent of women were satisfied with their partner's penis size. Only 14 percent wanted their partner to be larger, and 2 percent wanted their partner to be smaller. A much higher proportion of women were satisfied with their partner's penis size than the proportion of men who were satisfied with their own penis size (84 percent vs. 55 percent).

42. Bordo, *Male Body*; Melzer, *Manhood Impossible*; Helena M. Nutgeren, G. T. Balkema, Astrid L. Pascal, Weijmar Schultz, C. M. Willibrord, Johan M. Nijman,

Johan M., and Mels F. van Driel, "18-year Experience in the Management of Men with a Complaint of a Small Penis," *Journal of Sex and Marital Therapy* 36 (2010):109–117.

43. Connell, *Masculinities*; Christin L. Munsch and Kjerstin Gruys, "What Threatens, Defines: Tracing the Symbolic Boundaries of Contemporary Masculinity," *Sex Roles* 79, no. 7–8 (2018): 375–392; Orenstein, *Boys and Sex*; and Lisa Wade, *American Hookup: The New Culture of Sex on Campus* (New York: W. W. Norton, 2017).

44. Brooks, "Centerfold Syndrome"; Orenstein, *Boys and Sex*; and Wade, *American Hookup*

45. None of the women I interviewed for *Deserving Desire* expressed these desires or concerns about being in relationships with men based on penis size or spoke of breaking up with men due to penis size. Beth Montemurro, *Deserving Desire: Women's Stories of Sexual Evolution* (New Brunswick, NJ: Rutgers University Press, 2014)

46. Elliott and Umberson, "Performance of Desire"; Fahs, *Performing Sex*; Gavey, McPhillips, and Doherty, "If It's Not On"; and Montemurro, *Deserving Desire.*

47. See, for example, Elizabeth A. Armstrong, Paula England, and Allison C. K. Fogarty, "Accounting for Women's Orgasm and Sexual Enjoyment in College Hookups and Relationships," *American Sociological Review* 77 (2012): 435–462; Gavey, McPhillips, and Doherty, "If It's Not On"; Montemurro, *Deserving Desire*; Tine Vares, Annie Potts, Nicola Gavey, and Victoria Grace, "Reconceptualizing Cultural Narratives of Mature Women's Sexuality in the Viagra Era," *Journal of Aging Studies* 21 (2007): 153–164.

48. See also, Walker, *Chasing Masculinity.*

49. Fahs, *Performing Sex.*

50. Brooks, "Centerfold Syndrome."

51. Montemurro, *Deserving Desire.*

52. Stulhofer, Ferreira, and Landripet, "Emotional Intimacy."

53. I am grateful to Elizabeth Hughes for the idea of the imagined community of women partners.

54. Connell, *Masculinities*; Pascoe, *Dude*; and Richardson, "Youth Masculinities."

55. Flood, "Men, Sex, and Homosociality"; Melzer, *Manhood Impossible*; and Orenstein, *Boys and Sex.*

56. Bridges and Pascoe, "Masculinities and Post-Homophobias"; and Connell, *Masculinities.*

57. Chiara Bertone and Raffaella Ferrero Camoletto, "Beyond the Sex Machine? Sexual Practices and Masculinity in Adult Men's Heterosexual Accounts," *Journal*

of Gender Studies 18, no. 4 (2009): 369–386; Murray, "Heterosexual Men's Sexual Desire"; and Sweeney, "Masculine Status."

58. Linn Sandberg, "In Lust We Trust? Masculinity and Sexual Desire in Later Life," *Men and Masculinities* 19, no. 2 (2016): 197.

59. Armstrong, England, and Fogarty, "Accounting for Women's Orgasm."

60. Montemurro, *Deserving Desire.*

61. Bordo, *Male Body.*

62. Stulhofer, Ferreira, and Landripet, "Emotional Intimacy."

63. Montemurro, *Deserving Desire.*

CHAPTER 5 — HAVING IT: DESIRE, RELATIONSHIPS, AND SEX

1. Lisa Wade and Myra Marx Ferree, *Gender: Ideas, Interactions and Institutions*, 2nd ed. (New York: W. W. Norton, 2019), 403.

2. Scott Melzer, *Manhood Impossible: Men's Struggles to Control and Transform Their Bodies and Work* (New Brunswick, NJ: Rutgers University Press, 2018).

3. Melanie Hamlett, "Men Have No Friends and Women Bear the Burden," *Harper's Bazaar*, May 2, 2019, https://www.harpersbazaar.com/culture/features/a27259689/toxic-masculinity-male-friendships-emotional-labor-men-rely-on-women/.

4. Judith Chu, "Boys' Nature, Boys' Culture, and a Crisis of Connection," in *The Crisis of Connection: Roots, Consequences, and Solutions*, ed. Niobe Way, Alisha Ali, Carol Gilligan, and Pedro Noguera, 88–105 (New York: New York University Press, 2018); and Niobe Way, Jessica Cressen, Samuel Bodian, Justin Preston, Joseph Nelwo, and Diane Hughes, "'It Might Be Nice to Be a Girl . . . Then You Wouldn't Have to Be Emotionless': Boys' Resistance to Norms of Masculinity during Adolescence," *Psychology of Men & Masculinities* 15, no. 3 (2014): 241–252.

5. Way et al., "'It Might Be Nice.'"

6. Niobe Way, "Boys as Human," *Contexts* 12, no. 1 (2013): 16

7. Louisa Allen, "Girls Want Sex, Boys Want Love: Resisting Dominant Discourses of (Hetero)Sexuality," *Sexualities* 6 (2003): 215–236; Amy Schalet, *Not Under My Roof: Parents, Teens, and the Culture of Sex* (Chicago: University of Chicago Press, 2011); Andrew P. Smiler, "'I Wanted to Get to Know Her Better': Adolescent Boys' Dating Motives, Masculinity Ideology, and Sexual Behavior," *Journal of Adolescence* 31 (2008): 17–32; and Way et al., "'It Might Be Nice.'"

8. Allen, "Girls Want Sex"; Schalet, *Not Under My Roof*; Smiler, "'I Wanted to Get to Know Her Better'"; and Way et al., "'It Might Be Nice.'"

9. Schalet, *Not Under My Roof.*

10. Beth Montemurro and Christina Riehman Murphy, "Ready and Waiting: Heterosexual Men's Discourses on Decision Making in Initiation of Sexual Intimacy," *Men and Masculinities* 22, no. 5 (2019), 873.

11. Michael Flood, "Men, Sex, and Homosociality: How Bonds between Men Shape Their Sexual Relations with Women," *Men and Masculinities* 10, no. 3 (2008): 339–359; Melzer, *Manhood Impossible*; Erving Goffman, *The Presentation of Self in Everyday Life* (New York: Anchor Books, 1959); and Peggy Orenstein, *Boys and Sex: Young Men on Hookups, Love, Porn, Consent and Navigating the New Masculinity* (New York: Harper, 2020).

12. Orenstein, *Boys and Sex*; and Jane Ward, *The Tragedy of Heterosexuality* (New York: New York University Press, 2020).

13. Chiara Bertone and Raffaella Ferrero Camoletto, "Beyond the Sex Machine? Sexual Practices and Masculinity in Adult Men's Heterosexual Accounts," *Journal of Gender Studies* 18, no. 4 (2009): 369–386; and William Simon and John H. Gagnon, "Sexual Scripts," *Society*, November/December (1984): 53–60.

14. Bertone and Camoletto, "Beyond the Sex Machine?"

15. Gary R. Brooks, "The Centerfold Syndrome," in *Men and Sex: New Psychological Perspectives*, ed. Ronald F. Levant and Gary R. Brooks, 28–57 (New York: Wiley, 1997).

16. Elizabeth A. Armstrong, Paula England, and Allison C. K. Fogarty, "Accounting for Women's Orgasm and Sexual Enjoyment in College Hookups and Relationships," *American Sociological Review* 77 (2012): 435–462.

17. Allen, "Girls Want Sex"; Laura Hamilton and Elizabeth A. Armstrong, "Gendered Sexuality in Young Adulthood: Double Binds and Flawed Options," *Gender & Society* 23 (2009): 589–616; Michael Kimmel, *Angry White Men: American Masculinity at the End of an Era* (New York: Nation Books, 2013); Karin A. Martin, *Puberty, Sexuality, and the Self: Girls and Boys at Adolescence* (New York: Routledge, 1996); and Schalet, *Not Under My Roof.*

18. Montemurro, *Deserving Desire.*

19. See, for example, Allen. "Girls Want Sex"; Louisa Allen, "'Sensitive and Real Macho All at the Same Time': Young Heterosexual Men and Romance," *Men and Masculinities* 10, no. 2 (2007): 137–152; Mary Holmes, "Men's Emotions: Heteromasculinity, Emotional Reflexivity, and Intimate Relationships," *Men and Masculinities* 18, no. 2 (2015): 176–192; Schalet, *Not Under My Roof*; David Wyatt Seal, Lucia F. O'Sullivan, and Anke A. Ehrhardt, "Miscommunication and Misinterpretations: Men's Scripts about Sexual Communication and Unwanted Sex in Interactions with Women," in Kimmel, *The Sexual Self: Construction of Sexual Scripts*, ed. Michael Kimmel (Nashville, TN: Vanderbilt University Press, 2007),

141–161; Smiler 2008; Erin Watson, Lea J. Seguin, Robin R. Milhausen, and Sarah H. Murray, "The Impact of a Couple's Vibrator on Men's Perception of Their Own and Their Partner's Sexual Pleasure and Satisfaction," *Men and Masculinities* 19, no. 4 (2016): 370–383; and Way et al., "'It Might Be Nice.'"

20. Allen, "Sensitive and Real Macho," 141–142.

21. R. W. Connell, *Masculinities* (Berkeley: University of California Press, 1995).

22. See Linn Sandberg, "Just Feeling a Naked Body Close to You: Men, Sexuality and Intimacy in Later Life," *Sexualities* 16 (2013): 261–282; and Linn Sandberg, "In Lust We Trust? Masculinity and Sexual Desire in Later Life," *Men and Masculinities* 19, no. 2 (2016): 192–208.

23. Sandberg, "Just Feeling," 263.

24. I thank John Pruit for this idea that love and sex are separated by masculinity.

25. C. J. Pascoe and Sarah Diefendorf, "No Homo: Gendered Dimensions of Homophobic Epithets Online," *Sex Roles* 80 (2019): 123–136.

26. Ronald F. Levant, "Nonrelational Sexuality in Men," in Levant and Brooks, *Men and Sex*, 9–27.

27. Nancy Chodorow, *The Reproduction of Mothering: Psychoanalysis and the Sociology of Gender* (Berkeley: University of California Press, 1978), 165.

28. Levant, "Nonrelational Sexuality."

29. Hamlett, "Men Have No Friends."

30. David L. Bell, Joshua Rosenberger, and Mary Ott, "Masculinity in Adolescent Males' Early Romantic and Sexual Heterosexual Relationships," *American Journal of Men's Health* 9, no. 3 (2015): 201–208.

31. Ward, *The Tragedy of Heterosexuality.*

CHAPTER 6 — KEEPING IT UP: SEXUAL AND RELATIONSHIP PROBLEMS

1. See Christin L. Munsch and Kjerstin Gruys, "What Threatens, Defines: Tracing the Symbolic Boundaries of Contemporary Masculinity," *Sex Roles* 79, no. 7–8 (2018): 375–392. They found that almost half of their (heterosexual college-men) sample identified rejection as a chief marker of emasculation, so much so that they described strategies to avoid direct rejection.

2. David Grazian, "The Girl Hunt: Urban Nightlife and the Performance of Masculinity as Collective Activity," *Symbolic Interaction* 30, no. 2 (2007): 221–243; Diane Richardson, "Youth Masculinities: Compelling Male Heterosexualities," *British Journal of Sociology* 61 (2010): 737–756; and Brian Sweeney, "Masculine Status, Sexual Performance, and the Sexual Stigmatization of Women," *Symbolic Interaction* 37 (2014): 369–390.

3. See Linn Sandberg, "In Lust We Trust? Masculinity and Sexual Desire in Later Life," *Men and Masculinities* 19, no. 2 (2016): 197.

4. Sharron Hinchliff and Merryn Gott, "Intimacy, Commitment, and Adaptation: Sexual Relationships within Long-Term Marriages," *Journal of Personal and Social Relationships* 21 (2004), 605.

5. Linn Sandberg, "Just Feeling a Naked Body Close to You: Men, Sexuality and Intimacy in Later Life," *Sexualities* 16 (2013): 261–282; and Sandberg, "In Lust We Trust?"

6. Scott Melzer, *Manhood Impossible: Men's Struggles to Control and Transform Their Bodies and Work* (New Brunswick, NJ: Rutgers University Press, 2018).

7. Alexsandar Stulhofer, Luana Cunha Ferreira, and Ivan Landripet, "Emotional Intimacy, Sexual Desire, and Sexual Satisfaction among Partnered Heterosexual Men," *Sexual and Relationship Therapy* 29 (2014): 229–244.

8. Beth Montemurro, *Deserving Desire: Women's Stories of Sexual Evolution* (New Brunswick, NJ: Rutgers University Press, 2014).

9. Amy C. Lodge and Debra Umberson, "All Shook Up: Sexuality of Mid- to Later Life Married Couples," *Journal of Marriage and the Family* 74 (2012): 428–443.

10. Hinchliff and Gott, "Intimacy, Commitment, and Adaptation"; and Robynne Neugebauer-Visano, "Seniors and Sexuality? Confronting Cultural Contradictions," in *Seniors and Sexuality: Experiencing Intimacy in Later Life,* ed. R. Neugebauer-Visano, 17–34 (Toronto: Canadian Scholars' Press, 1995).

11. Chiara Bertone and Raffaella Ferrero Camoletto, "Beyond the Sex Machine? Sexual Practices and Masculinity in Adult Men's Heterosexual Accounts," *Journal of Gender Studies* 18, no. 4 (2009): 369–386.

12. Shawn Patrick and John Beckenbach, "Male Perceptions of Intimacy: A Qualitative Study," *Journal of Men's Studies* 17 (2009): 47–56; Lodge and Umberson, "All Shook Up"; Stulhofer, Ferreira, and Landripet, "Emotional Intimacy"; Neugebauer-Visano, "Seniors and Sexuality"; and Sandberg, "In Lust We Trust."

13. Melzer, *Manhood Impossible*, 5.

14. Hinchliff and Gott, "Intimacy, Commitment, and Adaptation," 605.

15. Stephen Katz and Barbara Marshall, "New Sex for Old: Lifestyle, Consumerism, and the Ethics of Aging Well," *Journal of Aging Studies* 17 (2003): 3–16.

16. Beth Montemurro, "'If You Could Just See Me': The Construction of Heterosexual Men's Sexual Selves and the Hierarchy of Desirability," *Sexualities* 24, no. 3 (2021): 303–321.

17. Sandberg, "In Lust We Trust," 199.

18. Sandberg, "Just Feeling."

19. Chelom Leavitt, Brandon T. McDaniel, Megan Maas, and Mark Ethan Feinberg, "Parenting Stress and Sexual Satisfaction among First-Time Parents: A Dyadic Approach," *Sex Roles* 76, no. 5–6 (2017): 346–355.

20. Sinikka Elliott and Debra Umberson, "The Performance of Desire," *Journal of Marriage and Family* 70, no. 2 (2008): 391–406.

21. Montemurro, *Deserving Desire*; Beth Montemurro and Jenna Marie Siefken, "Cougars on the Prowl? New Perceptions of Older Women's Sexuality," *Journal of Aging Studies* 28, no. 1 (2014): 35–43.

22. Leavitt et al., "Parenting Stress."

23. Amy C. Lodge and Debra Umberson, "Age and Embodied Masculinities: Midlife Gay and Heterosexual Men Talk about Their Bodies," *Journal of Aging Studies* 27 (2013): 227; Melzer, *Manhood Impossible*.

24. Melzer, *Manhood Impossible*.

25. Sandberg, "In Lust We Trust."

CHAPTER 7 — KEEPING *IT* UP: MAINTAINING AGING AND CHANGING BODIES

1. Linn Sandberg, "Just Feeling a Naked Body Close to You: Men, Sexuality and Intimacy in Later Life," *Sexualities* 16 (2013): 261–282; and Linn Sandberg, "In Lust We Trust? Masculinity and Sexual Desire in Later Life," *Men and Masculinities* 19, no. 2 (2016): 197.

2. Susan Bordo, *The Male Body: A New Look at Men in Public and Private* (New York: Farrar, Straus and Giroux, 1999); Meika Loe, *The Rise of Viagra: How the Little Blue Pill Changed Sex in America* (New York: New York University Press, 2004); and Scott Melzer, *Manhood Impossible: Men's Struggles to Control and Transform Their Bodies and Work* (New Brunswick, NJ: Rutgers University Press, 2018).

3. Stephen Katz and Barbara Marshall, "New Sex for Old: Lifestyle, Consumerism, and the Ethics of Aging Well," *Journal of Aging Studies* 17 (2003): 3–16; Stephen Katz and Toni Calasanti, "Critical Perspectives on Successful Aging: Does It 'Appeal More Than It Illuminates?'" *Gerontologist* 55, no. 1 (2015): 26–33; Amy C. Lodge and Debra Umberson, "All Shook Up: Sexuality of Mid- to Later Life Married Couples," *Journal of Marriage and the Family* 74 (2012): 428–443; Barbara Marshall, "Older Men and Sexual Health: Post-Viagra Views of Changes in Function," *Generations* 32, no. 1 (2008): 21–27; Sandberg, "Just Feeling"; and Kathleen Slevin, "'If I Had Lots of Money . . . I'd Have a Body Makeover': Managing the Aging Body," *Social Forces* 88, no. 3 (2010): 1003–1020.

4. Katz and Marshall, "New Sex for Old."

5. Sandberg, "In Lust We Trust?"

6. Laura Carpenter, *Virginity Lost: An Intimate Portrait of First Sexual Experiences* (New York: New York University Press, 2005).

7. Melzer, *Manhood Impossible*.

8. Bordo, *Male Body*; Toni Calasanti and Neal King, "Beware of the Estrogen Assault: Ideals of Old Manhood in Anti-Aging Advertisements" *Journal of Aging Studies* 21 (2007): 357–368; Katz and Marshall, "New Sex for Old"; Melzer, *Manhood Impossible*; and Slevin, "'If I Had Lots of Money.'"

9. Bordo, *Male Body*; Katz and Marshall, "New Sex for Old"; Loe, *Rise of Viagra*; Barbara Marshall and Stephen Katz, "Forever Functional: Sexual Fitness and the Ageing Male Body," *Body and Society* 8 (2002): 43–70; and Marshall, "Older Men and Sexual Health."

10. Bordo, *Male Body*.

11. Melzer, *Manhood Impossible*.

12. Michael S. Sand, William Fisher, Raymond Rosen, Julia Heiman, and Ian Eardley, "Erectile Dysfunction and Constructs of Masculinity and Quality of Life in the Multinational Men's Attitudes to Life Events and Sexuality (MALES) Study," *Journal of Sexual Medicine* 5 (2008): 583–594.

13. Lodge and Umberson, "All Shook Up"; and Loe, *Rise of Viagra*.

14. Loe, *Rise of Viagra*.

15. Vincent J. Del Casino and Catherine F. Brooks, "Talking about Bodies Online: Viagra, YouTube, and the Politics of Public(ized) Sexualities," *Gender, Place & Culture* 22, no. 4 (2015): 474–493; Lodge and Umberson, "All Shook Up"; and Marshall, "Older Men and Sexual Health."

16. Marshall, "Older Men and Sexual Health."

17. Karen Pyke, "Class-Based Masculinities: The Interdependence of Gender, Class, and Interpersonal Power," *Gender & Society* 10, no. 5 (1996): 527–549.

18. Amy C. Lodge and Debra Umberson, "Age and Embodied Masculinities: Midlife Gay and Heterosexual Men Talk about Their Bodies," *Journal of Aging Studies* 27 (2013): 225–232.

19. Rashawn Ray and Jason A. Rosow, "Getting Off on Getting Intimate: How Normative Arrangements Structure Black and White Fraternity Men's Approaches toward Women," *Men and Masculinities* 12, no. 5 (2010): 523–546; Jesus G. Smith, Maria Cristina Morales, and Chonh-Suk Han, "The Influence of Sexual Racism on Erotic Capital: A Systemic Racism Perspective," in *Handbook of Sociology of Racial and Ethnic Relations*, ed. Pinar Batur and Joe R. Feagin, 389–399 (New York: Springer, 2018); and Brittany C. Slatton and Kamesha Spates, eds., *Hyper Sexual, Hyper Masculine? Gender, Race and Sexuality in the Identities of Contemporary Black Men* (New York: Routledge, 2014).

20. See, for example, Jennifer Siebel Newsom, Regina Kulik Scully, and S. E. Johnson, producers, *The Mask You Live In* (DVD) (New York: Virgil Films, 2015); and Andrea Waling, "'We Are So Pumped Full of Shit by the Media': Masculinity,

Magazines, and the Lack of Self-Identification," *Men and Masculinities* 20, no. 4 (2017): 427–452.

21. Bordo, *Male Body.*

22. Melzer, *Manhood Impossible.*

23. Sandberg, "In Lust We Trust."

24. Melzer, *Manhood Impossible.*

25. Tristan Bridges and C. J. Pascoe, "Masculinities and Post-Homophobias?" in *Exploring Masculinities: Identity, Inequality, Continuity, and Change*, ed. C. J. Pascoe and Tristan Bridges, 412–423 (New York: Oxford University Press, 2016); and Sandberg, "In Lust We Trust."

26. Beth Montemurro, "'If You Could Just See Me': The Construction of Heterosexual Men's Sexual Selves and the Hierarchy of Desirability," *Sexualities* 24, no. 3 (2021): 303–321; and Sandberg, "In Lust We Trust."

27. Carpenter, *Virginity Lost.*

28. Lodge and Umberson, "Age and Embodied Masculinities"; Marshall, "Older Men and Sexual Health"; and Montemurro, "'If You Could Just See Me.'"

29. Lodge and Umberson, "Age and Embodied Masculinities"; Marshall, "Older Men and Sexual Health"; and Slevin, "'If I Had Lots of Money.'"

30. Slevin, "'If I Had Lots of Money.'"

31. Kristen Barber, *Gender, Class, and Inequality in the Men's Grooming Industry* (New Brunswick, NJ: Rutgers University Press, 2016).

32. Katz and Marshall, "New Sex for Old"; and Slevin, "'If I Had Lots of Money.'"

CONCLUSION: WRAPPING IT UP

1. Jane Ward, *The Tragedy of Heterosexuality* (New York: New York University Press, 2020).

2. Peggy Orenstein, *Boys and Sex: Young Men on Hookups, Love, Porn, Consent and Navigating the New Masculinity* (New York: Harper, 2020), 17.

3. Orenstein, *Boys and Sex*; and Ward, *Tragedy of Heterosexuality.*

4. Douglas Schrock and Michael Schwalbe, "Men, Masculinity, and Manhood Acts," *Annual Review of Sociology* 35 (2009): 281.

5. Schrock and Schwalbe, "Men, Masculinity, and Manhood Acts," 287.

6. Louisa Allen, "Girls Want Sex, Boys Want Love: Resisting Dominant Discourses of (Hetero)Sexuality," *Sexualities* 6 (2003): 215–236; Louisa Allen, "'Sensitive and Real Macho all at the Same Time': Young Heterosexual Men and Romance," *Men and Masculinities* 10, no. 2 (2007): 137–152; Michael Flood, "Men, Sex, and Homosociality: How Bonds between Men Shape Their Sexual Relations with Women," *Men and Masculinities* 10, no. 3 (2008): 339–359; Richard Mora, "'Do it for all your pubic hairs!' Latino Boys, Masculinity, and Puberty," *Gender &*

Society 26 (2012): 433–460; and C. J. Pascoe, *Dude You're a Fag: Masculinity and Sexuality in High School* (Berkeley: University of California Press, 2007).

7. Scott Melzer, *Manhood Impossible: Men's Struggles to Control and Transform Their Bodies and Work* (New Brunswick, NJ: Rutgers University Press, 2018), 103, 105.

8. Diane Richardson, "Youth Masculinities: Compelling Male Heterosexualities," *British Journal of Sociology* 61 (2010), 743.

9. Allen, "Girls Want Sex"; Judith Chu, "Boys' Nature, Boys' Culture, and a Crisis Of Connection," in *The Crisis of Connection: Roots, Consequences, and Solutions*, ed. Niobe Way, Alisha Ali, Carol Gilligan, and Pedro Noguera, 88–105 (New York: New York University Press, 2018), 88–105; Andrew P. Smiler, "'I Wanted to Get to Know Her Better': Adolescent Boys' Dating Motives, Masculinity Ideology, and Sexual Behavior," *Journal of Adolescence* 31 (2008): 17–32; and Niobe Way, Jessica Cressen, Samuel Bodian, Justin Preston, Joseph Nelwo, and Diane Hughes, "'It Might Be Nice to Be a Girl . . . Then You Wouldn't Have to Be Emotionless': Boys' Resistance to Norms of Masculinity during Adolescence," *Psychology of Men & Masculinities* 15, no. 3 (2014): 241–252.

10. Schrock and Schwalbe, "Men, Masculinity, and Manhood Acts," 282.

11. See, for example, Orenstein, *Boys and Sex*; Pascoe, *Dude*; and Richardson, "Youth Masculinities."

12. Erving Goffman, *The Presentation of Self in Everyday Life* (New York: Anchor Books, 1959).

13. Susan Bordo, *The Male Body: A New Look at Men in Public and Private* (New York: Farrar, Straus and Giroux, 1999), 55.

14. Breanne Fahs, *Performing Sex: The Making and Unmaking of Women's Erotic Lives* (Albany, State University of New York Press, 2011), 17.

15. Beth Montemurro and Christina Riehman Murphy, "Ready and Waiting: Heterosexual Men's Discourses on Decision Making in Initiation of Sexual Intimacy," *Men and Masculinities* 22, no. 5 (2019): 872–892.

16. Fahs, *Performing Sex*, 50.

17. See, for example, Janet Holland, Caroline Ramazanoglu, Sue Sharpe, and Rachel Thomson, *The Male in the Head: Young People, Heterosexuality, and Power* (London: Tuffnell, 2004), 136.

18. Montemurro and Riehman-Murphy, "Ready and Waiting."

19. Laura Carpenter, "Gendered Sexuality over the Life Course: A Conceptual Framework," *Sociological Perspectives* 53, no. 2 (2010): 155–177.

Index

About the Author

Beth Montemurro is a distinguished professor of sociology at Penn State University, Abington. She is the author of *Deserving Desire: Women's Stories of Sexual Evolution* and *Something Old, Something Bold: Bridal Showers and Bachelorette Parties*, as well as numerous journal articles in the areas of gender, sexualities, and popular culture.